Revival

CRITICAL CONDITIONS: FIELD DAY ESSAYS AND MONOGRAPHS

Edited by Seamus Deane

Critical Conditions: Field Day Monographs

Revival

The Abbey Theatre, Sinn Féin, the Gaelic League and the Co-operative Movement

P. J. Mathews

CORK UNIVERSITY PRESS
in association with
FIELD DAY

For Audrey,
with love

First published in 2003 by
Cork University Press
Crawford Business Park
Crosses Green
Cork
Ireland

British Library Cataloguing in Publication Data

A CIP catalogue record for this book is available from the British Library.

ISBN 1-85918-365-4

Typesetting by Red Barn Publishing, Skeagh, Skibbereen, Co. Cork

Printed by ColourBooks Ltd., Baldoyle, Co. Dublin

www.corkuniversitypress.com

CONTENTS

ACKNOWLEDGEMENTS

I am deeply indebted to Seamus Deane for his sound advice and insightful suggestions in the completion of this book. I would also like to express my heartfelt thanks to Declan Kiberd, who has been at different times an inspiring mentor, a steadfast colleague and a solid friend.

A special word of thanks to my colleagues at St Patrick's College, Drumcondra, and Dublin City University – Brenna Clarke, Pat Burke, Noreen Doody, Tom Halpin, Celia Keenan and Mary Shine Thompson – for their support, inspiration and forbearance during the closing stages. To Pauric Travers, Máirín Nic Eoin, Daire Keogh, Jimmy Kelly, John Devitt and Eddie Holt, I am thankful for their invaluable perspectives and generous willingness to address my queries. A special thanks to my colleague and long-time friend Derek Hand, with whom I have debated many of these issues for over a decade now without any sign of the conversation drying up.

Former colleagues Nick Daly, Darryl Jones, John Nash and Eve Patten at Trinity College Dublin and Anne Fogarty, Brian Donnelly, Jefferson Holdridge and Ron Callan at University College, Dublin have greatly enriched my thinking in many ways. I also wish to express my gratitude to Margaret Kelleher, Robert Savage, Michael Paul Gallagher, Donal McCartney, the Parnell Summer School Committee, the Boston University Dublin Programme and the New York University Summer Programme.

This book began life as a doctoral dissertation in the Department of English, TCD. I am thankful to have met along the way many inspiring fellow travellers whose irreverent company and wise scholarship (perhaps that should be the other way around!) have sustained and enlightened me over many years. I would like to remember, in particular, Colin Rothery, Des Fitzgibbon, Michael Egan, Beth Wightman, Greg Dobbins, Bernard Adams, Larry White, Elaine Sisson, Conor McCarthy, Lahney Preston-Matto, Julie Ann Stevens, Aaron Kelly, Alan Gillis, Fionnuala Dillane, Ronan Kelly, Jim Shanahan and Cormac McDonagh. My thanks to Sean Corcoran for insights into matters theatrical, much appreciated encouragement and friendship along the way. Padhraic Egan has been a special adviser, confidant and drinking partner all rolled into one.

To my brother Maurice, a font of knowledge on Irish history, I owe a particular debt of gratitude for inspiring this book in more ways than he will ever know; to my sister Andrea many thanks are due for support and encouragement throughout the years. My final and greatest debt is to my parents, Buddy and Marie Mathews: this book, in many ways, has its origins in the engaging cultural and political debates which are so much a feature of everyday life in the Mathews household in Newhaggard.

I wish to acknowledge the generous financial support of the research committee, St Patrick's College, Drumcondra, and of the Irish Co-operative Organisation Society Golden Jubilee Trust Fund.

Versions of sections of this book have appeared in *Éire-Ireland* 35.1&2 (Spring/Summer 2000) 173–87, the *Irish University Review* 33.1 (Spring/Summer 2003), and the *Irish Review* 29 (Autumn 2002) 22–37.

INTRODUCTION

The year 1899 marks a hugely significant moment, not only in Irish cultural history but also in terms of the development of Irish politics. In May of that year the Irish Literary Theatre staged its inaugural production, Yeats's *The Countess Cathleen,* in the Antient Concert Rooms in Dublin and set in motion a series of events that would culminate in the foundation of the Abbey Theatre five years later. In October 1899 the outbreak of the Boer War unleashed a new dynamic within Irish separatist politics which manifested itself in the establishment of the pro-Boer Transvaal Committee. Within six years this fledgling movement would develop into a new radical political party, Sinn Féin. Despite the contemporaneous evolution of two of the most important institutions in modern Irish history, there has been no scholarly attempt to map or analyse their comparative geneses. This is all the more remarkable given the importance of both to the Irish revival and the overlap in personnel, both at grassroots and executive levels, which existed between them. All too often, the years 1904 and 1905 are taken as the important iconic moments, as if theatre movements and political parties spontaneously appear.

This book takes the years 1899 to 1905 as its central focus, in an attempt to shed light on the nature of the relationships between those forces which gave birth to the Abbey Theatre and those energies which brought about the evolution of Sinn Féin. The aim, however, is not to posit a history of the origins of Sinn Féin as a secure 'background' against which the productions of the Irish Literary Theatre can be read and explained, but rather to highlight important moments of mutual significance. The extent to which the productions of the early theatre movement were inflected with the wider politico-cultural tensions of their moment will be a key preoccupation. Conversely, there is a concern here to investigate the ways in which these productions intervened materially in the political debates of the period. Much of the following analysis, therefore, sets out to disrupt the stable relationship between text and context, literature and history, art and politics which characterizes a great deal of the scholarly work carried out on the drama of the Irish revival. As Lionel Pilkington has recently noted, there is a need 'to counteract the long-standing assumption that Irish theatre exists outside politics[1]. Such an assumption necessarily forecloses the possibility that theatre 'takes part' in history and that dramatic performances provide a context for the mobilization of political energies in 'the real world'. Not only do prevailing political conditions have an impact on what playwrights write, but at any given time theatre can have a bearing on contemporary political ferment.

It will come as no surprise that the methodological approach employed here is avowedly materialist in its concern with the historical contexts in which dramatic texts originate and function. The broad aim is to open up the early productions of the Irish theatre movement to the discursive and material complexities of their historical moment and to explore the degree to which they were influenced by, and in turn influenced, the dynamics of the Irish revival. Central to this manoeuvre is the belief that the early Irish theatre initiative can be usefully understood as an important 'self-help' movement that has much in common with comparable projects such as the Gaelic League, the Irish Agricultural Organisation Society (IAOS) and Sinn Féin. Although operating in the cultural realm, the theatre movement not only produced plays by Irish writers intended to reflect Irish realities, but it also created the material conditions which allowed them to be staged before Irish audiences in an attempt to regenerate Irish narratives of cultural meaning, at a key moment in Ireland's decolonization. Notwithstanding the important points of contact between these self-help initiatives, they have generally been analysed as discrete and, at times, antagonistic groupings, to such a degree that their commonality of purpose has been obscured and their divergences emphasized. That the early theatre movement occasionally found itself at odds with elements within the Gaelic League and with the leadership of the nascent Sinn Féin is undeniable. However, it would seem to me that the sustained attention devoted to these disputes has worked to conceal the nature and extent of the co-operation across the self-help movements. The purpose of this book is to recover these connections and reveal the degree to which a progressive self-help ethos was subscribed to across a range of cultural and social initiatives during the Irish revival.

The placing of the Irish theatre movement within a wider self-help context, which is the central concern of the first chapter, is intended to work against orthodox notions of this period. The standard view of the revival sees it as a purely mystical affair of high culture characterized by a preoccupation with a backward-looking Celtic spirituality, a nostalgia for Gaelic Ireland and an obsessive anti-modern traditionalism. This dominant view stems, in large part, from a sustained interest in the literature of seminal figures such as W. B. Yeats, Lady Augusta Gregory, Douglas Hyde and J. M. Synge which is taken to represent the revival's Celtic *zeitgeist*. As we shall see in the opening chapter, however, such a construction of the Irish revival misrepresents the significance of the period by underplaying the degree of co-operation among the self-help revivalists and the important material advances for which they were responsible. Such material advances were not achieved by adopting colonial models of modernization which were largely antagonistic towards tradition. The 'alternative modernity' of the revival is distinctive in that it repeatedly understands the idea of tradition as a stimulus towards innovation and change rather than a barrier to it.[2] Within such a framework, the 'contradictions' of the major self-help revival projects begin to make sense. As we shall see, these 'contradictions' manifest themselves in: an Irish language league which worked to save 'the ancient tongue' by updating it and standardizing it; an organization for the modernization of farm methods which promoted traditional cultural and social practices; and a modern national theatre which drew heavily on the forms of the Irish folk tradition. If anything distinguishes the Gaelic League, the IAOS and the Irish Literary Theatre, it is the degree to which they 'emerge out of kilter with modernity but none the less in a dynamic relation to it'.[3]

The opening chapter, then, sets out the argument that the Revival can be understood as a progressive period that witnessed the co-operation of the self-help revivalists to encourage local modes of material and cultural development. The subsequent chapters test this hypothesis by using key productions of the Irish theatre movement as a focus for synchronic politico-cultural analysis. The plays chosen for in-depth treatment include: Yeats's *The Countess Cathleen,* Moore's *The Bending of the Bough,* Hyde's *Casadh an tSúgáin,* Moore and Yeats's *Diarmuid and Grania* and Synge's *The Shadow of the Glen.* This is not an exhaustive list of the major productions mounted between the inauguration of the Irish Literary Theatre and the opening of the Abbey Theatre, nor is it meant to be. My intention here is not to provide another 'blow by blow' account of the various mutations of the Irish theatre movement[4] but to dwell on productions which are interestingly inflected by their wider milieu or plays which themselves made significant interventions in the cultural discourse of their moment. Such a choice is necessarily subjective but none the less informed by a desire to understand the relationship between cultural practices and social, political and economic processes. One omission that may require some justification is the relative lack of attention paid to the Yeats–Gregory play *Kathleen ni Houlihan.* The main reason for this neglect is the sheer volume of attention that this play, particularly in its first production, has received. It would take a minor research project in itself to document the number of times this play has been cited in Irish cultural analysis and glossed inevitably by the ubiquitous Yeatsian line:

> Did that play of mine send out
> Certain men the English shot?[5]

A great deal of this scholarly work takes *Kathleen ni Houlihan* as *the* iconic moment of 'political theatre', as if the productions which surrounded it were somehow devoid of political resonance. In any event, the influence of contemporary affairs on the shaping of this play and the influence of this play on the shaping of nationalist discourse have been well attended to.[6]

The plays under consideration, therefore, or rather their first productions, will be taken as contexts within which a synchronic dialogue with a diverse range of contemporary debates and events can be opened. In chapter 2, the controversy surrounding *The Countess Cathleen* is examined in relation to the quarrel over the Irish language occasioned by two TCD professors' dismissal of that language as immoral and indecent. Chapter 3 examines the role of the

Boer War in the emergence of a non-clandestine separatist politics in opposition to the home rule aspirations of the newly reunited Irish Parliamentary Party. These developments are considered in relation to George Moore's critique of parliamentarianism in *The Bending of the Bough*. The penultimate chapter investigates the crystallizing antagonism between the civic-minded republicanism of William Rooney and the ethnic-minded nationalism of D. P. Moran. This is juxtaposed with the reception of *Casadh an tSúgáin* and *Diarmuid and Grania*. The final chapter reads Synge's *The Shadow of the Glen* as a timely critique of the *embourgeoisement* of Irish society at the very moment when Arthur Griffith began to nudge Sinn Féin politically to the right.

If this book seeks to prove anything it is that, between 1899 and 1905, Ireland was rapidly evolving and mutating both politically and culturally in all kinds of interesting ways. Yet much of the commentary on the early plays (especially the controversial ones) relies on the notion of a solidly homogenous entity denoted by the phrase 'the nationalist audience', which invariably occludes the complex range of political positions that were developing and competing within nationalism at this time. Similarly, in relation to leading literary figures such as W. B. Yeats and George Moore, much has been made of the strategic nature of their commitment to nationalist cultural politics. This book is less concerned with an author-centred examination of the consistency of such beliefs than with an appreciation of the material repercussions of the high-profile interventions they made.

REVIVAL CONNECTIONS
The Irish Literary Theatre, the Gaelic League and the Co-operative Movement

'We Don't Hear Much of Parliament Now'

In an essay on the condition of Ireland published in late 1898, Lady Augusta Gregory drew attention to the work being done by Horace Plunkett, 'whose name is now a household word in Ireland',[1] in relation to agricultural co-operation and scientific and technical instruction.

> This year a scarlet-spotted map of Ireland just published testifies to the extraordinary spread of the movement. There are now 243 societies, comprising about 30,000 members . . . As a result to the outsider one pound packets of excellent creamery butter are now to be had in every small town.[2]

In so doing, she documented the humble beginnings of what was to become one of Ireland's most significant industries of the twentieth century. Gregory, however, did not merely observe these important innovations in Irish agricultural practice but also played a part in bringing them about. As she indicated in the same essay, she actively encouraged the setting up of a co-operative society in her own parish. 'Mr. Plunkett came here for a day last year', she recalled, 'and I asked the farmers to meet him'.[3] It gave her a measure of satisfaction that, consequently, her neighbours had profited by cutting out the 'middleman' in the buying of seed and manure. It is quite possible that some of these neighbours were also in attendance eight months later when, at the invitation of Lady Gregory, Douglas Hyde and W. B. Yeats spoke at a meeting held by the recently founded Kiltartan branch of the Gaelic League.[4] Having listened to arguments in favour of the preservation of Irish as a spoken language, it is conceivable that post-lecture conversations could have turned to a controversy recently covered by Arthur Griffith's fledgling weekly newspaper, the *United Irishman*, and by the League's new journal, *An Claidheamh Soluis*.[5] The row in question was caused by the inaugural production of yet another new national initiative, the Irish Literary Theatre, which was the brainchild of Gregory and Yeats and staunchly supported by Plunkett and Hyde.[6] At stake here, in part, was the issue of whether English was a suitable language for an Irish national literature.

5

This vignette usefully suggests the complex network of relationships which was beginning to develop between the IAOS, the Gaelic League and the Irish Literary Theatre as the nineteenth century was drawing to a close. That this period marks the beginning of a profound transformation in the social, economic and cultural landscape of Ireland is beyond doubt. Yet the extent to which the leaders of these initiatives participated in and/or supported adjacent movements has yet to be fully appreciated. Likewise, the role of mass movements such as the IAOS and the Gaelic League in transmitting the major innovations of the Irish Revival needs to be more fully considered. Perhaps most significantly, the three movements in question were beginning to coalesce into a new 'self-help' consensus which would work steadily to provide a radical alternative to old-style parliamentary politics. As Lady Gregory, quoting the wise words of an old neighbour, reminded her readers in 1898: "'we don't hear much of Parliament now since Parnell died"'.7

From Parliamentary to Self-Help Politics

> The modern literature of Ireland, and indeed all that stir of thought which prepared for the Anglo-Irish war, began when Parnell fell from power in 1891. A disillusioned and embittered Ireland turned from parliamentary politics; an event was conceived; and the race began, as I think, to be troubled by that event's long gestation; Dr. Hyde founded the Gaelic League, which was for many years to substitute for political argument a Gaelic grammar, and for political meetings village gatherings, where songs were sung and stories told in the Gaelic language. Meanwhile I had begun a movement in English, in the language in which modern Ireland thinks and does its business; founded certain societies where clerks, working men, men of all classes, could study the Irish poets, novelists and historians who had written in English, and as much of Gaelic literature as had been translated into English. But the great mass of our people, accustomed to interminable political speeches, read little, and so from the very start we felt that we must have a theatre of our very own.
>
> W. B. Yeats, *Autobiographies* (pp. 559–60)

The centrality of this famous quotation to accounts by Irish historians of the period between 1891 and 1916 has been pointed out by Roy Foster. Many commentators, he argues, have taken the Yeatsian view that, in post-Parnell Ireland, political energy was diverted into cultural channels, creating a dynamic for political revolution:

> The torrent of 'politics' was seen suddenly to run into the channel of 'culture', in a curiously unquestioned way, creating a ferment which is automatically assumed to have been the necessary precondition of the 1916 rising.8

Foster challenges this orthodoxy by arguing that constitutional politics were working effectively at this time and that the imperative for revolution only came as a result of the unusual circumstances brought about by World War I. He sees the acceptance of what he calls Yeats's 'poetic version'[9] of history as a result of shoddy thinking, and very much a retrospective misreading. Literary activity, he contends, did not take over politics; in fact by 1900 'constitutional politics could be seen to be working'.[10] Yet Foster's revision still insists on a clear distinction between the lofty idealism of a literary movement and the practical concerns of parliamentary politics.[11] Surely, though, what is most striking about this period is not that literary activity *replaced* politics as Yeats implied (or that political activity was more effective than literary work as Foster argues), but that it was *accompanied* by a great deal of innovative 'political' activity – outside the purview of the main constitutional parties and within the domain of the new self-help movements. Although the self-help movements professed to operate beyond conventional party politics, their activities, as we shall see, clearly had political ramifications. If there is tension within Irish nationalism at this time, it is more useful to see it as a battle between a newly emerging self-help consensus and old-style parliamentary politics, rather than a struggle between clearly delineated 'cultural' and 'political' forces.

To return to post-Parnell Ireland, it seems as if too much significance has been accorded to 1891 – the year of Parnell's death – as a key turning-point in history. Much more important were the events of 1893, in which Gladstone's second home rule bill was defeated. Having deposed Parnell at Gladstone's request in 1890, the anti-Parnellite Irish Party had every reason to believe that home rule would be forthcoming. The passage of the bill through the Commons was smooth, however it failed miserably in the Lords, with a vote of 419–41 against. Such an overwhelming Lords veto virtually killed any chance of a revival of home rule. Furthermore, in the election of 1895 'the Tory-Unionists came in with a majority of 152 seats, making the most one sided House of Commons in sixty years'.[12] As a result, the probability of achieving home rule for Ireland receded even further into the distance. It was not until the Parliament Act of 1911 removed the power of the Lords to veto legislation (replacing it with a restricted delaying power) that the home rule cause could be revived with some hope of success.

Ironically, the Tory policy of conciliation was one of the factors which helped the revivalists to eclipse the parliamentary politicians. Perhaps the most radical reform instituted by the Conservative government was the introduction of local government. This initiative did not come about because of agitation by the Irish members, but was more a logical extension of the reforms already carried out in England and Scotland. Interestingly, local government was not enthusiastically canvassed nor supported by the Irish Party. This was because of a general feeling that these proposals were being advocated by unionists as an alternative to home rule:

Democratic local government, of which County Councils were the central example, was a virtually unwanted gift from the Conservative government to the Irish
people. There was no agitation in its favour. The Irish Party's feelings about
County government were soured by the belief, widely held, that the Irish Act
was a reward to Chamberlain and the other Liberal Unionists, for their help in
defeating Gladstone's (and Parnell's) first Home Rule Bills in 1886 . . . The new
Act was met therefore with suspicion and grudging acceptance. The Irish Party
looked on it as no substitute for national self-government, and as another Conservative attempt to kill Home Rule with kindness.[13]

It was within this climate of government concessions and Irish Parliamentary
Party indifference to anything but constitutional matters that the self-help
movements succeeded in making advances.

The upshot of all this is that the period between 1893 and 1911 represented a particularly dark and powerless period for constitutional politics in
Ireland in which the only way home rule could be achieved would be through
the benevolence of the Tory government. James Joyce caught this inertia perfectly in 'Ivy Day in the Committee Room' – a story which satirizes a political scene almost totally bereft of any commendable strategy to better Ireland's
lot and paralysed by a sodden nostalgia for Parnell. Ironically, it was this
macro-political stasis at a time of constitutional uncertainty which opened up
new possibilities for an alternative Irish politics. With the realization that little
could be achieved at Westminster and a weariness of the divisive squabbling
of Irish politicians, a new generation of Irish intellectuals came up with the
strategy of working for a form of *de facto* home rule despite its unattainabil-
ity *de jure*. The plan was to mobilize and apply the latent national intelligence
of the country to the practical needs of Ireland, a strategy conveniently encapsulated in the term 'self-help'. Central to the endeavour was the realization
that the Irish had accepted London as the centre of culture and civilization
for too long and that the time had come for the Irish people to regenerate
their own intellectual terms of reference and narratives of cultural meaning.
It is not an accident that the emergence of two of the most important self-help
movements to revolutionize the social, economic and cultural practices of Ireland – the Gaelic League (1893) and the IAOS (1894) – coincided with the
defeat of the second home rule bill. Yeats had already set the ball rolling with
the National Literary Society in 1892, the Irish Literary Theatre was founded
in 1899, and a women's movement – Inghinidhe na hÉireann – was established in 1901.

The loss of confidence in the tactics of the Irish MPs in London was neatly
reflected by the journalist D. P. Moran in a provocative essay published in
December 1898. 'Is the Nation Dying?' is in many ways a restatement of
Douglas Hyde's central thesis in his famous essay 'The Necessity for De-
Anglicising Ireland', in so far as it berated the Irish for imitating that which
they professed to detest – English customs and popular culture. We also find

here an early expression of Moran's hostility to the Anglo-Irish, and his belief in the power of an educated 'Gaelic' middle class to redeem Ireland. But what is perhaps most striking is his indifference to matters constitutional:

> Of course it is true that we cannot make our laws yet. That is a fact which we never forget, and, when we are playing at excuses, it is our trump card . . . Everything is to come straight when we can make those precious laws; in the meantime it would be futile to do anything. In other words all the national life is to bleed out of us, until we come by our right to make laws for the corpse.[14]

Moran had reached the same conclusion as W. B. Yeats, Horace Plunkett, Douglas Hyde, Lady Gregory and Arthur Griffith: if home rule was not a realistic political option, a new strategy should be adopted to improve the lot of the nation.

In many ways the evolution of the self-help movements bore many similarities to the home rule experience. Just as with home rule, a broad aspiration was subscribed to by many diverse groups with divergent political opinions. One could find liberal unionists, federal nationalists and separatists of various political hues willing to subscribe to the self-help ethos. Most of the self-help movements attempted to avoid political acrimony by consciously locating themselves outside the domain of party politics and beyond the reach of the constitutional parties. However, political differences often bubbled under the surface of the loose self-help coalition which emerged with the dawn of the new century. What is remarkable is how quickly the self-help revivalists succeeded in eclipsing the constitutional politicians in securing material and political gains for Ireland into the first decade of the century. It was out of the success of the co-operative movement that Horace Plunkett managed to secure a Department of Agriculture and Technical Instruction for Ireland in 1899, providing *de facto* home rule for Irish agriculture, and the Gaelic League through its agitation succeeded in attaining a higher recognition for the Irish language in the education system.[15] The open hostility of the *Freeman's Journal* and the *Irish Daily Independent* to the IAOS gives some indication of the extent to which this self-help movement was upsetting the status quo. The *Independent* criticized the IAOS for interfering with the legitimate interests of the traders by encouraging co-operation and an *Irish Homestead* editorial in December 1898 remarked that 'for several years we have had the spectacle of this feeble old paper [*Freeman's Journal*] shaking in decrepit rage at a movement which goes ahead in spite of its criticism'.[16]

Given the inertia of constitutional politics at this time, it is hardly surprising that the revival would eventually produce a movement which would take the self-help ethos to its most radical conclusion by advocating an alternative politics. Sinn Féin's answer to the home rule question was to give up seeking the sanction of the British and to get on with the business of setting up a parliament in Dublin by unilaterally withdrawing Irish members from Westminster. Significantly, by 1908 the major cultural, political and educational institutions of the 'post-British Irish state'[17] – the Gaelic League, the Abbey Theatre, Sinn Féin, and the National University of Ireland – had all been established, largely due to the efforts of the revivalists and with little help from mainstream politicians.[18] With the development of these national institutions and the emergence of a new wave of nationalist newspapers, an infrastructure was put in place which allowed the 'imagining' of the Irish nation.[19]

In the light of these advances, it is curious that this episode of Irish history is almost universally seen as a period of *cultural* nationalism, when cultural (specifically literary) activity is deemed to have taken over from mainstream politics. Such an analysis, however, disregards the substantial material gains and transformations made by the revivalists mentioned above. Even the most 'cultural' of the revivalist initiatives – the literary movement – succeeded not only in producing Irish literature and drama, but also in making material interventions, most obviously in the foundation of institutions such as the National Literary Society and the Abbey Theatre. What is not readily appreciated in appraisals of the revival is the extent to which cultural initiatives, like the theatre movement, not only produced a significant body of drama by Irish writers but also created the material context for these plays to be staged before Irish audiences. W. B. Yeats, Lady Gregory, George Moore and Edward Martyn were not only artists but also the 'arts planners' and 'arts administrators' of their day.

These cultural institutions mobilized the factors of cultural production in the same way as the IAOS encouraged peasant farmers to utilize the factors of material production. In this respect, the cultural aspect of the revival was profoundly political even though it happened, for the most part, outside the concerns of the parliamentary party. This drive towards cultural sovereignty proceeded by revising the imperial narrative of Ireland and relocating the nation at the centre rather than at the periphery of experience – a strategy which cannot be seen as apolitical. Luke Gibbons has written of how 'culture in Ireland became ineluctably bound up with politics' at this time:

> To engage in cultural activity in circumstances where one's culture was being effaced or obliterated, or even to assert the existence of a civilization prior to conquest, was to make a political statement, if only by depriving the frontier myth of its power to act as an alibi for colonization.[20]

Therefore, to accept a simple opposition between cultural and political forces at this time, as Roy Foster does – albeit to re-evaluate the advances made by constitutional politics – conceals the degree to which the self-help activists took over from the Irish Party MPs as the main innovators in Irish politics at this time.

There was a consensus among the revivalists that a more noble representation of Irishness was needed to displace colonial stereotypes and a shared willingness to put a rival cultural infrastructure in place to do so. But the matter of what should constitute such an 'authentic' Irishness would become a subject of intense debate. Not only did the revival involve a cultural struggle between Irish and British interests, therefore, but a battle would also take place within Irish nationalism for the leadership and articulation of the people-nation. In this great moment of national 'imagining', various different notions of Irish cultural identity began to crystallize and compete to become *the* emblem of Irish national identity. As we shall see in the following pages, the theatre was to become a pivotal site of this struggle. Looking back on this period, then, the question is not which conception of Irish identity represents *authentic* Irishness – as Benedict Anderson argues, all totalizing narratives of national identity are culturally produced – but rather how various notions of Irish identity came to be sanctioned, legitimized, challenged and to gain ascendancy in a nation that had not yet found full political expression.

Lady Gregory was perhaps the first to identify the new self-help *zeitgeist* as it was happening, in her remarkable essay published in the journal *Nineteenth Century* in November 1898 and quoted above. Following the passage of the Local Government Act in August and anticipating the announcement of the foundation of the Irish Literary Theatre the following January, 'Ireland, Real and Ideal' is a seminal piece which draws attention to the extent to which the self-help movements had eclipsed the national politicians as the major force for change in Ireland, both at a material and cultural level. What is striking is her awareness of the twin dynamics of the revival. She compares the double trajectory of the self-help movements to the materialist/idealist partnership of Sancho Panza and Quixote in *Don Quixote*.[21] In this respect, she corrects the then current Arnoldian view of the Celt, which was often used to represent the Irish as poetically gifted but materially inept.[22] In fact it was her belief that 'Irish Sancho has given a lead to English Hodge in the power of adaptation and of organising for a material purpose'.[23] Seeing in Westminster 'a confused crowd of politicians crying out to their opponents and to each other', Lady Gregory realized that the Irish MPs were not likely to achieve much. She looked with hope to the work of Horace Plunkett and to Douglas Hyde, being, perhaps, the first to make a connection between the work of the IAOS and the Gaelic League.[24]

Lady Gregory also showed her awareness of the powerful role of culture in reinforcing national stereotypes and was anxious to dispel English misconceptions of the Irish. 'There is', she wrote, 'a stage tradition and a literary tradition against [the Irishman]. The tourist who comes to Ireland finds in the country, like all other tourists, "what he brings with him," and a car-driver or professional beggar is called upon to supply the food he desires.'[25] In this analysis she presaged the thinking of later postcolonial theorists like Edward Said who would point out the limitations of a colonialist mindset which insisted on 'reading one culture in terms of another' and which 'left a legacy of diminished understanding of other cultures and their right to be known on their own terms'.[26] She believed that Ireland needed to break free of the identity foisted upon it and create itself anew. It was her view that 'we have worn the mask thrust upon us too long, and that we are more likely to win at least respect when we appear in our own form'.[27] In contrast to the situation in Westminster, this kind of thinking was optimistic, pointing out the possibilities for, rather than the limitations on, Ireland. Gregory evaded the determinism of the constitutional situation by configuring Irish identity as something yet to be created, yet to be imagined. There is no doubt that she had the Irish Literary Theatre (which would be announced just a few weeks after this article was published) in mind as the movement most likely to remake Irish identity in this way. Indeed, 'Ireland, Real and Ideal' gives us an insight into what Lady Gregory considered 'authentic Irishness' to be and how exactly 'our own form' would take shape. Her account of the spiritual visions of the peasantry in this article remarks on how their '"clasping hands with the Gods" has not been shaken by the Catholic teaching of future punishments'.[28] Clearly, then, she saw a residual paganism in the culture as the 'authentic' Irish spirit, and raw material for the creation of a new Irish identity. In this respect she anticipated the opening play of the Irish Literary Theatre. If Lady Gregory looked to this Celtic paganism as the source of true Irishness[29], she had another Anglo-Irish hero in mind to build on the work of the IAOS and the Gaelic League – the quintessential Sancho–Quixote, W. B. Yeats.

W. B. Yeats: Self-Help Pioneer

By the time of the announcement of the foundation of the Irish Literary Theatre, Yeats was well qualified to take on the mantle of chief propagandist for the new movement. Between the years 1886 and 1899 the young poet had come of age, not just as a writer, but as a skilled organizer and political activist as well. In *Autobiographies* he relates how, as a young man, he was so shy that he 'would often leave some business undone, or purchase unmade, because [he] shrank from facing a strange office or a shop a little grander than usual'. This timidity was soon overcome as the poet became more deeply involved in societies and movements, until eventually Yeats 'found the happiness that Shelley found when he tied a pamphlet to a fire balloon'.[30] The transformation from solitary aesthete to skilful agitator was swift and provided Yeats with an invaluable apprenticeship. In fact, by January 1899 he had gained extensive experience in founding literary societies and groups, sparring with formidable intellectual and political opponents and orchestrating street politics – experience that would stand him in good stead in his attempt to establish his own theatre.

It was only shortly after Yeats, under the influence of John O'Leary, had discovered literary fenianism, that he rather precociously attacked the criticism of his father's old friend, Edward Dowden, professor of English at Trinity College.[31] Dowden, a hero of the budding poet,[32] had praised the early efforts of the young Yeats. By the age of twenty-one, however, Yeats had outgrown the professor's guidance and had exchanged Dowden for John O'Leary as his chosen literary mentor. It was at this time that he also began to be troubled by the indifference of the professor to Irish influences in literature. In the course of a review of the poetry of Sir Samuel Ferguson, he berated Dowden for not taking more interest in Irish literature:

> If Ireland has produced no great poet, it is not that her poetic impulse has run dry, but because her critics have failed her, for every community is a solidarity, all depending upon each, and each upon all . . . It is a question whether the most distinguished of our critics, Professor Dowden, would not only have more consulted the interests of his country, but more also, in the long run, his own dignity and reputation, which are dear to all Irish men, if he had devoted some of those elaborate pages which he has spent on the much bewritten George Eliot, to a man like the subject of this article [Samuel Ferguson].[33]

Although this move by Yeats can be seen as an 'oedipal slaying', we can also recognize here the genesis of a whole series of ideas that were to inform his writing and agitation into the first decade of the twentieth century. Dowden saw his own criticism as imperial or cosmopolitan, whereas Yeats recognized it as quintessentially provincial in its deference to London taste and values. It is at this point that Yeats began to develop the idea that an Irish revival 'might be a revolt *against* imitative provincialism',[34] that it could in fact restore Ireland's cultural sovereignty by making the nation a centre of artistic excellence once again. This insight completely escaped Dowden, 'the grand old man of literary Unionism'.[35] Furthermore, Yeats began to realize that his own class, far from being the guardian of high cultural values, was in fact cut off from the source of Ireland's cultural vitality. This was his first, but by no means his last, dispute with a professor of Trinity College over Irish cultural matters. More than a decade later, Yeats would berate Professor Atkinson for his attempt to denigrate the educational and cultural worth of the Irish language.

Yeats's disagreement with Dowden brought home a wider truth to him — that literature was intimately bound up with the institutions of criticism, and that there was no standard of criticism in Ireland essential for the cultivation of a prosperous Irish literature. Quite simply, there was no well-informed periodical press dedicated to Irish matters. He lamented the fact that educated men, particularly among the Anglo-Irish, did not buy Irish books,[36] and that Dowden, 'the one man of letters with an international influence', was noted for recounting 'that he knew an Irish book by its smell, because he had once seen some books whose binding had been fastened together by rotten glue'.[37] It was to remedy this situation that Yeats set up the Irish Literary Society of London with T. W. Rolleston in December 1891, and the National Literary Society in

Dublin[38] with John O'Leary five months later on 24 May 1892. Yeats clearly stated that the purpose of the new Dublin society was to halt denationalization. In a letter to *United Ireland* he pointed out that this was the reason the Irish Literary Society of London was founded and not to 'do anything so absurd and impossible as to make London "the intellectual centre of Ireland"'.[39] It is possible that Yeats had these schemes in mind since the time of his quarrel with Dowden, but no doubt the death of Parnell the previous October instilled a sense of urgency into the enterprise. By the time the second home rule bill was defeated in 1893, both these societies were well established as important forums for Irish letters. The main objective was ostensibly to publicize the literature, folklore and legends of Ireland, but quite clearly an important function was also to create an audience and a market for Yeats and his literary cronies, not just in England but in Ireland as well. As Conor Cruise O'Brien remarked, Yeats had 'a politician's eye and a politician's sense of timing'[40] and young recruits 'flocked to a movement which did not require them to take sides in the Parnell dispute and had no direct interest in politics'.[41] With such a high level of support, mostly from interested men of letters, it became possible to plan various projects and schemes including: cultural agitation through lectures, concerts and poetry readings; the establishment of a network of nationalist reading rooms throughout the country; and the mass distribution of a series of new nationalist books. Furthermore, Yeats hoped to organize a travelling theatre company to perform to peasant audiences.[42] The intention was to create as much impact as possible on national opinion and national taste by encouraging Irish readers to look on Ireland rather than England as the epicentre of cultural value. In many respects, therefore, Yeats's societies can be seen as pioneering self-help movements, anticipating the work of the Gaelic League and the IAOS in their attempt to achieve a measure of cultural sovereignty for Ireland by restoring the intellectual traditions of the nation. Douglas Hyde, in fact, was the first president of the National Literary Society in Dublin and delivered his famous lecture 'The Necessity for De-Anglicising Ireland' to the newly formed group in 1892. His call for Irish people to cease imitating English customs and habits and to cultivate native ones instead built on Yeats's critique of Dowden and galvanized the emerging self-help spirit.

Hyde emerged out of the fervour of the Dublin society to found the Gaelic League the following year[43] – a movement that was to carry out work that was in many ways comparable to, and in other ways different from, the literary societies. The distinctions stemmed from a fundamental difference of approach between Yeats and Hyde. Both men believed that Ireland was being culturally drained as a result of the union with Britain. Yeats, however, felt that 'the trend could be reversed even if the Gaelic language itself did die out',[44] while Hyde believed that a restoration of the Irish language was the only hope for Ireland's cultural salvation. These distinctions were to become extremely important several years later when the foundation of the Irish Literary Theatre provoked a debate on whether or not an Irish literature in the English language could be truly national.

Yeats's intention in setting up the literary societies in London and Dublin was to combat the indifference and provincialism of Anglo-Irish intellectuals like Dowden and create a standard of criticism for Ireland yet his aims were soon thwarted by a provincialism of another kind. As Malcolm Brown has pointed out, Yeats 'lifted the machinery for the new Irish cultural movement bodily from Young Ireland's literary organization of 1843'.[45] Although quite happy to inherit the infrastructure of the Young Irelanders, Yeats was not all that keen on their literary standards. He had learned his lesson well from John O'Leary and believed in protesting against 'the right of patriots to perpetrate bad verses'.[46] The weakness of the Davis school of poetry for Yeats was that it professed to be national but was clearly imitative of English poetry, both in form and style, just as Dowden's criticism claimed cosmopolitan status but was really quite provincial. As far as Yeats was concerned the Davis school turned its back on Irish poetic traditions, 'borrowed the mature English methods of utterance and used them to sing of Irish wrongs or preach of Irish purposes'. Consequently, 'their work was never wholly satisfactory, for what was Irish in it looked ungainly in an English garb and what was English was never perfectly mastered, never wholly absorbed into their being'.[47] It is hardly surprising that Yeats found it difficult to tolerate those elements within nationalist Ireland who viewed such poetry 'as certain enlightened believers look upon the story of Adam and Eve and the apple'[48] – sacred truths, impervious to criticism.

Yeats, however, was to take on the chauvinism of old-style nationalists as readily as he had confronted Dowden's ignorance of Irish literature. In so doing, he opened up a new position within Irish cultural discourse which at once eschewed ascendancy indifference to matters Irish and nationalist apathy towards literary standards. In many ways, then, Yeats set a new tone for the revival period by rejecting the intransigence of entrenched cultural positions. This strategy also suited his own literary ends and helped set him up as the self-styled arbiter of taste, particularly at a time when artists and intellectuals all over Europe were becoming increasingly conscious of a distinction between high art and popular culture.

It was the famous controversy with Sir Charles Gavan Duffy that enabled him to adopt this new position. This well-documented dispute, on the surface, centred on the choice of books to be made available for the National Literary Society's library scheme.[49] However, at a deeper level it was a dogfight over the establishment of a canon of Irish national literature. The dispute has been seen as a straightforward battle between art and nationalism, with Yeats playing the role of 'the artist of integrity' and Gavan Duffy 'the propagandist nationalist'. Such an analysis, however, is based on a false dichotomy: particularly when one considers that Yeats himself *was* a nationalist, who had just recently established the National Literary Society, and was very much aware of the role of culture in advancing the claims of nationalism, both at home and abroad. It is more useful instead to see this controversy as an early manifestation of the sea change taking place in Ireland, which was, in many important ways, a generational revolution. The ageing Gavan Duffy, who had just returned after years in exile and was still psychologically in tune with the Ireland of Thomas Davis, championed the poetry of the Young Irelanders, while the young Yeats, disillusioned with the squabbling of politicians and caught up in the spirit of self-help, insisted that contemporary poetic output be represented.

In the end Yeats was defeated, but he was in no doubt that the entire project was 'killed by its first volume, Thomas Davis' dry but informing historical essay'.[50] Nevertheless, the affair marks an important moment in Yeats's development. This was his first experience of public controversy and, although ultimately defeated, one cannot but be struck by the confidence and skill with which he confronted as formidable an opponent as Sir Charles Gavan Duffy. What is particularly noteworthy is the way in which the young poet dictated the terms of the debate, a skill he would draw on in many future controversies.

Yeats may have established himself as a defender of Irish poetry, but such a lofty position was not secured without cost. Because he had had the audacity to interrogate the orthodoxies of Young Ireland, Yeats had to countenance jibes from Duffy's supporters that he was 'under English influence'.[51] Such a slur might also have something to do with the fact that, during these years when Yeats was developing his ideas on Celticism, he was 'willing to extend his interpretation of Anglo-Irish letters not only to embrace his good friends Lionel Johnson and Arthur Symons', but that he also sensed a certain Celtic affinity 'in such opposite forces as William Blake and Maurice Maeterlinck'.[52] However, the notion that his commitment to nationalism should automatically preclude him from engaging with these influences was anathema to him. In retrospect, Yeats saw his intervention in the Gavan Duffy affair as vital to changing opinion in Ireland. In *Autobiographies* he makes the claim that, if he had not made some headway against 'old fashioned nationalism' in 1892 and 1893, 'it might have silenced in 1907 John Synge, the greatest dramatic genius of Ireland'.[53] As a result of the controversy, Yeats grew in confidence as a formidable public figure and gained valuable experience in speech-making – a skill he would draw on in the early years of the Irish Literary Theatre.

Yeats continued his crusade to set standards for the Irish Literary movement with the publication of *A Book of Irish Verse*, which he edited in 1894. In this farewell to the Gavan Duffy controversy he gave more prominence to the literature of living writers like T. W. Rolleston, Douglas Hyde and Katherine Tynan than to old favourites like Davis and Moore. The next four years, however, were to witness his most intense period of political commitment. In 1895 he joined the Irish National Alliance, an offshoot of the Irish Republican Brotherhood, perhaps in an attempt to renew his nationalist credentials after the fracas with Duffy.[54] For whatever reason, this is the period in which he came closest to understanding the complicated relationship between class and culture in Ireland. He temporarily dropped his aristocratic pose to accept what he would call 'the baptism of the gutter'. He had finally come to the understanding that, 'in a battle like Ireland's, which is one of poverty against wealth', prominent Anglo-Irish figures like himself needed to prove their sincerity 'by making ourselves unpopular to wealth'.[55] Yeats chose one of the most visible means possible of siding with the underdog – organized street politics.

This form of political agitation was becoming increasingly popular and was to play an important role in the political development of Ireland over the coming decades. The Fenians were past masters of this particular form of publicity, making great capital out of the funerals of their leaders.[56] In an era when the right to picket and demonstrate peacefully had not yet been established, street demonstrations guaranteed confrontation with the authorities and, as a result, widespread publicity.[57] The year 1897 marks an important date in the evolution of street politics in Ireland, marking, as it does, the popular celebrations for Queen Victoria's Diamond Jubilee and the counter-demonstrations organized in June by James Connolly's Irish Socialist Republican Party. If the British authorities were beginning to use street theatre to harness popular sentiment, nationalists were quickly learning how to use such methods to oppose these manifestations.

Yeats chose the anti-Jubilee demonstration as the moment for his 'baptism of the gutter', with James Connolly playing a rather unlikely John the Baptist. It was Yeats who persuaded Maud Gonne to speak at Connolly's anti-Jubilee demonstration and both of them joined Connolly's march the following evening behind a mock coffin representing the British empire. A riot ensued when the police attempted to clear the crowd, and '200 people were treated for injuries and one woman subsequently died'.[58] Undoubtedly, Yeats retrospectively exaggerated the degree of his acquiescence in the violent protests. In *Autobiographies*, he relates of this incident that he had lost his voice and, 'thus freed from responsibility', shared in the emotion of the crowd and 'perhaps even [felt] as they [felt] when the glass crash[ed]'.[59] In reality, he was terrified and insisted that he and Gonne 'remain in the National Club during the police charge, much to her fury'.[60] The commonplace that Yeats's involvement in advanced politics was motivated by his infatuation with Maude Gonne and his desire to impress her at this time is often used to gloss incidents like this. Yet the fact remains that his presence as a high-profile public figure added legitimacy and gravitas to this important moment of anti-monarchist protest and represented a significant intervention in the political ferment of the time. Whether or not Yeats's public actions were disingenuous and belied his private opinions is a moot point, especially in this era when authorial intentions have proven to be slippery and indeterminate. The tendency to dwell on the integrity or otherwise of his actions, however, necessarily deflects attention from the public impact they may have had. Clearly, the Jubilee protest represented Yeats's most outward defiance of the British

authorities in Ireland up to that point. Significantly, by the turn of the century opposition to royal visits would become a recurring tactic of nationalist
protest to which he would contribute in no small measure with his propa-
gandistic letters to the press.

On the day he had taken part in Connolly's demonstration, Yeats had also
been at a meeting of the Centenary Committee. As president of the '98 Commemoration Association of Great Britain and France[61] he was given the opportunity to take part in some street politics of his own, but on a much larger
scale and in a context of his own making. The highlight of the centenary celebrations was to be the laying of the cornerstone for a Wolfe Tone Memorial
at the head of Grafton street on 15 August 1898. The wider political aim, however, was to use the occasion to unite both Parnellites and anti-Parnellites and
the warring factions of the Irish Republican Brotherhood (IRB). All parties
were present at the mass demonstration, however little progress appeared to
be made on the question of unity. Yeats recounted in *Autobiographies* how:

> Our movement became a protest against the dissensions, the lack of dignity, of
> the Parnellite and Anti-Parnellite parties, who had fought one another for seven
> or eight years, till busy men passed them by, as they did those performing cats
> that in my childhood I used to see, pretending to spit at one another, on a table
> outside Charing Cross station.[62]

Those 'busy men' (and women) Yeats referred to were self-help activists such
as Douglas Hyde, Horace Plunkett, Lady Gregory (and indeed himself), who
in the seven years since Parnell's death had effected more change in Ireland
than the constitutional politicians. There may have been some truth to his
recollection that, on the day of the Wolfe Tone Centenary demonstration,
'Maud Gonne [was] cheered everywhere' and 'the Irish members march[ed]
through street after street without welcome'.[63]

Clearly then, Yeats, in his early career was heavily involved in what might
broadly be termed 'self-help activities'. He was a pioneering self-help organizer
in his work with the literary societies and had a profound influence on later
activists such as Douglas Hyde. By rejecting the provincialism of both Dowden and Gavan Duffy and the inertia of the Irish Parliamentary Party, Yeats created a new position within Irish cultural discourse and initiated the eclipse of
constitutional politics by self-help organizations. By the turn of the century,
however, he had become aware of the limitations of poetry in influencing public opinion in Ireland, believing that 'the great mass of our people, accustomed
to interminable political speeches, read little'.[64] As a result of this, he decided
to turn his attention to the foundation of his next self-help movement – an
Irish theatre – believing, as he did, that 'in the theatre the mob becomes a
people'.[65]

Staging the Nation: The Irish Literary Theatre

From the 1890s onwards there was a rising sense within Irish cultural circles that the nation was being swamped by what were clearly seen as alien cultural forms from England, and that the Irish people had acquiesced in accepting these forms to their detriment. This sentiment was widely expressed by a self-conscious rejection of English culture, especially in its popular forms, as having anything positive to contribute to Ireland. Douglas Hyde was one of the first cultural commentators to articulate this. As the title of 'The Necessity for De-Anglicising Ireland' would suggest, many of these ideas were advanced in this famous essay:

> That is the necessity for encouraging the use of Anglo-Irish literature instead of English books, especially instead of English periodicals. We must set our face sternly against penny dreadfuls, shilling shockers, and still more, the garbage of vulgar English weeklies like *Bow Bells* and the *Police Intelligence*. Every house should have a copy of Moore and Davis . . . We must create a strong feeling against West-Britonism for it . . . will overwhelm us like a flood, and we shall find ourselves toiling painfully behind the English at each step following the same fashions, only six months behind them; taking up the same fads, after they have become stale *there*, following *them* in our dress, literature, music, games, and ideas only a long time after them and a vast way behind. We will become what, I fear we are largely at present, a nation of imitators, the Japanese of Western Europe, lost to the power of native initiative and alive only to second-hand assimilation.[66]

For Hyde, then, English cultural forms had been adopted too readily by the Irish people and their easy transferability had been detrimental to Irish initiative. He was concerned by the absence of cultural innovation in Ireland, which he blamed on the eagerness of the Irish to adopt English customs. One can detect here not only a hostility to 'alien' cultural forms but also a deep-seated opposition to the homogenizing influences of mass culture. In many interesting respects, though, Hyde's thesis was a reiteration of Yeats's critique of Dowden's imitative provincialism, but one that extended the analysis into the realm of popular culture. Whereas Yeats chided Dowden for slavishly following the literary fashions of London to the disadvantage of Irish letters, Hyde rebuked the Irish people for their unthinking embrace of popular British culture and disregard for local cultural forms.

Another consistent critic of the widespread adoption of English customs in Ireland was D. P. Moran, who wrote countless articles and essays for the *New Ireland Review*, *An Claidheamh Soluis* and *The Leader* on this theme. What was significant about Moran's work was his clear identification of English *cultural* influence as a form of dominance. It was his view that British control of Ireland was aided by importing supportive forms of culture from England. He also realized the difficulties faced by a small nation like Ireland in generating its own narratives of cultural meaning in the vicinity of a larger and more powerful offshore imperial presence. One of his earliest expressions of these sentiments was published in an essay entitled 'English literature and Irish Humbug'.[67] Moran expressed the view that the imports were 'demoralising and corrupting, giving us literature which is not real, standards which are false, even in England, and utterly unfitting to the social and intellectual condition of Ireland'. He argued further that no nation can adopt 'the literature of another as its staple mental food' and lamented the fact that Ireland chose to live on 'the dregs of the printed output of another country'.[68] Moran went further than Hyde by identifying such imports as a form of cultural domination directly associated with England's economic control of Ireland:

> Be that as it may, one of the great causes – we meet it whenever we look below the surface of things in Ireland – is an economic one. The English penny and other periodicals supply a home demand of some hundreds of thousands of copies of each publication. The cost of running off an extra ten or twenty thousand for Irish consumption is comparatively infinitesimal. An amount of paper and reading matter – the original of which was heavily paid for – can be sold in Ireland – by London firms for a penny that could not be produced in Ireland for Irish circulation only – at probably threepence. And if a good Irish paper were produced at that price it would be difficult to get 500, not to talk of 20,000, people to pay the price.[69]

Moran's analysis of the poverty of Irish cultural infrastructure identified the relative economies of scale of British publishing and the lack of a reading public in Ireland as central problems.

From an initial suspicion of cheap periodicals and popular literature, the attention of the revivalists was focused on the pernicious influence of English theatre on the Irish stage. As Mary Trotter has observed, 'during the nineteenth century, Dublin theaters provided much of the same dramatic repertoire as that found in England; the Irish city was often a stop on British company tours. Thus, Irish dramas – and stage Irish stereotypes – found themselves on the boards of Dublin's theaters'.[70] Arthur Griffith, in one of the first editions of the *United Irishman*, was quick to criticize these Dublin theatres for hiring English touring companies to put on stage-Irish comedies:

> We think the lessees of the Queen's would be well advised to cease placing such travesties of Irish life on the stage as 'Muldoon's Pic-Nic' which holds the boards this week. The thing is merely pantomic [sic] and as a representation of Irish character beneath contempt. Really it is time that the citizens of Dublin, who after all have these matters in their own hands, made a determined stand against this persistent caricaturing and libelling of their nation.[71]

Unlike Griffith, who was worried by the unpatriotic demeanour of Irish theatre, the Catholic Church was concerned by the forces of immorality that it saw being unleashed there. However, the criticisms of the Church were often couched in the rhetoric of nationalism, with England being invariably identified as the source of evil. In a speech in 1900 on the state of the Dublin stage, the Catholic archbishop of Dublin stated his belief that such evil would 'never really be checked as long as Dublin [was] left dependent for its theatrical representations, as it now is, upon the weekly visits of roving companies of players with their imported plays.'[72] Inghinidhe na hÉireann, led by Maud Gonne, was also explicit in its rejection of English theatrical productions. Although this society for women was set up to encourage the study of Irish literature and to support Irish manufacture, the third and most detailed objective was 'to discourage the reading and circulation of low English literature, the singing of English songs, the attending of vulgar English entertainments at the theatres and music-halls, and to combat in everyway English influence, which is doing so much injury to the artistic taste and refinement of the Irish people'.[73]

What is noteworthy about much of the nationalist sentiment of the 1890s, therefore, is that it was inspired by what would be recognized today as a growing sense of resistance to cultural imperialism, rather than by a positive assertion of a single Irish identity. In fact, on closer examination of the cultural discourse of the time it is easy to pinpoint those forces that are perceived to be threatening native culture, but there is a lack of specificity as to what actually constitutes native culture. This holds true, surprisingly, for Hyde's 'De-Anglicising' essay. Although he lays emphasis on arresting the decay of the Irish language and on securing its position in the education system, Hyde does not provide an unequivocal endorsement of a singular Gaelic identity. In fact, the essay is remarkable for its lack of specificity as he counterpoises the various loose categories 'Anglo-Irish', 'Irish', 'Gaelic' and 'Celtic' with the category 'English' throughout. But what is clear is Hyde's interest in fostering a spirit of cultural innovation in Ireland and his assertion of the right of the Irish nation to produce its own narrative and cultural forms, rather than have them imposed from outside.[74] Likewise, in the work of D. P. Moran there is a palpable uncertainty as to what actually constituted Irish literature. In the essay referred to earlier, he asked '[w]hat is Irish literature and if we are to pay for it where are we to get it?' and conceded that 'we are in a period of rapid transition in regard to this matter'.[75] Again there is a very clear sense of the cultural influences which needed to be combated but uneasiness on the matter of what was actually threatened by them.[76] Even W. B. Yeats, reviewing this period of Irish cultural history, was aware of it as a time of few cultural fixities and many possibilities and remembers contemplating 'how one might seal with the right image the soft wax before it began to harden'.[77]

Much of the cultural criticism of the 1890s, therefore, stemmed from the growing recognition of imported English culture as alien, imperialistic and detrimental to Irish initiative. Yet such an exclusion and disapproval of certain cultural products presupposes the existence of an authentic national culture under threat by the alien influence. However, as we have seen, in the late

1890s what constituted such an 'authentic' national culture was, in many respects, 'yet to be imagined' and was to be severely contested throughout the revival – most vigorously on the stage of the 'national theatre'.[78]

Contrary to Benedict Anderson's theory, it was the theatre rather than the novel that was to play a more crucial role in 'imagining Ireland'. As we have seen, Yeats quite deliberately turned from poetry to drama rather than fiction in the belief that 'in the theatre the mob becomes a people'. This was, perhaps, an astute response to the reality of Ireland's minuscule reading public as much as an appreciation of the nation's distinct oral traditions.[79] With the foundation of the Irish Literary Theatre in 1899, there was a widespread expectation that the new movement would be broadly nationalist in ethos. At last, it was hoped, Ireland would express itself in a way that would depend solely on Irish suffrage. The success of the project would depend on the ability of Irish playwrights and the support of an Irish audience. Unlike Anglo-Irish poetry and fiction up to this point, which was, for the most part, published in Britain for the consumption of a British audience, the new theatre was designed to bolster the nation's impoverished cultural infrastructure and to stimulate intellectual debate at home. Important too was the fact that the English stage had long been very influential in fashioning the negative image of the stage-Irishman. The hope was, therefore, that the new Irish Literary Theatre would play an important part in displacing such a negative image with a more positive representation of the nation.

The Irish Literary Theatre was very much a self-help initiative in that it represented the first serious attempt by a group of Irish artists to consciously replace English cultural imports with a home-grown alternative. Dedicated to performing Irish plays for Irish audiences, the new project was conceived as another attempt to shift the Irish gaze from London to Dublin. The nurturing of new Irish playwrights and later the fostering of an Irish school of acting were central objectives. Like other self-help movements, the Irish Literary Theatre proposed to operate outside the political faction-fighting of unionist and nationalist, Parnellite and anti-Parnellite. In an initial request for financial backing, Yeats, Lady Gregory and Edward Martyn managed to secure cross-community support from figures with such diverse political beliefs as W. E. H. Lecky, Douglas Hyde, J. P. Mahaffy, T. M. Healy, John O'Leary, Lord Castletown and Maud Gonne, among others. The new venture also disrupted Dublin's theatrical *status quo*: when the Abbey Theatre attempted to secure a patent in August 1904, it was the managers of Dublin's commercial theatres who objected. Significantly the patent was secured with the help of Horace Plunkett who saw the theatre as an important anti-emigration agent.[80]

During the first decade of the twentieth century, drama more than any other form dominated Irish cultural discourse and commanded an unprecedented and perhaps unsurpassed level of comment, scrutiny and criticism in the national press.[81] Much of this was occasioned by the inception of the Irish Literary Theatre, which was perhaps one of the first movements to provide, in

any detailed way, a positive assertion of Irish identity in the most explicit manner – on stage. There were high expectations of the new movement: de-Anglicization, moral prudence, high artistic aspirations, Celtic folklore and positive
national image would all compete to be included as governing influences on
the new theatre. These often mutually exclusive forces in Irish society collided
in at least three major controversies during this period – *The Countess Cathleen*
(1899), *The Shadow of the Glen* (1903) and *The Playboy of the Western World*
(1907). Several plays caused minor skirmishes including *Diarmuid and Grania*
(1901) and the *Saxon Shillin'* (1903). Controversy was never far from the surface during this decade and even though the audience was quite small, num-
bering in thousands, these theatrical disagreements became issues of national
importance, with the most minute details of the plays and controversies being
mediated via the national press. In this respect the theatre, by creating such
contested events, became a central arena where notions of national identity
could be fashioned, legitimized and disputed.

The Gaelic League: Modernizing on Irish Terms

The Gaelic League was by no means the first organization to dedicate itself to
the Irish language; however, its foundation does mark a fundamental shift in
attitudes towards the language. 'Precursors of the Gaelic League, such as the
Society for the Preservation of the Irish Language and the Gaelic Union, had
limited, largely preservationary, objectives and made little impact on Irish life.'[82]
These earlier societies tended to be antiquarian, scholarly and concerned with
the collection of the ancient lore of Ireland before its disappearance with the
death of the language. Right from its inception in 1893 the Gaelic League disregarded the basic assumption of the previous societies – that Irish was a dying
language which needed to be documented before its passing – and insisted that
the language could be revived as a means of mass communication in Ireland.
Its aims therefore were 'the preservation of Irish as the national language, its
propagation as a spoken tongue and the cultivation of Gaelic letters'.[83] Not only
did the League place an emphasis on the spoken language for the first time but
it also fostered and encouraged a modern Gaelic literature. Like the theatre
movement, the Gaelic League grew out of the rise in opposition to imported
English culture during the 1890s which, in the words of Hyde, led to Irish
people 'ceasing to be Irish without becoming English'.[84] As a result, one of its
main objectives became the reinvention of the Irish language and its intellectual inheritance as the cornerstone of Irish identity.

   Another important difference between the Gaelic League and previous Irish
language organizations was that the League was a popular movement rather
than an exclusively scholarly one. The aims of the movement were furthered
by setting up small branches at parish level all over the country. These branches
provided informal instruction in the language outside the formal education system, which was hostile to Irish language studies. Although it was founded in

1893, it was not until the turn of the century that the Gaelic League became an important influence on national life. 'By 1897 only 43 branches had been formed, and real progress was made only after 1901. In the following year the number of branches practically doubled to 227 and a similar increase occurred in 1902–3. By 1904 there were almost 600 branches with a total membership of the order of 50,000 people.'[85] As with the theatre movement, there was a lot of support for the League from other movements and sections of Irish society. The Catholic Church, which had been hostile to the language earlier in the nineteenth century, came out in support of it towards the end. Catholic bishops and priests were particularly instrumental in setting up the first branches of the League throughout the country. *An Claidheamh Soluis* of 5 May 1899, for example, offers its 'warmest thanks to his Eminence the Cardinal Primate to their Graces the Archbishops of Dublin and Tuam, and to their Lordships the Bishops of Elphin, Raphoe and Clogher, for their outspoken advocacy of the claims of our ancestral tongue'.[86] However, much of the credit for setting up the nationwide network of branches is due to the League's *Timirí* – voluntary organizers who travelled the country to co-ordinate classes and activities.[87] Their work, in many respects, was analogous to the efforts of co-operative enthusiasts who set up IAOS branches in a similar fashion.

There was also considerable support from the leaders of the theatre movement. Speaking at the inaugural meeting of the Kiltartan branch of the Gaelic League that he attended with Lady Gregory and Edward Martyn, Yeats opined that 'every nation has its own duty in the world, its own message to deliver and the message is to a considerable extent bound up with language'.[88] Notwithstanding his support for the Gaelic League, Yeats was adamant that 'no man can write well except in the language he has been born and bred to'.[89] It was his belief that it was possible to produce Irish literature in the English language and that such a literature had an important role to play in national revival:

> In Ireland, too, it may be those very men, who have made a subtle personal way of expressing themselves, instead of being content with English as it is understood in the newspapers, or who see all things reflected in their own souls, which are from the parent fountain of their race, instead of filling their work with the circumstance of a life which is dominated by England, who may be recognised in the future as being most Irish, though their own time entangled in the surfaces of things may think them lacking in everything that is Irish.[90]

These words turned out to be quite prophetic – especially in relation to Synge – as Irish literature in the English language did indeed prosper and was eventually embraced as part of the national literature, but not, as Yeats alluded, without quite a degree of controversy. This question of whether an Irish literature in the English language was possible would become a major point of contention between elements within the Gaelic League and leading figures within the Irish Literary Theatre.

In many respects the claims of the Gaelic League to be a non-political orga-nization have been widely misunderstood. Certainly the organization remained above party politics from its inception until the historic Dundalk Ard Fhéis of 1915. At that event a resolution was passed calling on the League to work 'to free Ireland from foreign rule'.[91] The organization, at this point, formally came under the sway of Sinn Féin and the IRB, which prompted the resignation of Douglas Hyde as president. Yet the activities of the Gaelic League in the intervening years could hardly be described as 'non-political'. As an organization engaged in the promotion of a language not recognized in law by the British state at a key moment in Ireland's decolonization, its *raison d'être* was, by nature, political. That the League was perceived by the state as a sedi-tious movement is demonstrated by the fact that as early as 1903 'Dublin Cas-tle had identified [it] as a subversive organisation and had begun to keep a file on its activities'.[92]

Like the theatre movement, the Gaelic League organization became an important focal point around which firm notions of Irish identity and the true native culture of Ireland began to crystallize. The Irish language was consid-ered to be the national language, while English was seen as a foreign tongue which had been imposed forcefully through British coercion. This Irish iden-tity was also expressed through traditional music, dance and costume, which were fostered by the League and unequivocally linked to the Gaelic past. The notion that the authentic culture of Ireland was an assimilative Gaelic one that absorbed the influences of the Vikings, the Normans and the English is also directly attributable to the Gaelic League. Clearly this was intended as a response to the British imperial apparatus in Ireland, which worked both to confirm Britain rather than Ireland as the origin of culture and civilization and to deny the moral integrity of forms of indigenous culture. If the Gaelic League's attempt to posit a rival cultural identity did not at this stage embody political separatism, it did foster the belief that Irish problems could only be solved by Irish people with a belief in themselves and their culture rather than by paternalistic British governments. One of the obvious ways it advanced this line was by forcefully aligning itself against the British state's exclusion of the language from public discourse.

As the movement grew throughout the first decade of the new century, so too did its ambition and influence. Broadly speaking, the League concerned itself with fashioning change within three general spheres of influence during this period. Firstly, there was a concerted attempt to dismantle many of the state biases against the Irish language that were built into the education and legal systems. Secondly, the Gaelic League became a major source of influence on Irish education policy. Although it began modestly outside the official edu-cation system providing adult classes on an informal basis, the League quickly focused its attention on securing a central position for the Irish language within that system. Thirdly, within the realm of cultural discourse the League became active in promoting the idea that the only true Irish literature was a

Gaelic literature.[93] In vigorously pursuing these aims it is hardly surprising that the organization became embroiled in many controversies in its heyday between 1899 and 1909. During this time the League crossed swords with three formidable opponents: the British administration and supportive institutions (the Post Office, the legal system, TCD); the Irish Literary Theatre, which some elements within the League considered to be promoting a rival conception of Irish literature; and the Catholic Church, which wanted to retain its dominant influence over education policy and to promote the Catholic religion, rather than the Irish language, as the central badge of Irish identity.

The first major controversy was occasioned by the Vice-Regal Inquiry into Irish and Intermediate Education in 1899. During the proceedings, the merits of the Irish language and literature were dismissed by the Trinity College academics Mahaffy and Atkinson. The language was stoutly defended by Hyde, among others, who won a decisive moral victory. However, the role that Irish was to play in the education system was to be hotly contested for the rest of the decade. Over the next few years the organization went on to challenge other state and institutional biases against the language.[94] In a matter of months after the Atkinson/Mahaffy affair, the Gaelic League found itself at odds with the fledgling Irish Literary Theatre over its inaugural production, *The Countess Cathleen*. The objections of the League were not based on moral or artistic bases but on the grounds that this so-called national theatre was conducted through the medium of English. As an event, *The Countess Cathleen* affair had quite an influence on the Gaelic League. It was largely in response to it that the organization began to articulate more clearly its own ideas on Irish literature in a series of editorials and articles which ran for up to two months afterwards.

The first sign of tension between the Gaelic League and the Catholic Church manifested itself in 1902 when 'An Claidheamh Soluis attacked priests for their reluctance to allow Irish to be taught. For example, it named Father White of Arainn, who had told his parishioners to speak to him in English if they wanted him.'[95] Later, in 1905, a distinctly local dispute betrayed underlying tensions between the two groups and developed into a national issue. The parish priest of Portarlington, preaching in church, was vigorous in his condemnation of the mixed-sex classes organized by the League. 'A public protest in church, the expulsion of the parish priest and curate from the League, the foundation in the neighbourhood of a rival, clerically-controlled, branch of the League, an appeal to the local bishop all led ultimately to accusations of anti-clericalism against the League executive.'[96] This episode illustrated very clearly the threat felt by the Catholic Church from the Gaelic League. The language revival movement, after all, was one of the first nationally organized groupings outside the Catholic Church to exercise considerable control over social intercourse. It is hardly surprising, then, that the Catholic hierarchy should make a concerted attempt to graft their moral concerns onto the language revival project.

Despite such attempts to link the Church and the language movement, a bitter row was to be fought between the Catholic hierarchy and the Gaelic League in 1908 – the year of the foundation of the National University of Ireland (NUI). Although this row was caused by differing views of what the position of the Irish language in the new university should be, at another level it was a struggle to determine whether the Irish language or the Catholic religion were to be the most important markers of national identity. Also at issue was the matter of which group could exercise most control over education policy. The League's position was that Irish should be made compulsory[97] for matriculation to the NUI as a strategy for reversing the decline of the language. Douglas Hyde was one of the leading exponents of compulsory Irish:

> I believe that as the Irish language did not die naturally but was killed by force, so a little gentle pressure is necessary for its restoration. I am persuaded that nothing less than the national language essential [sic] in the national university can convince the Irish-speaking population that they really and truly possess in their language a great asset of the highest national importance and that nothing short of this will bring home to the mind of the Gaelic Irishman that after 300 or 400 years of oppression he is at last ceasing to be the underdog in Ireland. I firmly believe that until he loses the sense of inferiority that has been so long and so sedulously impressed upon him that the Irish nation can neither thrive nor prosper.[98]

The Catholic hierarchy, on the other hand, opposed mandatory Irish on the basis that Catholic students without Irish would have no other option but to go to the 'apostate' Trinity College. On the surface this was a debate about education policy; however, at a deeper level this was a dispute about the fundamentals of national identity. Central to this dispute was Father Michael O'Hickey,[99] professor of Irish at St Patrick's College, Maynooth. O'Hickey was brave enough to support compulsory Irish against the wishes of the hierarchy and was dismissed from his chair for his trouble. The decision to sack O'Hickey deepened the controversy, which culminated in a mass demonstration of 100,000 people packing the streets of Dublin in support of the professor of Irish. Nine months later, in June 1910, the senate of the NUI decided that Irish would be compulsory for matriculation from 1913 onwards.

Although the Gaelic League professed to revive the ancient Irish tongue and traditional Irish cultural practices, the movement was, curiously, a modernizing force in Irish cultural life. Its attempt to construct a Gaelic national identity was, in theory, posited on a rigidly fixed notion of the pre-colonial Gaelic past, which precluded the idea that all cultures are essentially dynamic. As Tomlinson puts it: 'how we live is never a "static" set of circumstances, but always something in flux, in process'.[100] In practice, however, the League's activities embodied a perfect example of such cultural flux. Many of the rediscovered 'traditions', while appearing to be well established practices reaching back to the immemorial past, were, at best, loosely based on earlier customs and, at worst, really of recent origin. Paradoxically, then, the process of reviving 'ancient' cultural practices was always already complicit in a process of modernization. In this respect a 'revived' practice such as the Oireachtas,[101] although very loosely based on ancient cultural festivals, was, in practice, a modern cultural phenomenon not unlike the Irish Literary Theatre. If the aim of the Irish theatre movement was to foster playwriting and acting, the Oireachtas encouraged playwriting in Irish, traditional music and dance, singing and storytelling. By setting out elaborate rules for these practices, it also codified and standardized them. Compounding the paradox was the fact that the League's main activity – reviving the ancient language – was also dependent on a programme of standardizing and modernizing it.[102]

However, rather than seeing these 'new traditional practices' as fraudulent or bogus, it is possible to view them as examples of an alternative modernization process that was informed by a belief in the dormant potential within pre-colonial Irish cultural forms. Kevin Whelan describes this process as 'the creation of an Irish radical memory that sought to escape the baneful binary of modernisation and tradition – the Hegelian view that all that is lost to history is well lost'. This stands in contrast to colonial modes of development, which invariably configured tradition as a direct antithesis to modernity. 'By contrast, radical memory deployed the past to challenge the present, to restore into possibility historical moments that had been blocked or unfulfilled earlier.'[103] Far from being a hopelessly nostalgic movement, therefore, the Gaelic League actively concerned itself with the material problems of the Irish nation and recognized a link between the language revival and the regeneration of the Irish economy. To this end it instituted its own industrial committees, whose members included Arthur Griffith, W. P. Ryan and George Russell. Furthermore, the pages of *An Claidheamh Soluis* were frequently used to drum up support for 'native manufactures' and to advance the argument that there was a link between the decline of the language and the loss of industry in rural Ireland in the nineteenth century.[104] At times the campaign for Irish industry was pursued to the point of absurdity: in 1901 a directive was passed ordering that no prize be awarded to a competitor in the Oireachtas unless they were dressed in clothes of Irish manufacture. Directives like these betrayed the middle-class tendencies of the Gaelic League, which became a source of irritation for socialists like James Connolly and Sean O'Casey – both Irish language enthusiasts. Notwithstanding the Gaelic League's blind spot in relation to class, it was a modernizing force within Irish society during the Revival. Yet, crucially, its programme for development was, for the most part, informed by a desire to follow an alternative path to modernization – on Irish terms.

Ireland in the New Century: The Irish Agricultural
Organisation Society

The Irish Agricultural Organisation Society was founded by Horace Plunkett in 1894. Just as Yeats's literary societies aimed to mobilize the factors of cultural production to improve the intellectual condition of the nation, so Plunkett's co-operative movement was founded to better the material circumstances of the emerging class of small farmers. Although a unionist MP for eight years, Plunkett was very much a maverick figure who was often out of step with conventional parliamentary politics.[105] In fact his own party, threatened by his radical co-operative proposals, ran a candidate against him in the general election of 1900, thus forfeiting the seat to the nationalist candidate.[106] Like Yeats and Hyde, therefore, he had no qualms about turning his back on his ascendancy elders or the interests of his own class in the cause of national revival. As Trevor West has noted:

> Yeats shared with Plunkett a belief that the explosion of pent-up energy released by the fall of Parnell heralded a regeneration in Irish cultural and economic life, but shared adversity was also a bond between them. The Parliamentary Party and the Trinity College establishment were among their common enemies and Yeats crossed swords with the two men [Dowden and Ardilaun] who spearheaded the opposition to Plunkett in the South Dublin election of 1900.[107]

At this time the position of Irish tenant farmers had improved considerably, thanks to a sequence of land acts which was transforming a country of tenant farmers into one of landowners within the short span of thirty years.[108] With the settling of the land question, attention was now focused on how the land would be used. This was an issue that Plunkett became deeply involved in and over which he was to have a profound influence during the course of the coming decade. Having been a member of the government-sponsored Congested Districts Board, Plunkett was unhappy with its paternalistic ethos and believed strongly that the problems of rural Ireland could only be solved by encouraging self-help. Although the majority of Irish farmers now enjoyed fixity of tenure, most of them lacked the expertise to compete in an increasingly sophisticated and mechanized agricultural market. For this reason the IAOS was set up to educate farmers in modern agricultural practices and to encourage them to benefit from economies of scale by forming co-operative societies and credit unions. In this way they could break the economic stranglehold of the shopkeepers, who, particularly in the congested districts, were not only the main suppliers of consumer items and the only buyers of many home-produced goods, but were also engaged in usurious money-lending practices. These 'gombeen men' were notoriously dishonest in their business dealings and wielded considerable power in rural Ireland. As George Russell memorably wrote:

In congested Ireland every job which can be filled by the kith and kin of the
gombeen kings and queens is filled accordingly and you get every kind of inef-
ficiency and jobbery. They are all publicans, and their friends are all strong
drinkers. They beget people of their own character and appoint them lieu-
tenants and non-commissioned officers in their service. All the local appoint-
ments are in their gift, and hence you get drunken doctors, drunken rate
collectors, drunken JPs, drunken inspectors – in fact, round the gombeen system reels the whole drunken congested world.[109]

Despite opposition from conservative nationalism and unionism alike, the
co-operative movement spread rapidly – within twenty years 1,023 co-operative societies had been founded all over the country. The rapid success of the
movement may be partly explained by the fact that 'the land agitation had given
[Irish tenant farmers] the habit of combining and had familiarized at least some
of them with the working of committees'.[110] Another important factor was that
the IAOS, like the other movements examined, professed to operate outside
party politics. This is evidenced by the eclectic team of organizers assembled
by Plunkett. Senior figures in the movement included: Fr Tom Finlay, the Jesuit
economist and philosopher; the poet and mystic, George Russell; T. P. Gill, a
former landleaguer; and R. A. Anderson, a skilled administrator. Notwithstanding the movement's strategic disavowal of conventional politics, however,
there can be no doubt that it was the agent of profound material change, bor-
dering on the revolutionary.

Plunkett, too, taking a lead from Yeats and Hyde, was firm in the belief that
Ireland could only recover economically if it was culturally self-assured. To this
end he endorsed and repeatedly drew attention to the work of the Gaelic
League and lent his support to the theatre movement.[111] He also employed the
services of the poet George Russell in the cause of agricultural co-operation.
Russell was, in many respects, an archetypal revivalist figure, who, at once,
embraced the literary mystique of Celtic Ireland and worked to advance the co-
operative ethos as editor of the *Irish Homestead*. The IAOS, therefore, had a significant cultural dimension to its activities, both in the sense of wanting to
change the home and social life of the rural Irish peasantry and to encourage
their intellectual and artistic development. Significantly though, Plunkett's
modernization programme was informed by a desire to embrace and encourage traditional cultural practices. 'There is in the Irish mind today', he wrote, 'a
yearning for a national life and dignity which the Irish believe existed long ago,
and which they know has not existed, at any rate for centuries'. 'It is remarkable', he added, 'that in all my work having a purely agricultural aim, my
friends and I succeeded by appealing to those old national instincts'.[112] Once
again the revival's alternative modernity, in which agricultural development and
traditional culture are not cast as mutually exclusive terms, is clearly in evidence. Although drawing heavily on the thinking and experiments of Robert
Owen and William Thompson, the success of Plunkett's co-operative idea in

Ireland may, in some measure, be explained by its contiguity to the pre-existing practices of 'meitheal' in rural areas. Writing in 1904 about the new co-operatives, Padraic Colum noted that 'mutual aid was once a great factor in the social and economic life of the Irish cottage' and that the tradition 'still survives in mahils [sic] for outdoor work that needs many hands'.[113]

The idea that the 'defeat' of the landlords and the transfer of land to tenants marked the beginning of a new Irish civilization was quite a radical one for a member of the ascendancy to espouse, nevertheless it was enthusiastically promoted by Plunkett and Russell as they spread the gospel of co-operation:

> But all fine civilisations begin at the bottom and not at the top, at the cottage and not at the castle. The Greek temples, we are told, were glorified expansions of the huts of the primitive herdsmen, and the Pyramids repeat the outline of the Arab's tent. Whatever worth or beauty there is in the final splendid display is a repetition of qualities which have their birth and exit close to the earth. To have an Irish civilisation worthy of the name, we must begin at the cottage, and build round and about and evolve from its life, its necessities and desires, a civilisation of national character which will suit us, which we can be proud of, and which will make us respected among other races.[114]

This was quite a progressive model of cultural development for its time, which would contrast sharply with Yeats's later view that a healthy peasant society is best achieved through the patronage and example of the aristocracy, rather than the other way around. The extent to which the co-operative movement worked to transform the cultural practices of rural Ireland 'from the cottage up' is neatly illustrated by the following description of the prize-winning achievements of the Dromahair society in County Leitrim in 1901:[115]

> Lectures were delivered on such subjects as poultry, horticulture, veterinary science, domestic economy, bee-keeping, electricity and elementary science, with magic lantern entertainments after every lecture. They encouraged the attendance at night schools by offering prizes . . . A farmers' circulating library was established, and scores of books were sold as well at cost prices. Hundreds of fruit trees and flowering shrubs were distributed free to school children to encourage cottage gardening and good attendance at schools. A parish *feis ceoil* (music festival) was held, a concert and cinematograph exhibition. Two temperance societies were formed; a cattle show was held, and also spinning contests and athletic sports; loom and home spinning were revived together with horse-hair and fish-scale work; a stall was obtained at the Cork Exhibition for the display of cottage industries; a crusade was directed against badly-kept homesteads, hundreds of white and purple lilacs, laburnums, rose trees and other flowering shrubs were sold at cost price and others distributed free . . . This is an amazing record of social activity in a poor country parish.[116]

In many respects, therefore, the co-operative societies, with the help of the *Irish Homestead*, provided an extensive cultural infrastructure through which revivalist initiatives could be transmitted to a mass audience. Once again, the key revivalist aim of making Ireland a place of innovation rather than passive cultural consumption was paramount.

The IAOS also concerned itself with the intellectual and artistic development of rural areas on a macro-scale. 'With the assistance of the Carnegie Trust Plunkett established village libraries all over Ireland.'[117] The *Irish Homestead* too was influential in this respect, devoting space to new Irish writing and book reviews. In this remarkable publication it was not uncommon to see a poem by Yeats or a short story by James Joyce published side by side with an article on fertilizers or foot-and-mouth disease. From December 1897 the *Homestead* published a special literary Christmas number, with contributions by W. B. Yeats, Douglas Hyde, Emily Lawless, Standish O'Grady, Nora Hopper, J. B. Yeats, Edith Somerville, Padraic Colum and Lady Gregory, among others. The aim of this initiative was 'to illustrate the sympathy between these two "streams of tendency" in Ireland, the economic and the spiritual'.[118] Joyce was just one of numerous budding Irish writers to grace the pages of the *Homestead*. In commissioning Joyce's story, 'The Sisters', for the co-op journal, George Russell prompted what was to become the opening story of *Dubliners*.

There was an acute awareness, therefore, within the IAOS that the 'defeated' landlord class as the self-appointed 'bearers of culture' had to be replaced by promoting cultural activity in the small towns and villages of Ireland:

> We think libraries of general literature will supply the lack in the present system of national education, and by awakening a general all-round intelligence, make people far more receptive of the ideas on special subjects inculcated by lecturers and instructors under the country scheme. Even apart from this it is of the greatest importance that the farmers in Ireland should have a culture suited to their class. Culture of some kind we must have in a country or it becomes barbarous, and the standard of life, morals and civilisation sinks lower and lower. When land purchase has been completed, and the great families, who, however inadequately, kept up the tradition of a cultured class in Ireland, are gone, as they will go for the most part, for families with wealth untied by local possessions will inevitably gravitate to other countries – what kind of country will it be from the intellectual point of view?[119]

There was a strong belief within the organization that a new era had begun for Ireland, with the decline of landlordism and the emergence of the small farmer. How this new society should articulate itself culturally was a question of the utmost importance to the co-operative movement.

Given the radical interventions of the IAOS, it is inevitable that the movement would become embroiled in disputes and controversies. There was tension between Plunkett's Department of Agriculture and Technical Instruction and the Catholic Church when the former revealed its plans to introduce a secular system of technical education, but this was defused on the intervention of William Walsh, Catholic archbishop of Dublin. It was Plunkett's *Ire-*

land in the New Century, however, which ensnared the author and the IAOS in a storm of protest when the book was published in 1904. Ostensibly an apologia for the self-help movements, his analysis was an 'attempt to argue that the Irish problem was neither political, nor economic, nor religious but primarily a matter of character'.[120] The book made many references to defects in the Irish disposition, but, not surprisingly, it was his section on religion and the churches which caused the greatest uproar:

> I have learned from practical experience amongst the Roman Catholic people of Ireland that, while more free from bigotry, in the sense in which that word is generally applied, they are apathetic, thriftless, and almost non-industrial, and that they especially require the exercise of strengthening influences on their moral fibre.[121]

These comments overshadowed Plunkett's trenchant critique of the history of British misrule, of Protestant bigotry, of the political parties for their lack of constructive thought, of the educational authorities for their neglect of technical instruction and of Trinity College for contributing little to economic thought. Many influential figures took part, including Cardinal Logue and Monsignor Michael O'Riordan, who was prompted to reply to Plunkett in a book entitled *Catholicity and Progress in Ireland* (1905). Ultimately this affair caused considerable damage to the IAOS and led to Horace Plunkett's disengagement from the movement for a number of years.

It is hard not to object to the overtly sectarian terms within which Plunkett configured the Irish problem in this small passage of a quite substantial book. As Trevor West has noted, 'for a member of the ascendancy (however lukewarm his own religious affiliation) to cast aspersions on Irish Catholicism was . . . an unforgivable sin. Unfortunately the furious reaction completely overshadowed the author's incisive commentary on Irish affairs . . . and his blueprint for Ireland's future.'[122] On balance, however, Plunkett's diagnosis of Irish ills was progressive, if somewhat unconventional. His central argument held that Ireland's problems stemmed from a lack of independent thought and self-reliance and he pointedly contrasted the moral timidity of nationalist Ireland with its physical courage. The solution lay, he argued, in a project that would change Ireland's material condition but not one motivated solely by individual gain – hence the emphasis on co-operation and collective self-help. The co-operative movement was, after all, intent on mitigating the exploitative practices of naked capitalism associated with the gombeen class of publican-shopkeepers. James Connolly, for one, saw in it an Irish socialist republic in embryo.[123] It is hardly surprising, therefore, that the movement was viewed suspiciously by the Catholic hierarchy, middle-class nationalism and the unionist establishment.

Ireland Awakes

On 14 May 1901 George Russell wrote to congratulate his friend Charles
Weekes, then living in London, on his recent marriage. Russell was keen for
his friend to return to Ireland to witness the great changes that were taking
place there:

> Surely you have heard rumours even in London that Ireland is growing alive
> steadily, with immense waves of new ideas, Gaelic Leagues, Literary Theatres,
> music, art even business – the spirit of business – has opened a sleepy eye after
> long slumber, and won't be allowed to go asleep again.[124]

The poet and co-op organizer was quite accurate in his appraisal of the extraordinary revival that was taking place in Ireland at the turn of the century, both
among the nation's leading intellectuals and at grassroots parish level. One of
the most remarkable features of this period is the extent to which the dynamic
energies of a loosely aligned self-help revivalism emerged as an alternative
sphere of influence to the realm of crisis-ridden parliamentary politics. All of
the movements examined here professed to operate outside the concerns of
party politics, yet, in their joint concern to turn Ireland into a centre of both
cultural *and* material innovation again, their activities were inherently political and played an important role in Irish decolonization. Furthermore, the theatre movement, the Gaelic League and the IAOS were at one in their strategies
of revival. All of these groups subscribed to a variant programme of development in which traditional cultural forms were considered central to progress
rather than anathema to it. As a result of the traffic between grassroots movements like the Gaelic League and the IAOS and radical intellectuals such as W.
B. Yeats, Horace Plunkett, Lady Gregory, George Russell, Tom Finlay and Douglas Hyde, the self-help revival succeeded in effecting a quasi-revolutionary
influence on the cultural, economic and social practices of Ireland at the turn
of the century.

GAEL, CATHOLIC, CELT OR COMRADE?
The Countess Cathleen and the Battle for Irish Identity

Representing Ireland

Any student of Irish cultural history will be aware that the first decade of the twentieth century was marked by an intense and at times heated debate over attempts to define the essential nature of Irish identity. Interestingly enough, it was on the stage that the debate became most animated as objections to plays such as Yeats's *The Countess Cathleen* (1899) and Synge's *The Shadow of the Glen* (1903) and *The Playboy of the Western World* (1907) bubbled to the surface. Undoubtedly much of the criticism directed at these plays was due to an anxiety within sections of nationalist Ireland to display the inherent morality of Irish culture in the face of colonial stereotypes. Yet in many ways this need for the projection of an idealized Ireland was to prove as disabling as the racial slurs. What is little appreciated, however, is that these anxieties of representation, ever-present in the first decade of the theatre movement, were prefigured and to some degree precipitated by one of the most important, though largely forgotten, controversies in modern Irish history – the Irish language controversy of 1899.

The Mahaffy/Atkinson affair (as it has come to be known) marks a crucial moment in the development of the Gaelic League in that it galvanized national support for the organization for the first time. More significantly, this controversy represents both a watershed in the breakdown of colonial sanction over cultural value in Ireland, and the inauguration of a new nationalist phase of cultural and intellectual authority. Interestingly, the defeat of the old ascendancy hegemony also initiated a struggle *within* nationalism over the formulation and legitimization of representations of national identity. This contest over the right to sanction images of Ireland would be precipitated by the opening production of the Irish Literary Theatre in May 1899.

'I Would Not Allow Any Daughter of Mine to Study It': The Irish Language Controversy of 1899

Four months before *The Countess Cathleen* and *The Heather Field* inaugurated the Irish Literary Theatre, a row was developing that would place the Gaelic

35

League in the spotlight as a major national institution for the first time. The occasion was the Vice-Regal Inquiry into Irish and Intermediate Education, which sat from 11 January to 23 February 1899 to examine the state of secondary education in Ireland. The Gaelic League, which was eager to influence the state education system to achieve its objectives, looked on this as the perfect opportunity to improve the status of Irish in the curriculum. Indeed 'it became a primary objective of the League to ensure that the teaching of Irish would find a place in the normal educational system of the country, at both primary and secondary level, and if possible at university level as well'.[1] Although Irish had been smuggled into the system as an optional subject under the less offensive title 'Celtic' in 1878, it was only allotted 600 marks (500 in first year), compared to 700 for French and German and 1,200 for Greek, Latin and English – a schema which reflected the priorities of the colonial state. In this regime the adoption of Irish 'as a subject for examination or for scoring marks in, was distinctly and strongly discouraged, rendering its study almost impracticable'.[2] The modest hope of the Gaelic League was that Irish should attain a position 'intermediate between that of English and other Modern Languages'.[3]

The Anglo-Irish élite of Trinity College, however, had other ideas. Clearly upset by the concessions being made to nationalists by a conciliatory British government, they felt the threat of a better educated, more culturally aware and self-confident nationalist population, advancing materially and, moreover, with the active support of some of the most talented of a new generation of Anglo-Irish intellectuals, including W. B. Yeats, George Russell, Lady Gregory, Horace Plunkett and Douglas Hyde. Any attempt to legitimize the Irish language was undoubtedly perceived as threatening to their position. But just as the Gaelic League was emerging as a significant force in the revision of the imperial narrative of Irish cultural barbarism by restoring interest in Irish as a language of culture, senior academics in Trinity College were beginning a vicious attack on the language and its literature. They seized on the Vice-Regal Inquiry as an opportunity to remove Irish from the education system once and for all. The ensuing controversy led to one of the most significant battles in Irish academic history and embroiled many of the country's leading intellects in heated dispute.

The opening shots in this row were fired by Dr John Pentland Mahaffy, Professor of Ancient History at Trinity College. A former tutor to Oscar Wilde, he had made his antipathy to the Irish language well known before 1899. In an essay on education in Hungary published in 1882, he had included the remark: 'we are to be much congratulated that in Ireland the national system [of primary education] ignored Celtic, and this tended strongly to the destruction of that equally out-of-the-way and troublesome language'.[4] Now, before the Vice-Regal commission, he elaborated on his ideas with the self-confidence of an academic well accustomed to influencing public opinion. However, it was his tone of smug self-assuredness as much as the content of his remarks that caused so much offence. When asked if Irish had any educational value as a living language, Mahaffy candidly replied, 'None', and proceeded to speak of Irish literature as 'silly [and] indecent'. Pushed to outline a positive aspect of the language he stated sardonically, 'It is sometimes useful to a man fishing for salmon or shooting grouse in the west. I have often found a few words very serviceable.'[5] Finally he confessed that he would be pleased if the board diminished the marks for Irish and admitted that he would not 'fret over' the death of the language.

Needless to say, Mahaffy's testimony enraged Irish language enthusiasts. George Russell was later to denounce him as a 'blockhead of a professor drawn from the intellectual obscurity of Trinity and appointed as a commissioner to train the national mind according to British ideals'.[6] But it was Douglas Hyde who stepped in as the most competent and best-informed defender of the language. As president of the Gaelic League, translator of Irish poetry and folklore and author of the soon to be published *Literary History of Ireland* (November 1899), Hyde was well placed to put forward the virtues of Irish as a worthy subject of intermediate education. If Mahaffy's rejection of Irish depended to a large extent on a cavalier dismissal, Hyde's apology was well argued, scholarly, backed by respected opinion and clearly infused with the zealousness of an enthusiast.[7] His strategy was to argue for the revival of Irish as a living language that was vital to the process of national regeneration. In his evidence he noted the propensity of the peasantry to defer to figures in authority. He attributed this to their perception of traditional cultural forms as inferior when confronted with more dominant metropolitan forms, rather than to priestly domination, as another Trinity academic and future Provost, Anthony Traill, had argued elsewhere.[8] Hyde himself had experienced this at first hand:

> We found, wherever we went, and we went over about ten or eleven counties of Ireland, whenever we entered a house, the parents speaking one language and the children speaking another. We found that if you addressed the children in their parents' language they hung their heads for shame, and they slunk out of the cabin like whipped hounds, as if you had pointed [out] some blot on the escutcheon, or some crime that they had been guilty of.[9]

Placing a value on the Irish language through the education system would, in Hyde's view, go a long way towards getting over this self hatred, and would engender a capacity for self-reliance in the Irish people. Hyde was careful to point out that it was in the 'national' interest to encourage Irish, but 'national' in 'a non-political sense'.[10] Just as the Catholic Church had promised the British that a legitimate expression of Catholicism would mollify the patriotic vigour of the Irish, so too the Gaelic League officially put forward the language for similar reasons.

Hyde's defence of Irish, therefore, revolved around its acceptance as a living language with an important literature which had a fundamental role to play in the revival of the nation. To avoid charges of provincialism, the Gaelic League

president recruited the opinions of some of the most respected scholars in
Europe with an interest in Irish studies including: York Powell, regius professor
of history at Oxford; Dr Ernest Windisch of Leipsic and Professor Zimmer of
Griefswald – 'two of the greatest Celticists in Europe'; Dr Kuno Meyer of Liverpool, editor of *Celtische Philologie;* Dr Stern of Berlin; Dr Holger Pedersen of
Copenhagen; and Alfred Nutt, 'one of the greatest living authorities on folk-lore'
[*sic*].[11] Before closing his argument, Hyde pointed out that Mahaffy was not an
authority on the Irish language and had based his remarks on the opinion of an
expert. This expert, Dr Robert Atkinson (professor of Sanskrit and comparative
philology at Trinity College), was unexpectedly called to give evidence before
the commission and succeeded in turning a heated exchange of views into a full-
blown national controversy. Atkinson and Hyde had had acrimonious dealings
in the past. In March 1896 Hyde had applied for a professorship of Irish at Trinity College, being confident that his work in the field would make him a strong
candidate for the position in his *alma mater*. His application was opposed, however, by Provost Salmon and Robert Atkinson. Salmon objected on the basis that
'Hyde's chief interests were known to be political rather than philological'. Atkinson's opposition was more circumspect: 'He knew nothing whatever of Hyde's
political position, he maintained, but the language Hyde spoke was simply
"baboon Irish", not anything that could be taught in a classroom.'[12]

In the battle between Mahaffy and Hyde, the Irish scholar had come out
the clear winner. Atkinson, however, was hastily summoned to strengthen the
anti-Irish case.[13] His role was to debunk the Irish language and its literature
as a subject unworthy of study except from a philological point of view. That
Atkinson was a philologist is worth noting. As Edward Said has pointed out,[14]
language and race are inextricably linked in this discipline, which emerged at
the end of the eighteenth century in response to the needs of European imperialism. In its concern with comparative grammar and the reclassification of
languages into families, philology effectively placed the practitioner in the role
of 'harsh divider of men into superior and inferior races'.[15] In this way the
respectability of an academic discipline could be used to support a colonial
agenda. Atkinson was no exception and used philology to implicitly support
English interests in Ireland. He attacked Irish on the basis that it was not 'in a
settled state' – that it had not yet evolved a standard of speech that was
accepted by everybody. Furthermore, he contrasted it with Greek and Latin,
which had 'perfectly definite spelling, definite declensions, definite form, a
definite syntax',[16] whereas Irish, in his opinion, did not. Atkinson, therefore,
chose to categorize Irish as a *patois* rather than a language. But what he failed
to admit was that such was the case with all European vernaculars until the
process of print-capitalism transformed them. As Benedict Anderson has
pointed out, it was print-capitalism that 'gave a new fixity to language'.[17] English, having been transformed by print-capitalism, was standardized and
emerged as a metropolitan 'language of power', while Irish as a language of the
colonized periphery never made it into print and as a result never underwent

the process of modern standardization.[18] Much of the work of the Gaelic League was an attempt to drag the Irish language into the era of print-capitalism by publishing newspapers and encouraging literature, particularly fiction, in Irish. Hence the confusion and squabbling over the standardization of the language, a process which needed to be accelerated to ensure the survival of Irish in the modern world.[19]

Having written off the language as a *patois*, Atkinson continued his attack by recourse to the well-worn colonial strategy of pointing out the fundamental immorality of Irish literature. *Tóraíocht Dhiarmada agus Gráinne* was, he said, 'not fit for children', and he admitted that he 'would allow no daughter of [his] of any age to see it'. He refused to offer the commission any examples of this 'intolerably low'[20] literature, but did offer to verify his opinions at the convenience of the commission:

> Now, all I can say is that no human being could read through that book, containing an immense quantity of Irish matter, without feeling that he had been absolutely degraded by contact with it – filth that I will not demean myself even to mention. Instances, no doubt, are not numerous in it, but they are there; and if you will call at any time upon me in my rooms, I will show you them.[21]

He continued by pouring scorn on one of the main enthusiasms of the literary revival – folklore – making a link between Irish culture and that of another British colony:

> All folk-lore [sic] is at the bottom abominable. You have to send your children back from India, not solely because of their health, but because the language of the people in the streets is at times so defiling in its nature that they cannot be allowed to hear it. I know what folk-lore is, and I would not allow any daughter of mine to study it . . . I have asked our Irish speakers 'Won't you translate "Robinson Crusoe", or some book of that kind, and let the people have something that they can read?' but they will not do it.[22]

For Professor Atkinson, then, the content of the Irish language was as offensive as its form.

Hyde, not surprisingly, was infuriated by Atkinson's submission and forwarded a written statement to address in detail the outrageous claims made by the professor. With regard to the charge that the language was in an 'unsettled state', Hyde countered by deflating the pretensions of standard English. Quite perceptively he pointed out that the English spoken in England was every bit as 'unsettled', containing as it did 'many different patois'. He recalled hearing people speaking in Yorkshire who 'would have been absolutely unintelligible to an American, an Australian, an Irishman, or a Londoner'.[23] Since England was a larger country than Ireland, remarked Hyde, 'the differences of the dialects spoken over its area are far and away greater than any that exist in Ireland'.[24] In many respects, then, Hyde exposed the hidden assumption behind Atkinson's attack – that English was an inherently regular, and therefore superior, language, while Irish was without structure and worthless. Although he does not state it outright, one can detect in his analysis an awareness of an English folk tradition that was also being repressed by the standard English of the centralized imperial state.

The Gaelic League president was equally robust in his defence of Irish literature. Taking the example of Standish Hayes O'Grady's *Silva Gadelica*, one of the books attacked on moral grounds by Atkinson, Hyde argued that '[i]f anyone could feel degraded by coming into contact with "Silva Gadelica", that person would feel degraded by coming into contact with the Bible'.[25] Having succeeded in portraying the Trinity professor as a hyper-sensitive Victorian moralist,[26] Hyde went on to attack his ego. He quoted from a letter from Dr Pedersen in which the Danish academic attacked Atkinson's 'intolerable boasting, his speaking with the utmost contempt about everyone and everything in the world except himself, [and] his manifest tendency to try to crush us all under the weight of his authority'.[27]

In the weeks following Atkinson's evidence to the commission, a huge body of opinion built up against the Trinity professors. Not surprisingly the Gaelic League newspaper reacted angrily. In its first ever editorial, *An Claidheamh Soluis* represented the controversy as a battle between the Anglo-Irish dominated Trinity College and the Irish people:

> It is the worst attack ever made on the whole Irish race, on all Irish thought, on the genius of the people. It stamps the race as gross, and lacking in creative and imaginative power, it deprives us of our inheritance, our past. It says, in effect, the thoughts and deeds of the Irish people for over a thousand years are not worth the reading.[28]

What incensed the Gaelic League was the attempt by Atkinson and Mahaffy to downgrade and discredit the native Irish cultural inheritance as immoral and worthless at a time when they were trying to rekindle interest in it.

Gaelic scholars in sympathy with Hyde's position subjected Atkinson's work in the field of Irish studies to the most detailed scrutiny and found it alarmingly wanting. In a lively series of articles in *An Claidheamh Soluis* entitled 'The Dismal Swamp', an tAthair Peadar Ó Laoghaire examined Atkinson's treatment of the Irish verb *is* in his edition of Keating's *Trí Bior-Ghaoithe an Bháis* and found it amazingly faulty for an Irish scholar. In fact the only few sentences which 'he had penned in Irish were shown to be abominable'.[29] He was also embarrassed by the publication of earlier pronouncements of his which praised the merits of Irish literature. Dr Michael O'Hickey, professor of Irish at Maynooth, further highlighted Atkinson's spurious knowledge of the language, remarking that 'it would be difficult to find anywhere a more slip-shod or misleading piece of grammatical work than his treatment of the so-called Infinitive in the Appendix to the "Three Shafts of Death"'.[30] In the end, however, the Gaelic League won a modest victory, as Irish was given an improved status in the education act of 1900 subsequent to the Vice-Regal Inquiry of the previous year. This had an almost immediate effect on the numbers of students presenting for the intermediate Irish exam: between 1899 and 1902 the numbers trebled; in 1904, 30 per cent of students took the Irish exam; and by 1908 the figure had risen to 50 per cent.[31]

In many respects, one can see in the Irish language controversy of 1899 many interesting parallels with the Yeats–Dowden debate over the importance of encouraging Irish writing, with Hyde and Atkinson occupying the positions of chief protagonists in this instance. In both cases, emerging Anglo-Irish intellectuals chided senior ascendancy academics over their colonial disdain for matters Irish. Yeats himself, who believed that 'a writer or public man of the upper classes is useless to this country till he has done something that separates him from his class',[32] was quick to come to Hyde's defence. In an important essay, 'The Academic Class and the Agrarian Revolution', he rightly located the source of Atkinson's prejudice in recent political developments:

> The true explanation is that Dr Atkinson, like most people on both sides in politics of the generation which had to endure the bitterness of the agrarian revolution, is still in a fume of political excitement and cannot consider any Irish matter without this excitement . . . Ireland will have no dispassionate opinion on any literary or political matter till that generation has died or has fallen into discredit.[33]

Yeats was firm in his belief in the need for a generational shift of opinion within Anglo-Ireland. This he felt was absolutely essential to national revival. If there had been a tendency for the older generation to 'set its face against all Irish enthusiasms',[34] he saw himself and Hyde as being to the forefront in reversing the tide.

Mahaffy, true to form, countered in an essay written several months after the Vice-Regal Inquiry. Here he tried to play down the significance of the row while reiterating his objections to Irish:

> . . . are we to spend our lives learning the various jargons which have either absolutely or relatively no literature, in order to humour foolish people whose pride consists in provincial isolation? Surely, even those whom these objections cannot convert must at least recognise that there is something to be said for imperialism, not only in politics, but in language, and that the advantages of a common and ready means of Communication in speech are not less than those of a ready Communication by high roads and railways.[35]

His strategy now was to configure his intervention in the Irish language debate as a brave fight against the 'provincialism' of the revival, which would be won by spreading the gospel of cosmopolitanism to the unenlightened Irish. But it was just such a deference to metropolitan values that Hyde objected to. His essay, the 'Necessity for De-Anglicising Ireland', had shown how an uncritical acceptance of the forces of Anglicization had had a debilitating effect on the Irish people, causing them to become slavish imitators of English fashions and incapable of cultural innovation. In such a scenario the Irish were for ever destined to be consumers rather than producers of modernity. From Hyde's point of view it was the loss of the language rather than its revival which condemned the Irish to be for ever provincial. Following the example of Yeats in his tiff with Dowden, he realized that the importance of the Revival lay in its 'revolt against the imitative provincialism'[36] espoused by the Trinity dons.

If the Mahaffy/Atkinson affair exposed dissension among the Anglo-Irish, it also registered a shift of opinion that was taking place within the Catholic Church in relation to the revival of Irish. As Kevin Nowlan pointed out, 'in contrast to earlier in the nineteenth century, there was now a rather widespread interest in the language question in Catholic circles'.[37] Reports in *An Claidheamh Soluis* show 'how important were the Catholic bishops and priests in organising the first branches of the league throughout the country'.[38] However, in contrast with Hyde's motives, this awakening of interest in the language had as much to do with the Church's fear of the onslaught of what it saw as the debilitating influences of modern popular culture as it had with nationalist sentiment. In this respect the Irish language, which had 'fallen out of history', offered a position of retreat from the vulgar threat of modern culture. The Catholic primate of all Ireland, Cardinal Logue, was not reticent in offering a staunch defence of the language in the wake of the allegations of Mahaffy and Atkinson. Logue came from an Irish-speaking region of Donegal and was to figure prominently in the controversy over Yeats's play, *The Countess Cathleen*, some weeks later. He was upset by the charges that the Irish language was somehow indecent, and was vocal in his defence of the native tongue and of the movement to restore it. In a letter to *An Claidheamh Soluis* on 1 April he responded to the charges against the language:

> I have no doubt the efforts now being made, with such promise of success, to restore our venerable and beautiful old tongue to the place which it has lost through past indifference, will contribute to, renew and strengthen not only the spirit of nationality, but also the spirit of piety and morality. It is a well known fact that nowhere in Ireland is faith stronger, religious feeling deeper, innocence of life more conspicuous, than in those districts where the Irish language still lingers and is lovingly cherished.[39]

Logue was particularly worried by the charges of indecency and immorality, since they related to the language and literature historically associated with the Catholic section of the population. Such taunts he would have interpreted as veiled attacks on the Catholic religion.

Yet Logue's defence of the Irish language is far from a sophisticated appraisal and in the end does little more than replicate the crude tendency to stereotype of Atkinson and Mahaffy, but in this case arguing for the undisputed piety and moral purity of the language. What we witness here is an early attempt to idealize the Irish-speaking peasantry as innocent, intensely religious and impervious to the morally degrading influences of the modern world – an idea that Yeats also found attractive in ways. Ironically, at the very moment this mythical version of the Irish-speaking peasantry was being constructed, one of the best accounts we have of contemporary Gaeltacht life was being written by J. M. Synge. Synge's Aran does not confirm Logue's conception of the Irish-speaking district as a place where 'innocence of life is more conspicuous'. Rather, any reader of *The Aran Islands* cannot but be struck by the extent to which the society Synge describes with affection and sympathy is informed by an unashamed carnivalesque energy. This is a place of bawdy good humour, where the women 'are as wild and capricious as the women who live in towns',[40] and where a disrespect for the law is manifested in the universal 'impulse to protect the criminal'.[41] Logue's inclination to edit out the carnivalesque in Gaelic culture is hardly surprising, given the Catholic Church's policy since the mid-nineteenth century of centralizing and standardizing Church practices by discouraging local forms of Catholicism, such as patterns and wakes, and importing new forms of devotion from Rome.[42] Such a need to reconfigure these cultural forms undoubtedly owes a lot to a post-colonial insecurity that the colonial conception of 'native' culture may in fact be true. This need to prove at all costs the morality of Irish culture, however, would prove to be almost as restrictive as the colonial attempts to degrade it. What is perhaps most revealing about Cardinal Logue's response to the controversy is his conception of the Irish language, the Catholic religion and Irish nationality as coterminous. By constructing the native Irish speaker as inherently virtuous and beyond reproach, the Catholic Church could successfully carry out its own moral agenda while harnessing popular nationalist sentiment.

This propensity to foreground the unquestionable virtue of the Irish language and its literature, however, was by no means peculiar to the Catholic Church. Indeed the same impulse is present in Hyde's written reply to Atkinson:

> My own experience is, that the Irish-speaking population are infinitely more clean and less ribald in their language than the English-speaking population . . . To insinuate that these people tell indecent stories or use indecent language is grotesque, and could only be done by an ignorant man, who does not know the conditions of life about which he speaks.[43]

In Dr O'Hickey's contribution to the language debate, the tendency to idealize reaches a crescendo:

> I tell the Professor – and I know modern Irish literature far better than he does – that this same peasant literature which he despised is the most vigorous, the most imaginative, the most playful, the most healthy, the most graceful, the finest and most perfect literature of its kind that the world has ever seen – vastly

superior to any literature ever produced under similar conditions – a perfectly marvellous emanation of the mind, intellect, and imagination of the Gael during a period of enforced illiteracy.[44]

It is this moment, then, which marks the beginning of the idealization of the Irish-speaking peasant as a noble and pious character enriched with a pure folk imagination. From this time onwards the mobilization of this image as a defining constituent of national identity would become a central preoccupation within nationalist Ireland. But whether this ideal countryman should be configured as a Catholic peasant, a Gaelic peasant or a Celtic peasant was to fuel the major controversies of the national theatre over the next decade.

The 1899 Irish language controversy, then, marks a crucial moment in Irish history, for many reasons. Firstly, it represents the coming of age of the Gaelic League as a significant force in Irish national life. Although Hyde insisted that the League was strictly non-political, the language controversy did place the organization in direct collision with the forces promoting English interests in Ireland and 'massed public opinion throughout the country solidly behind the Gaelic League for the first time'.[45] Just as the university question placed the Catholic Church to the fore in the fight for nationalist advance, the Mahaffy/Atkinson row placed the Gaelic League at the centre of the nationalist struggle. Although the fight for a university and for the language brought the Gaelic League and the Catholic Church into an unofficial alignment on the national front, it also opened up the potential for friction between both organizations. For 1899 also saw the Gaelic League step into a field that was traditionally seen as the exclusive preserve of the Catholic Church – education. Having achieved a modest victory in the area of intermediate education, the League was to become a significant player in Irish education over the next decade. This development was to lead to many bitter disputes between the Church and the League, most spectacularly in 1908, when the controversy over compulsory Irish for NUI matriculation broke out.

Secondly, the language controversy was not merely a battle over the merits or demerits of the Irish language, it was also a battle for academic ascendancy between Trinity College and an emerging generation of nationalist intellectuals. In an unprecedented move, Trinity College, so long the centre of gravity of Irish intellectual life, was effectively overlooked by a Vice-Regal Inquiry. This of course was consistent with the government's policy of conciliation, but it is more significant than that. The Trinity professors had lost the intellectual battle. In their self-assuredness and in their utter disregard for the formidable foreign evidence assembled by Hyde, they had shown themselves up to be hopelessly provincial. In short they were 'out-cosmopolitaned' by the Gaelic League president. As Hyde pointed out in his last word on this controversy, Trinity College had fallen behind the most significant national developments and was occupying an ever-diminishing role in Irish affairs.[46] Beyond the walls of Trinity, the old guard[47] could only resort to a trenchant restatement of their colonial beliefs in defence of their position. Undoubtedly this attack on the language was hugely significant in earning the college the reputation of an anti-national institution in the popular mind.[48] Nevertheless, the language row did highlight a clear-cut split within Anglo-Ireland as a younger generation of intellectuals and artists stood up to their elders in a valiant defence of the language.[49]

Finally, and perhaps most significantly, the dismissal of the Irish language and its literature as inherently immoral by Atkinson and Mahaffy and the knee-jerk response of those who could only countenance an idealized Irishness set the terms within which the major cultural debates of the coming decade, particularly those sparked off by the theatre movement, would take place. In this classic post-colonial situation, emerging nationalists felt obliged to refute the imperial conception of Irish culture by idealizing it and exaggerating its inherent morality, but in the process often replicated in nationalist guise the very colonial thinking which they sought to dislodge. There is no doubt that the Irish language row had a huge influence on the negative reception of Yeats's *Countess Cathleen* three months later, when the playwright was accused of representing the peasantry as 'a sordid tribe of black devil-worshippers and fetish-worshippers on the Congo or the Niger'.[50] The ghosts of Atkinson and Mahaffy also haunt Lady Gregory's *Cuchulain of Muirthemne*. In her anxiety not to verify the claims that Irish literature was indecent, she took the liberty of 'sanitizing' material she thought might cause offence.[51] Synge unquestionably did more than anyone to break the tyranny of stereotype – both colonial and nationalist – by offering a more complex and liberating exploration of the Irish psyche, which was deeply informed by his knowledge of the Gaelic tradition. It was his refusal to see Gaelic culture through the lens of a narrow Victorian morality that fuelled so much opposition to his *Shadow of the Glen* and *Playboy of the Western World*.[52]

Pagan Ireland: Erasure and Revival

In the essay 'Ireland, Real and Ideal' Lady Gregory made the point that the Irish had worn the mask thrust upon them for too long, and that they were more likely to win respect when they appeared in their own form.[53] What exactly 'our own form' should be was decidedly uncertain as the nineteenth century drew to a close, due to the steady abandonment of Irish cultural practices and the rapid assimilation of colonial cultural forms. Nevertheless, the Catholic Church throughout that century had worked hard to situate Catholicism at the defining core of Irishness. The project to modernize the religious practices of Catholic Ireland can be traced back to Cardinal Cullen's attempt to centralize and nationalize the Church by wiping out older, local independent forms of Catholicism and importing new 'more respectable' forms of devotion from Rome. This eradication of local and traditional practices (a task made easier by the decline of the language) was a bid by the Church to institute a modern, 'civilized' Catholic identity as the defining constituent of Irish nationalism and to get rid of older 'pagan' elements within Irish Catholicism. This modern Catholic identity was successfully mediated via the temperance and other Church societies.[54] As early as 1852, Sir William Wilde recorded in his book *Irish Popular Superstitions* that:

> The native humour of the people is not so rich and racy as in days of yore . . . Well-honoured be the name of Theobald Mathew – but, after all, a power of fun went away with the whiskey . . . The pilgrimages formerly undertaken to holy wells and sacred shrines for cures and penances have been strenuously inter- dicted . . . The fairies, the whole pantheon of Irish demigods are retiring, one by one, from the habitations of man.[55]

The zeal with which this project was undertaken and its rapid success in reconfiguring the popular practices of Irish Catholicism undoubtedly reflected a post-colonial anxiety to distance the beliefs and practices of the religion from 'pagan superstition', as well as a concerted desire to consolidate the position of the Church in Irish society.[56] This pathological fear of a residual paganism within Irish culture lasted well into the twentieth century to become one of the hallmarks of modern Irish Catholicism.[57] In the aftermath of the Mahaffy/Atkinson affair, however, the Church's attempt to institute a Catholic Irishness was being challenged by the rapidly growing Gaelic League. By imag- ining Ireland as an essentially Gaelic nation, the League effectively opened up the category 'Irish' to all religions on the island.[58] Furthermore, with the emer- gence of the Irish Literary Theatre in May 1899 a third category was posited as a central badge of national identity – Celticism.

The idea of a Celtic Ireland appealed in particular to Yeats and Lady Gre- gory and other writers from an Anglo-Irish background. It enabled those Anglo-Irish writers keen to separate themselves from the prejudices of their class but lacking obvious markers of cultural identity, such as Catholicism and the Irish language, to express their indigeneity. An engagement with Celticism, therefore, enabled them to establish a connection with the ancient Irish past which elided the sectarian divisions of the reformation. Furthermore, the work of scholars[59] across Europe and the commentaries of Renan and Arnold had drawn attention to the primitive richness of Celtic myth and folklore at a time when European artists were being reinvigorated by non-European primitive art and becoming conscious of separating their work from mass-produced popular culture. Celticism was particularly amenable to Yeats, who saw it as a perfect way of reconciling his nationalism with his aesthetic ideals.

Having been introduced to folklore by Lady Gregory, Yeats began to mod- ify his own ideas on Celticism in the 1890s.[60] Earlier his Celtic encounters had been bookish and abstract, as exemplified by his early narrative poem 'The Wanderings of Oisin'. But, as he became more interested in folklore, he began to make connections between the ancient myths and the lore of the peasantry, constructing a link between the ancient Celtic past and the contemporary peasantry. This he configured as the essence of Irishness. Yeats's thinking on this can be traced in a series of articles he wrote in 1898 based on the folk materials he had gathered with Lady Gregory. The second of these articles – 'The Prisoners of the Gods', published in *Nineteenth Century* in January 1898 – opens as follows:

> None among people visiting Ireland, and few among the people living in Ireland, except peasants, understand that the peasants believe in their ancient gods, and that to them, as to their forebears, everything is inhabited and mysterious. The gods gather in the raths or forts, and about the twisted thorn trees, and appear in many shapes, now little and grotesque, now tall, fair-haired and noble, and seem busy and real in the world, like the people in the markets or at the crossroads. The peasants remember their old name, the *Sheagh Sidhe*, though they fear mostly to call them by any name lest they be angry, unless it be by some vague words, 'the gentry,' or 'the royal gentry,' or 'the army,' or 'the spirits,' or 'the others' . . . and they believe, after twelve Christian centuries, that the most and the best of their dead are among them.[61]

Folklore was an exciting revelation to Yeats and, for him, represented a form of authentic popular culture in contrast to the propagandizing of the ballad tradition and the homogenizing influence of British imports. The Celtic world of legends, spirits and visions which he had studied now came alive in the stories and lore of the peasantry, perhaps all too readily for one who did not need much convincing of the existence of a Celtic otherworld. For Yeats, then, the real voice of Ireland could be heard in folklore 'because it preserved a tradition predating English, and often even Christian influence upon Irish life'.[62] Although modern life discounted the possibility of a spirit world beyond the senses, the Irish country people lived in constant touch with that world, in the opinion of Yeats and Lady Gregory. Both saw the strong pagan undercurrent in Irish peasant ways as being reconciled to some extent with Christianity and yet saliently present as the vital informing force in Irish culture.

With the launch of the Irish Literary Theatre, the Celticism of Yeats, Lady Gregory and, to a lesser extent, Edward Martyn surfaced as an alternative vision of national identity to that of the Gaelic League and the Catholic Church. The founding document of the new movement pledged 'to build up a Celtic and Irish school of dramatic literature' which would 'express the deeper thoughts and emotions of Ireland' and prove that Ireland was 'the home of an ancient idealism'.[63] This was not a language-based identity but one founded on an empathy with the Celtic past. It was also very different from the world of Cardinal Logue's spiritual peasantry. As we have seen, there was never any doubt that Logue viewed the peasantry as anything other than Christian, and that the spirituality and pious devotion which marked them off as distinctive was nothing more than a manifestation of their allegiance to the one holy Catholic and apostolic church. Yeats's peasant, on the other hand, was a very different breed – spiritual certainly, but pagan rather than Christ-ian in impulse, and with a significant dark side.[64] Yeats's fashioning of the Irish peasant as a Celtic pagan allowed him to bypass the complexities of post-refor-mation Christianity, but it also embroiled him in other complications which would ultimately precipitate the *Countess Cathleen* controversy. In an Ireland where, as we have seen, anti-nationalist forces were making much of the 'immorality' and unsuitability of literature in the Irish language, any attempt to advocate an essentially pagan (albeit Celtic) Irish identity was bound to meet with resistance. To put this another way, the Irish Literary Theatre pro-posed to revive and reinvigorate the ancient vestiges of pre-Christian Ireland at the very time that the Catholic Church was investing so much energy in purging itself of them in the name of progress and modernity. A further irony stems from the fact that, at the very moment that Yeats discovered folklore as a creative source, the peasantry, as cultural agents, were actively embracing the benefits of modernity. As a result of the land acts, local government, better education and the self-help movements, a nation of tenant farmers was being rapidly and willingly transformed into a nation of small landowners, middle-class in outlook and with little nostalgia for the Ireland they were leaving behind. With these contradictions bubbling under the surface, the seeds of the *Countess Cathleen* controversy had already been sown by the time the new the-atre initiative was announced.

Lady Gregory was instrumental in persuading Ireland's most influential public figures to support the Irish Literary Theatre, but it was Yeats who took on the responsibility of informing and educating the public in advance of the inaugural performance. He worked tirelessly between January and May 1899 to promote the aims of the new theatrical venture and proved to be quite a skilful manipulator of the media, opening up many points of entry into pub-lic discourse for himself. By means of countless newspaper articles, interviews and letters,[65] pamphlets (*Beltaine*), public lectures and reviews of his poetry and drama, he was seldom out of the national press, and he deftly used this position to publicize and further the aims of the Irish Literary Theatre.

Yeats's propaganda crusade began with a letter to the *Daily Express* on 12 January 1899 in which he advertised the advent of the new movement. The hope was, he stated, to do for Irish dramatic literature 'what the Théâtre Libre and the Théâtre L'Oeuvre have done for French dramatic literature' and 'to per-form plays upon Irish subjects, which would at any rate aim at being litera-ture'.[66] Right from the start, therefore, he signposted his commitment both to the nation and to high art – he was, after all, beginning to reconcile these twin aims through Celticism. The initial announcement was followed up two days later by a more detailed article, which spelt out the aspirations of the new ven-ture and also, pointedly, contained a scathing attack on the state of contem-porary drama. As far as Yeats was concerned, the theatre was characterized by 'vulgarity and triviality'. 'Now and then a play is better than the others', he wrote, 'and when it is nearly as good as a good, but still ephemeral novel, the critics, who are men of letters, call it a great play, and common playgoers believe them, because it does not accuse them of want of wit, being but the image of a passing fashion.'[67] He also regretted the marginalization and deterioration of literary drama, which he claimed, when revived, was spoiled by elaborate scenery and costume to such a degree that very little attention was actually paid to the words spoken.

Although he plays it down, it is clear from this article that Yeats was anticipating some hostility to his literary theatre from old-style nationalists as a result of his stance on the poetry of the Young Irelanders. In an attempt to garner support from a group who might not understand or be interested in his aesthetics (as was the case in 1892 – the year of his clash with Gavan Duffy), Yeats made much of the importance of 'national feeling' to the success of the Irish Literary Theatre.

> We believe that common playgoers will *not dislike us very much* . . . and that they will come *in time* to like us; for even if they do not understand that we offer them plays *written in a more sincere spirit* than plays which are written to please as many people as possible, they will understand that *we are writing about the country in which they live*, and re-telling those ancient, heroic tales which are chief among its treasures.[68] [emphasis added]

Furthermore, he contended, perhaps in response to the concerns of John Eglinton,[69] the importance of 'national feeling' to the new movement would save it from falling foul of the excesses of *belles lettres*. 'There is no feeling except religious feeling', he argued, 'which moves masses of men so powerfully as national feeling'. This, he felt, was Ireland's strength, and what would keep his movement 'out of the shadow of dilletantism [sic]'. Yeats, therefore, clearly advertised the new theatre as a project committed to the nationalist cause, claiming that 'all literature and art is national'.[70] It is also clear that he had in mind a more sophisticated national literature than the poetry of the Young Irelanders and that he was not interested in repeating the well-worn platitudes of *The Spirit of the Nation*.

The *United Irishman*, encouraged by the self-help impulse of the project but obviously sceptical of Yeats's plans for an art theatre, gave the Irish Literary Theatre a guarded welcome. Unlike *An Claidheamh Soluis*, it did not insist on an Irish literature in the Irish language.[71] However, it could not go along with Yeats that a national theatre would be 'at once literary and popular':

> Mr. Yeats's project, of course, is an attempt to produce a really high class Anglo-Irish drama; but such plays as he meditates can never be popular. They are too far above the people's heads, and while they shall not want for an audience, they will not appeal to the taste of the multitude, for whom melodrama is for a long time yet the best field to work. If the Irish drama is to be, as all such undertakings should be, educational, it must make due allowance for the deficiencies which still exist in our tastes. The Young Irelanders justly grasped the necessities

of their time when they made the tone of their writings simple, vigorous, and strong, looking less to style than to spirit and sentiment. A healthy national drama would educate the people far quicker, far easier, and more permanently than any number of histories or lectures.[72]

Griffith's paper clearly attached itself to the tradition of Thomas Davis and the Young Irelanders who believed in the power of popular culture to promote the aims of nationalism. Griffith was concerned with the educational 'deficiencies' of the Irish people and could not conceive of a popular literature emanating from the lofty heights of Anglo-Irish aesthetics. He was also worried that Yeats would substitute one form of cultural domination – English popular culture – with another – élitist poetics.[73]

As well as playing up the commitment of the Irish Literary Theatre to Irish nationalism, Yeats also returned to what had become an important theme for him since his critique of Dowden – the creative paucity and hostility of the ascendancy in regard to things national:

> The curious imaginative sterility of what are called the Irish educated classes has its source in that spirit of antagonism to the life about them, which until recently has cut them off from the foundations of literature, and left their imaginations cold and conventional. That small minority which from time to time has divided itself from its class, has been so fruitful in imagination that one understands how much evil has been worked by a bad theory and how great the flood may be once the flood gates have been lifted.[74]

If Yeats was forthright in his criticism of the ascendancy he was also careful, by alluding to the memory of Swift, Grattan and Parnell, not to rule out this group from involvement in the national revival. He certainly conceived of himself as part of the vanguard of a new generation of ascendancy intellectuals committed to working against the interests of their class. In this opening essay on the Irish Literary Theatre, then, Yeats again adopted a position which allowed him at once to criticize the popular nationalism of Thomas Davis and the hostility of the ascendancy to things Irish, just as he had done in the Gavan Duffy affair.

About three weeks after this article was published, almost to validate Yeats's description of the 'imaginative sterility' of the ascendancy and to confirm the extent to which Yeats, Hyde and others had divided themselves from their class, the Irish language controversy involving Mahaffy and Atkinson broke out. Yeats, as we have seen, was quick to defend Irish literature and Douglas Hyde against the outrageous claims of the academics, and located the source of the prejudice in recent political developments. If there had been a tendency for the older generation to 'set its face against all Irish enthusiasms', he saw himself and Hyde[75] as being to the forefront in discovering their indigeneity. Again he had shown himself to be as implacably opposed to ascendancy die-hards as he was to narrow-minded nationalists. He was particularly annoyed at Atkinson's dismissal of folklore as 'essentially abominable' and singularly denounced the academics of Trinity College as promoters of philistinism.[76]

'Souls for Gold': The *Countess Cathleen* Controversy

The standard account of the *Countess Cathleen* affair is given in Hogan and Kilroy's *The Irish Literary Theatre 1899–1901*. In an attempt to explain the controversial opening of the new theatre they contend that:

> Ireland was, and to some extent still is, in the grip of a hyper-sensitive, hyper-puritanical public morality, that was quick to sense slights, whether intentional or not and whether blatant or obscure, against religion and a rather narrow morality. Second, this tender moral sensitivity was paralleled by a patriotic sensitivity that was just as quick to take offence.[77]

Such an analysis, however, ignores the cultural and political complexities of Ireland in 1899 as they have been examined above. Matters of religion and national identity *were* sensitive at this time. One could hardly dismiss the reaction to the claims of Atkinson and Mahaffy as 'hyper-sensitive', since they attacked the very possibility of an Irish culture. Furthermore, in terms of moral sensibility, it was the Trinity academics who opposed the Irish language because of its indecent and immoral literature. Hogan and Kilroy's argument also temporarily strips Yeats of his nationalist credentials and construes the row as a 'battle of two civilisations' between Catholic nationalism and the Anglo-Irish ascendancy. This is far too simplistic and ignores the complexity of the power struggle taking place within nationalism.

By choosing *The Countess Cathleen* as the inaugural play of the new national theatre, Yeats sought to legitimize a residual Celtic paganism as the essential hallmark of Irishness.[78] Although based on a well-known folktale, the play is infused throughout with Yeatsian Celtic mysticism. Set during an unspecified time of famine, this is not a recognizably Catholic or Gaelic Ireland, but an Ireland where Christianity functions uneasily inside the wider, albeit nebulous, parameters of Celtic spirituality. The play tells the simple story of a peasantry who, in a time of dire famine, turn from God to the Devil for material gain.[79] They are saved, however, by the heroine – the Countess Cathleen – who pledges her soul to the Devil to redeem her peasantry. In the end, she too is saved from hell, as we are told that God 'looks always on the motive, not the deed' (p. 105).

The play is full of supernatural visions and occurrences, many of them reminiscent of the essays written by Yeats and Lady Gregory on peasant folklore, and the playwright makes it clear from the very beginning that Christianity has only a tenuous hold over the peasantry:

> TEIGUE: God, and the Mother of God, have dropped asleep,
> For they are weary of the prayers and candles;

> But Satan pours the famine from his bag,
> And I am mindful to go pray to him
> To cover all this table with red gold. (p. 18)

There is no hint in the play that the famine is politically motivated: instead it is seen by the peasantry as an act of a remiss and unjust God. Such a view of famine in Ireland ran counter to the received view within nationalist Ireland. John Mitchel had set the tone when 'he attacked the act of God theory of the famine and substituted for it a theory of mass murder masked as charity'.[80]

The peasantry are not the main focus of *The Countess Cathleen* and serve merely to provide a context for the benevolence of the heroine – the aristo-cratic Countess. She, in many ways, embodies the Yeatsian fantasy of an Irish nation led by the spiritual guidance of the aristocracy. 'Certainly, the chief virtue in the ethical scheme of the play is *generosity*, a quality most accessible to the rich. The main virtue to which the poor may aspire is gratitude – as in the one blameless peasant character, Maire, who shows exaggerated respect and thankfulness to the Countess, then dies of starvation.'[81] In fact one could see the play as an allegorical commentary by Yeats on the changing role of the ascendancy after the Land War. The Countess is, after all, a returning absen-tee landlord. We are told that she is 'the owner of a long empty castle in these woods' to which she is returning (p. 15). Just like Yeats and his Anglo-Irish counterparts, she separates herself from the interests of her class by taking up the cause of the people. She does everything in her power to save the people from the material corruption of the merchants from the east, in the same way as the revivalists warned against the dangers of English materialism. Also, in a gesture which carries some echoes of the post-1882 land acts, the Countess sells off her land to help her people:

> CATHLEEN: Keeping this house alone, sell all I have
> Go barter where you please, but come again
> With many herds of cattle and with ships of grain. (p. 47)

Flanked by the poet Aleel and her foster-mother Oona, the Countess Cathleen is, in many ways, a precursor of Kathleen ni Houlihan as a symbolic repre-sentation of Ireland. Her relationship with these companions reveals a lot about Yeats's vision of Ireland. Aleel is very much an autobiographical figure who is in love with the unattainable Countess. He owes his soul to the time-less world of Celtic myth and in Act III attempts to woo the Countess to escape to the otherworld with him. This is in direct contrast to Oona, who represents a more orthodox Christian, perhaps Catholic, position. The Countess is tempted by Aleel's invitation to the spirit world, but in the end she rejects the individual pleasure of the otherworld and reconfirms her commitment to Christianity and to relieving the suffering of her dependants:

> CATHLEEN: [*she goes to the chapel door;* ALEEL *holds his clasped hands towards her for a moment hesitatingly, and then lets them fall beside him*]
> Do not hold out to me beseeching hands.

This heart shall never waken on earth. I have sworn,
By her whose heart the seven sorrows have pierced,
To pray before this altar until my heart
Has grown to Heaven like a tree, and there
Rustled its leaves, till Heaven has saved my people. (p. 56)

The Countess, then, becomes the central Christian presence in the play whose one soul, redeems all of those sold by the peasants, and earns 500,000 crowns to feed them 'till the dearth go by' (p. 93).

In contrast to the Countess Cathleen, the peasantry seem to embody all that Yeats despised about Irish bourgeois nationalism. Seamus Rua is a particularly despicable character. He is a selfish, grovelling, unprincipled philistine who feigns despair to extract maximum alms from the Countess Cathleen:

SHEMUS: shut the door
And call up a whey face and a whining voice,
And let your head be bowed upon your knees. (p. 20)

Unlike the heroine who is given the opportunity by Aleel to escape to a Celtic otherworld, the only extra-Christian option extended to the people is to join forces with the Devil. Again, in contrast to the Countess who chooses to affirm her Christianity, the peasantry readily indulge when tempted by the forces of darkness. In the end they can only gratefully accept the benevolence of the Countess.

From this analysis of The Countess Cathleen we can begin to understand the causes of the controversy surrounding it. There is no doubt that the play – notwithstanding Yeats's efforts to distance himself from the prejudices of his class – worked to confirm the supremacy of the aristocracy as the spiritual leaders of the Irish people at a time when political control was slipping from their grasp. Despite the fact that the theatre initiative marked another bold step on the road to self-help, The Countess Cathleen, in its portrayal of a dependent peasantry, conveyed a contrary message. Furthermore, the play as the inaugural production of a new national theatre worked to further Yeats's agenda of locating a pagan Celtic otherworldliness at the heart of an Irish identity. However, his representation of the peasantry as superstitious, immoral and unchristian could be seen to confirm the opinions of Mahaffy and Atkinson that had caused such outrage weeks before. The seeming proximity of Yeats's vision of Ireland to the worst colonial stereotypes was quickly pointed out by rival forces who were separately promoting the Irish language and Catholicism as the essence of Irishness.

It was the protestations of Frank Hugh O'Donnell that precipitated the Countess Cathleen controversy. O'Donnell, a past rival of Parnell for the leadership of the Irish Parliamentary Party, was rather a flamboyant character and no stranger to controversy. He managed to attack at one stage or another nearly all sides and parties involved with Irish politics. As a former constitutional politician and anti-Parnellite he certainly did not share Yeats's view that Ireland was awakening culturally with the coming of age of a new generation. This is quite clear from his reaction to *The Countess Cathleen* (based on a reading of the play), which took the form of a letter to the *Freeman's Journal* published in advance of the opening production. A further letter was refused publication; however, O'Donnell made both available in a pamphlet called *Souls for Gold! Pseudo-Celtic Drama in Dublin*.

O'Donnell began by undermining Yeats's self-appointed status as a national dramatist. He contended that, although *The Countess Cathleen* purported to be a national drama, it was in fact 'alien to all our national traditions'.[82] O'Donnell, no doubt, expected a positive and morally upstanding celebration of Irishness to answer the racial slurs of Mahaffy and Atkinson. Instead, *The Countess Cathleen* depicted the Irish peasantry not as faithful Catholics but as a materialistic people ready to sell their souls to the Devil for selfish gain. He believed, perhaps rightly, that Yeats was trying to dislodge Catholicism from the centre of the Irish moral outlook and complained that Yeats had chosen 'precisely the baseness which is utterly alien to all our national traditions, the barter of faith for gold', as 'the fundamental idea of his Celtic drama!'[83] Taking issue with Yeats's conception of Celtic Irishness, O'Donnell saw in *The Countess Cathleen* a condescending degradation of the Irish character by a decadent ascendancy writer out of touch with the beliefs and sensibilities of the majority of the Irish people:

> Mr. Yeats's notion of what is Celtic is everywhere illustrated by his harpings on his pet 'Celtic idea', that the Gaels of Erin have and had only the thinnest veneer of Christian religion and civilisation, and really reserve their deepest beliefs for demons, fairies, leprachauns, sowlths, thivishes, etc., [sic] whom he loves to describe in the stilted occultism of a Mrs. Besant or a Madame Blavatsky, and that 'Catholic shrines', 'Catholic priests' and Catholic prayers and places are little more than sport for the pranks of the devil's own.[84]

Clearly the line between colonial stereotype and Yeats's Celtic devil-worshipping peasantry was too thin for comfort. What we witness here is a clash of two separate conceptions of national identity that was to be repeated many times over the coming decade in the national theatre. While Yeats focused on the pagan past because it was romantic and spiritual rather than scientific and analytical, there was a tendency among conservative nationalists in their quest for bourgeois respectability to suppress recalcitrant elements within Irish culture.[85] This cultural need to appear 'civilized' was certainly heightened in the wake of the Mahaffy/Atkinson affair.

O'Donnell's arguments were taken on board and blown into a national controversy by the *Daily Nation*. Significantly, this newspaper was controlled at the time by William Martin Murphy – a wealthy and strongly anti-Parnellite Member of Parliament – and was known as 'Healy's mouthpiece'.[86] A *Daily Nation* leader virulently condemned *The Countess Cathleen* on the Saturday before the first performance, based on a reading of the play.[87] Many of the criticisms were taken from O'Donnell's pamphlet, stressing, as he did, the anti-Catholic and anti-national nature of the play. It registered its protest 'in the names of morality and religion and Irish nationality' and condemned the Irish Literary Theatre as an attempt to deceive the Catholic and nationalist audience into accepting Yeats's evil doctrines. The paper implied that the theatre movement was an Anglo-Irish conspiracy by noting 'the effort that [was] made to give the play the appearance of the patronage of Catholics and nationalists'. In the end it was unambiguous in its rejection of the play and its contribution to national literature, and went so far as to urge those Irish Catholics who would attend the performance to voice their disapproval at anything they found offensive.[88] In many ways the reaction of 'Healy's mouthpiece' was a measure of the threat felt by constitutional politicians, particularly the anti-Parnellites, of another innovative self-help initiative beyond its control. But, more than that, what was particularly upsetting to the *Daily Nation* was the manner in which Yeats disturbed the equation of nationalism with Catholicism in the inaugural play, at a time when Healy's anti-Parnellites were attempting to locate a conservative Catholic ethos at the heart of Irishness.

It was the Catholic students of University College who took up the promptings of the *Daily Nation* and caused a disturbance during the opening performance of *The Countess Cathleen*. Joseph Holloway records how 'an organised claque of about twenty brainless, beardless, idiotic-looking youths did all they knew to interfere with the progress of the play by their meaningless automatic hissing and senseless comments'.[89] T. W. Rolleston, on the other hand, felt that 'they expressed their sentiments with vigour, but in a perfectly gentlemanlike manner'.[90] They elaborated on their objections to the play in a letter published in various national newspapers on 10 May – a letter which James Joyce famously refused to sign.[91] The letter expressed the view that Yeats had broken a contract which he had concluded with the Irish people some months previously. By the terms of that contract the playwright had promised, if sufficiently supported, to put on the stage plays dealing with Irish subjects or reflecting Irish ideas and sentiments. In the view of the Catholic students the performance did not live up to the expectations of the promise:

> Why, if this is a true portrait of Irish Catholic character, every effort of England to stamp out our religion and incidentally our nationality is not merely to be justified, but to be applauded ... when Mr. William Butler Yeats is, apparently, treated as the leader, the pattern and the despair of the modern Irish intellectual movement ... we feel it our duty, in the name and for the honour of Dublin Catholic students of the Royal university, to protest against an art, even a dispassionate art, which offers as a type of our people a loathsome brood of apostates.[92]

This was yet another attempt to undermine Yeats's self-ordained position as a national dramatist. For these students, who were at once the emerging intelligentsia of the Irish nation and second-class citizens within an imperial university system, Yeats's Celtic Ireland was not sufficiently distinguished from prevalent racial stereotypes.[93] In their analysis of the play, as in Cardinal Logue's defence of the Irish language, the burden of having to prove the moral integrity of one's culture and religion to the colonial powers-that-be was never far from the surface. Once more the concept of Irish nationality became inextricably bound up with religion, as the Catholic students strained to distance themselves from Yeats's 'loathsome brood of apostates'. The hostility of the Catholic students was a sign of things to come.

What also caused annoyance was the manner in which Yeats manipulated the historical record.[94] As Frazier has pointed out, the nationalists 'looked upon an Ireland with an irresponsible aristocracy and a rebellious tenantry struggling for equality and independence [but Yeats] exhibited for their admiration an Ireland with a conscientious aristocracy and a suffering, misguided tenantry at last happy to settle back down into their position in the hierarchy . . . This was neither what Ireland really was nor what they wanted it to be.'[95] All the overtures to 'national sentiment' that Yeats had made since January now appeared to ring hollow to a nationalist audience eager to display the inherent morality of its culture. He now found himself cast in the role of an ascendancy writer who appeared to exploit the Irish rather than express them, and was judged to have confirmed the views of Mahaffy and Atkinson rather than refuted them.

The controversy over *The Countess Cathleen* was further deepened by a letter sent by Cardinal Logue to the *Daily Nation* in condemnation of the play, even though, as he freely admitted, he had not read it or seen it. As far as he was concerned, 'an Irish Catholic audience which could patiently sit out such a play must have sadly degenerated, both in religion and patriotism'.[96] It was not just the theological issues that exercised him, but also the questioning of the position of Catholicism at the centre of Irish *national* life. On 15 May the *Irish Daily Independent* published a reply by Yeats to Cardinal Logue. Yeats optimistically cast Cardinal Logue as one of the old guard, in the same way as he did Gavan Duffy and Mahaffy and Atkinson. He was amazed at the Cardinal's recklessness at not having read the play and saw it as 'part of that carelessness and indifference which the older generation in Ireland has too often shown in the discussion of intellectual issues'.[97] Yeats tried to maintain that Logue in no way represented the opinion of the younger and more intellectual Catholics, but, given that the playwright had just been denounced by the Catholic students of University College, this was little more than wishful thinking on his part.

Malcolm Brown has noted that Yeats's relationship to Irish peasants was 'abstract and literary rather than immediate and personal, and his knowledge of Irish historical motion, the source of both servility and the loss of servility, was . . . minimal by any standard'.[98] Clearly the playwright was motivated by a wish to institute an Irish identity not centred on Catholicism. However, in the choice of *The Countess Cathleen* as the inaugural production of the Irish

Literary Theatre he betrayed an alarming lack of empathy with the historical experience of Catholic Ireland, and a blindness to the sensibilities of that section of the population which was burdened by the need to proclaim the morality of Irish culture in a way he and his Anglo-Irish companions were not. However, the controversy was seized on by constitutional political forces who detected the threat of yet another innovative self-help initiative outside its control. 'Healy's mouthpiece', the *Daily Nation*, in particular, was quick to discredit Yeats's Celticism as a threat to what it saw as the central tenet of Irishness – Catholicism.

An Irish Drama in English? 'Let Us Strangle it at Its Birth'

As well as the hostility to *The Countess Cathleen* from forces outside the informal self-help alliance of the IAOS, the Gaelic League and the Irish Literary Theatre, there were also signs of dissension from within its ranks. In advance of the inaugural production there was evidence of antipathy within some sections of the Gaelic League towards the direction the theatre movement was taking and to the level of national publicity it was receiving, particularly in the wake of the Mahaffy/Atkinson attempt to discredit the Irish language and its literature. In fact it is in this context that the first major debate on whether an Irish national literature should be written in Irish or English took place.

On 29 April, ten days before the opening performance of the Irish Literary Theatre, D. P. Moran wrote an important article in *An Claidheamh Soluis* entitled 'English literature and Irish Humbug'.[99] Moran expounded the standard revivalist line on the way Irish society was being overwhelmed by cheap imported English publications. But more significantly he admitted the uncertainty which abounded over what exactly constituted Irish literature, and moved to discount the possibility of an Irish literature in any language other than Irish.

> What is Irish literature and if we are to pay for it where are we to get it? We are in a period of rapid transition in regard to this matter . . . The great body think – or rather they don't think but have a hazy idea – that Irish literature is to be discovered in the English language . . . or nebulous twaddle labelled 'the Celtic note' . . . Any man may be safely defied to define what is Irish literature in the English language.[100]

This was yet another attack on Yeats's Celticism, but by a figure who wanted to establish the Irish language as the defining feature of Irishness. The article went beyond an analysis of *The Countess Cathleen* and, significantly, marked the beginning of a period of intense discussion about the nature of Irish literature – undoubtedly occasioned by the foundation of the Irish Literary Theatre. For the first time, but by no means the last, the theatre movement precipitated a debate on the fundamentals of Irish identity which was to reach an audience far greater than that present in the theatre for the performances, via the national press. In the light of Moran's article it is hardly surprising that *An Claidheamh Soluis* would condemn *The Countess Cathleen* outright the following week:

> The subject matter is based on a German legend discovered by John Augustus O'Shea, transferred by him to *The Shamrock* whence the story found its way to English-speaking, English reading people in the west of Ireland. There Mr. Yeats rediscovered it, and here it is – the foundation of what is to be our national the-atre. The management of the theatre is English and the cast is English – the actors hailing from London theatres. One of the guarantors in this genuine Irish undertaking is Prof. Mahaffy . . . It has been objected that this tale is pagan. It is enough for us that it is un-Irish.[101]

This was another attempt to deny Yeats the status of a national dramatist by highlighting the 'inauthenticity' of *The Countess Cathleen*. The reference to Mahaffy was obviously an attempt to link the Irish Literary Theatre with the professor's hostility towards Irish, which conveniently ignored Yeats's valiant defence of the language.

The extent to which the foundation of the Irish Literary Theatre was to impact on the Gaelic League can be measured by the level of debate that occurred in *An Claidheamh Soluis* in the aftermath of the first season of the new theatrical venture. Articles and letters relating to the Irish Literary Theatre were to be found in the League's paper for up to two months afterwards. In the edition of 20 May, Patrick Pearse wrote a letter reiterating the Gaelic League's outright rejection of the Irish Literary Theatre. His main problem with the new venture was that it was founded on the heresy 'that there can be an Ireland, that there can be an Irish literature, an Irish social life, whilst the language of Ireland is English'.[102] As far as he was concerned at this point, the Celtic Revival amounted to little more than a superficial sham:

> Apparently, the only thing necessary to make a man or an institution Irish is a little dab of green displayed now and again to relieve the monotony, a little elo-quent twaddle about the 'children of the Gael' or a little meaningless vapouring about some unknown quantity 'termed Celtic glamour'.[103]

Pearse went as far as representing the Irish Literary Theatre as a threat to the language revival, seeing the influence of Yeats as negatively as that of Mahaffy and Atkinson. He saw the new theatre movement as more dangerous, 'because less glaringly anti-national than Trinity College'. He feared that the theatre would 'give the Gaelic League more trouble than the Atkinson–Mahaffy com-bination'. 'Let us strangle it at its birth', he implored.[104]

Ten days after Pearse had argued the case for an Irish literature in the Irish language, Yeats was promulgating the idea of an Irish literature in English in Trinity College.[105] The occasion was a Historical Society debate on the motion – 'that any attempt to further an Irish literary movement would result in provincialism'. Here Yeats expressed his delight at the controversy that the Irish Literary Theatre had provoked, interpreting this positively as a willingness of people to take an interest in the movement. He also urged Trinity College to 'watch over all that was distinctive and racial in this country',[106] arguing that a literature rising out of racial characteristics was not necessarily provincial. Returning to a familiar theme of his, Yeats defined provincialism as the propensity to imitate without discrimination. ('The small shopkeeper in the country town dressed in the costume of London or Paris was provincial.') Provincialism, according to Yeats, amounted to 'the cast off fashion, the cast off clothes, the cast off thoughts of some active centre of creative minds'.[107]

At this meeting Yeats referred ironically to some of the criticism[108] of him by extreme nationalists. He had read in an extreme organ of patriotic opinion that he would only be acceptable as long as he wrote for English readers and English critics, 'but now that he tried to establish an Irish Literary Theatre it was time to crush him'.[109] More significantly, Yeats proceeded to argue in favour of a distinctly national literature in the English language:

> It was impossible that those nations which spoke for good or for ill, the English tongue would accept perpetually the ideas of one city, which was no longer moved by any high ideal. America had a national literature, and America wrote in English. Ireland would have a national literature which would be written to a very great extent in English. Scotland would probably begin again to expose herself in a way personal to herself, and Australia and South-Africa and the other English speaking countries would sooner or later express their personal life in literature . . . Every Irish writer for many years, every Irish person who had taken up any intellectual Irish question whatever, had found his coldest welcome in his own city.[110]

Yeats envisaged a specific role for Irish national literature 'to lift up its voice for spirituality, for identity, for simplicity in the English speaking world . . . He believed that Ireland with its legends, its profound faith with its simplicity, with its sincerity, would lift up its voice for an empire of the spirit greater than any material empire.'[111] This is truly a landmark speech, prophetic in its anticipation of the emergence of post-colonial literatures and pioneering in its apology for an Irish national literature in the English language.

Predictably enough *An Claidheamh Soluis* continued to pour cold water on Yeats's plan for an Irish literature in the English language. However, he was stoutly defended in the next edition of the same paper by T. C. Murray, who in time was to become a successful Abbey playwright. Murray challenged the narrow definition of Irishness proposed by elements within the Gaelic League.[112] He could not accept that 'the term "National" should apply merely to those works which are written in the Gaelic language'. In his opinion this was 'too narrow, if not a false use of the term'.[113] Ironically Murray defended literature in English on the basis that this was the medium through which we received 'the half-inspired utterances of Davis himself'. His main point was

that millions of Irish people were educated in the principles of Irish nationality through the English language. To jettison the English language, therefore,
would mean a loss of the writings of Mangan, Ferguson, Griffin and Kickham
from the canon of national literature. As far as Murray was concerned, these
men deserved 'to be spoken of with at least as much reverence as the most
eager enthusiasts in the Gaelic revival'.[114] What is notable, though, is that he
does not see a literature in Irish and a literature in English as mutually exclusive. He admitted to taking an interest in the Irish language movement but felt
that it did not prevent him from 'appreciating the efforts of those who are
working in another, but, perhaps equally effective groove'.[115]

Not surprisingly Murray's sentiments were savagely attacked in the next
edition of *An Claidheamh Soluis*. A leading article effectively knocked the
notion of an Irish literature in English on the head and outlined a strategy of
Gaelicization which would become central to much of the League's thinking,
despite its stated commitment to bilingualism:

> No confusion of thought, no weak compromise of principle no lingering han-
> kering after the broad and smooth and seductive middle way must be allowed
> to remain in our midst, deadening our energies and clogging our advance, nay
> dragging us steadily back into the land of bondage.[116]

Yeats's attempt to create a national literature that was at once recognizably Irish
and written in the English language was judged to have produced a useless
hybrid, ultimately damaging to Irish nationality and to the project of recon-
structing Irish intellectual traditions. The acceptance of this literature, it was
argued, would fulfil 'the destiny which Trinity College was founded by Elizabeth and Adam Loftus to impose on Ireland, and the more rapid fulfilment of
which Drs. Mahaffy and Atkinson have lately been in such a hurry to assist'.[117]

Just as the *Daily Nation* had rubbished Yeats's theatre in the name of
Catholicism, so too did *An Claidheamh Soluis* debunk *The Countess Cathleen*
in the name of the Irish language. Not only did Yeats's play inaugurate the
Irish Literary Theatre, therefore, but it also precipitated the first major debate
on the nature of Irish identity since the Young Irelanders. Yeats gained a lot
from these debates and learned that support from Catholic nationalists and
the Gaelic League was vital to the success of the theatre venture. Before the
year was out, he began to 'make amends'. Writing to the editor of the *Gael* in
December 1899, he disclosed: 'I have taken up Gaelic again, and though I
shall never have entire mastery of it, I hope to be able to get some feeling of
the language.'[118]

Yeats's Fairies and Plunkett's Dairies

Despite the heated controversy over Yeats's *Countess Cathleen*, the aftermath of
the first season of the Irish Literary Theatre actually witnessed a consolidation

of the self-help coalition. On the evening of 12 May the *Daily Express* hosted
a dinner in honour of the new Irish Literary Theatre in the Shelbourne Hotel.
This function took place at the instigation of Horace Plunkett and marks an
important moment during which some of Ireland's greatest minds, including
most of the leaders of the revival, gathered to give their first considered
response to the new Irish Literary Theatre. Among those present were John
O'Leary, George Moore, W. B. Yeats, Standish O'Grady, George Sigerson, Douglas Hyde, J. F. Taylor, George Russell, T. W. Rolleston, R. A. Anderson,
William Larminie and John Eglinton. Significantly, most of the speakers
referred to the theatre movement in relation to other movements for national
revival, chiefly the Gaelic League and the IAOS. There was a palpable sense at
this gathering that, for the first time, these various groups had now become
affiliated and were working towards the same goal of national revival. As Lady
Gregory had pointed out several months beforehand in 'Ireland, Real and
Ideal', the dynamic for change in Ireland was coming from the material/cul-
tural alliance of the IAOS, the Gaelic League and the Irish Literary Theatre,
rather than from within constitutional politics. Significantly, one could see the
proceedings of this function as an important precursor, however informal, to
the formation of the Cumman na nGaedheal federation the following year.

Horace Plunkett, although unable to attend the meeting due to illness, set
the tone for the evening with his letter of apology:

> . . . as one who has chosen the humbler service of promoting the development
> of material resources, I am always glad to emphasise the paramount impor-
> tance from a purely economic standpoint of simultaneously developing our
> national life in the higher regions of literature and art. We practical folk keep
> a poet in the office of our Agricultural Organisation Society from whom our
> most fruitful inspirations are derived. It is on the friendly relations and mutual
> help subsisting between the two classes of workers for Ireland's regeneration
> that I rest my hopes for the future.

This notion that cultural self-belief was fundamental to economic prosperity
was to become a vital informing principle of the revival. In the same way, the
economic self-help ethos was to become central to most of the new cultural
movements that actively advocated support for Irish industry. The swiftness
with which Plunkett moved to embrace the Irish Literary Theatre demonstrated his belief in the contribution the new movement would make to a
national revival.

By far the most remarkable speech of the evening was delivered by George
Moore. Recently returned to Ireland, he was clearly intoxicated by the new
artistic and intellectual awakening of the country he had left because of its
stagnation:

> . . . if the revival of interest in the ancient language and the myths and tradi-
> tions of the ancient people mean more than a flitting apparition of art, then the

peaceful economics and policy of social reconstruction of Mr. Horace Plunkett, rather than the revival of old animosities, may be expected to fill the near future. Mr. O'Brien and Mr. Dillon, if I rightly interpret their utterances, do not pretend to any new ideas – they seem to believe in repetition of the old ideas; possibly they are right. Mr. Horace Plunkett, however, comes with a new set of ideas, with a new system of economics, especially adapted to the needs of modern Ireland . . . The analogy between a system of rural banking and co-operation dairies and the poetry of Mr. Yeats is not obvious at first sight; but I think anyone who has listened to the little historic account which I have given of the rise and fall of artistic movements from the Greeks BC450 to the romantic movement in France in 1830 will see that there is a connection. It would seem that the time has come for putting all the old ideas, whether of land agitation or of literature behind us. When I say old, I really mean those of the last two generations.

Like Lady Gregory, therefore, Moore was eager to point out the strength of the self-help movements in contrast to the inertia of the parliamentarians. Recognizing the connection between artistic and material success, he attributed the renaissance to the coming of age of a new generation.[119] The *Daily Nation*, however, was quick with a witty attempt to deflate what it saw as the pretensions of the leaders of the Irish Literary Theatre in their attempt to link economic revival with artistic renewal during the after-dinner speeches. Some days later it published the following skit on the Shelbourne Hotel proceedings:

> The banquet was fine and the speeches delicious:
> Indeed, 'tis admitted on every hand
> That nothing so high-toned, sublime, and auspicious
> For many a year has been known in our land.
> No wonder the scene has been highly commended,
> For everyone knows 'tis the richest of treats
> To get intermixed and judiciously blended
> The wisdom of Plunkett, the genius of Yeats.
>
> With much that was mystic, sublime, and symbolic,
> And truly enchanting – when once understood –
> Came sober suggestions on matters bucolic
> That many believed to be equally good.
> There thoughts were expressed 'twas a glory to utter,
> And facts were set forth that no scoffer can blink.
> Making plain to the world that aesthetics and butter
> Have closer connection than some people think.
>
> Awhile we were whirled into regions ideal,
> By lofty emotions our spirits were swayed:
> Again a few words brought us back to the real,
> And turned all our thoughts to legitimate trade.
> The evening, in fact, brought such charming elation,

> Such promising projects, such brilliant conceits,
> That now we include in the joys of our nation
> The dairies of Plunkett, the fairies of Yeats.[120]

Notwithstanding the wit of these verses, it is important to point out that they were published in the newspaper which was owned by that giant of Irish capital, William Martin Murphy, and which was soon to become the *Irish Independent*. The same newspaper, of course, had also led the campaign against *The Countess Cathleen* some weeks earlier. This is hardly surprising given the fact that for years the main organs of parliamentarianism had been trying to discredit the co-operative project by casting aspersions on the movement, at times on the basis of Plunkett's ascendancy background and at other times by charging that it was responsible for the spread of 'alien' socialist ideas.[121] There seems little doubt, therefore, that the coming together of some of Ireland's most progressive thinkers and the leaders of the mass co-operative movement outside the sanction of parliamentary politics posed a significant political threat to the interests of Irish capital at this time. Indeed, the radical possibilities of the co-operative movement had been identified in the socialist republican thinking of James Connolly the previous year.

Writing in the *Workers' Republic* Connolly argued that 'the same shrewd sense which has inspired the Irish farmers to appreciate the advantages of agricultural co-operation in dairies and banks, with only their little savings to finance the enterprise, will also lead them to appreciate the advantages which might be derived from co-operation on a national scale with the entire resources of the nation to equip it'. Such co-operation, he believed, could provide a foundation for 'the future socialist republic'.[122] Notwithstanding Connolly's admiration for the efficacy of the mass co-operative movement, he remained deeply sceptical of the culturally based agenda which characterized much nationalist thinking and which was so much in evidence during the *Countess Cathleen* controversy. The battle over whether the Irish nation was essentially Catholic, Gaelic or Celtic was little more than a bourgeois nationalist distraction to someone of Connolly's socialist republican beliefs. Not surprisingly, within weeks of the *Countess Cathleen* he began to articulate an alternative vision based on the solidarity of the working classes rather than on any defining ethnic, national or racial category:

> We mean to be free, and in every enemy of tyranny we recognise a brother, wherever be his birthplace; in every enemy of freedom we also recognise our enemy, though he were as Irish as our hills. The whole of Ireland for the people of Ireland – their public property, to be owned and operated as a national heritage, by the labour of free men in a free country.[123]

Although broadly supportive of attempts to revive the Irish language, Connolly never lost sight of the fact that 'you cannot teach starving men Gaelic'.[124] Nor did he forget the simple reality that the Catholic Church 'always accepts the established "order" even if it has warred upon those who had striven to establish such order'.[125] Likewise, Celticism was of interest to Connolly not in terms of its ancient mystique but only in so far as it was useful in explaining socialism to the Irish.[126] Much of Connolly's efforts, therefore, were invested in making 'socialists see the importance of anti-imperialist struggles' and in making 'nationalists see the importance of tying their anti-imperialism to the socialist movement'.[127] As Gregory Dobbins astutely puts it, Connolly challenged 'those dimensions of the Irish Revival circumscribed by the cultural politics of identity without abandoning an insistence upon Irish cultural specificity'.[128]

War of Position

The year 1899 has never stood out as a landmark in Irish history; however, both the Mahaffy/Atkinson affair and the *Countess Cathleen* controversy stand out as important, if related, politico-cultural moments. The row over the Irish language marks the last flourish of a moribund colonial intelligentsia and, at the same time, the coming of age of a new generation of nationalist intellectuals. The foundation of the Irish Literary Theatre, on the other hand, represents not only an important cultural moment but also a significant political juncture in Irish history, when the battle for the control of cultural discourse within nationalism was recognized as a vital concomitant to the wielding of political power. In other words the debate over the forms and subjects of Irish drama at this time is as much a debate over the forms and subjects of the nation itself.

Although the majority population had to confront the grand narrative of English imperialism, which saw them as degraded and superstitious, radical Anglo-Irish artists like Yeats had to confront established thinking within Irish nationalism, which saw them as evil colonial West Britons. This mismatch of cultural needs was an important contributory factor to the *Countess Cathleen* debate. An even more crucial factor, however, was the intra-nationalist war of position taking place over who had the right to define 'authentic Irishness' in a nation without a political expression. Yeats's Celtic Irishness was amenable to his imagination and his cultural sensitivities, yet his attempt to institute it via *The Countess Cathleen* betrayed a disregard for the historical experience of Catholic Ireland. Other nationalist organs such as the *Daily Nation* and *An Claidheamh Soluis* were quick to generate a national controversy in order to pursue their own agendas. It was the performance of *The Countess Cathleen*, however, which brought Celticism, Catholicism, the Irish language and republican socialism into dispute, making the theatre the central arena for the formulation and contesting of Irish identity – a position it would occupy for most of the next decade.

If nations are 'imagined political communities', then those in a position to imagine the community or construct a national identity occupy a position of considerable power. Put another way, the construction of a national culture is not only a 'literary judgement as to what might exemplify national identity, but a political one as to what national identity consists in'.[129] Clearly, the various cultural disputes which surrounded the inaugural production of the Irish Literary Theatre a matter of months after the Mahaffy/Atkinson affair were symptomatic of a wider contest beginning to erupt within nationalist Ireland over who should do the constructing.

STIRRING UP DISLOYALTY
The Boer War, the Irish Literary Theatre and the Emergence of a New Separatism

England's Difficulty . . .

Thus far we have seen how the Irish Literary Theatre consciously located itself at the heart of a wider extra-parliamentary self-help movement, forming an implicit coalition with the Gaelic League and the IAOS. However, while following this broadly nationalist agenda, the theatre also became a pivotal arena for vigorous intra-nationalist debate. One can read the *Countess Cathleen* affair as an event which struck a blow for Irish cultural sovereignty and at the same time exposed the power struggle within nationalism for the right to sanction Irish identity. Although the Irish language and the theatre preoccupied nationalist minds in 1899, the outbreak of the Boer War towards the end of the year was to have a seismic effect on the Irish cultural and political landscape. This event greatly assisted the emergence of a new non-clandestine separatist politics outside the Parliamentary Party which was to win a significant level of popular support and lay the foundations of Sinn Féin. The Boer War also witnessed the emergence of a wider theatre of organized politico-cultural events which were consciously orchestrated to mobilize nationalist and loyalist sentiment. All the important figures of the Irish Literary Theatre played a significant role in these developments and it is noticeable how W. B. Yeats, Edward Martyn and George Moore became more aggressively involved in nationalist politics at this time. Not surprisingly the theatre programme of 1900 would become implicated in the ideological ferment generated by the outbreak of war.

Theatre of War

Much has been made of the importance of the '98 demonstrations to the reawakening of the cause of advanced nationalism and to the uniting of the Irish Parliamentary Party. Yet Maud Gonne remarks in her autobiography that the 'centenary commemorations, for which such great preparations had been made, seemed to me a little disappointing'.[1] In fact the occasion failed to draw the warring factions together. Furthermore, the attempt to raise funds for a Wolfe Tone memorial costing £14,000 realized only £561.[2] In many respects, then, the '98 project failed to live up to expectations. It may be more useful to see the activity of 1898 as part of a broader continuum of nationalist protest

66

which began with the jubilee riot of 1897, culminated in the massive pro-Boer street protests and continued until the visit of Edward VII in 1903. This wave of street protest is important in that it marks the beginning of the shift of nationalist agitation from rural Ireland to the urban locale, building up momentum for the subsequent Sinn Féin movement. Furthermore, it occasioned the deployment of staged publicity stunts as a central nationalist tactic. As the century draws to a close, the use of choreographed public events, often leading to confrontation with the authorities, becomes a key strategy for subverting the colonial agenda in Ireland. Central to these developments was the figure of Maud Gonne, whose organizational skills, forceful personality and theatrical flair contributed much to such events.[3] However, just as crucial were the energies she harnessed and the friendships she cultivated. She was the vital linking figure between such diverse personalities as W. B. Yeats, Arthur Griffith, William Rooney, James Connolly and Michael Davitt, and brought them together as co-workers for Irish separatism.[4] Indeed the short period during which they co-operated represents one of the most innovative phases of Irish separatist agitation.

The outbreak of the Boer War on 11 October 1899 provided a perfect opportunity for Irish nationalists to advance their cause subliminally as public opinion divided predictably between unionist supporters of the war and nationalist critics of it. More specifically, it provided the Irish Parliamentary Party, shell-shocked from almost a decade of in-fighting, with an opportunity to unite around an issue which had no direct bearing on Irish affairs and was, therefore, less likely to cause dissension. In many respects the war provided Irish nationalist MPs with a common cause and held the various factions together long enough for a degree of mutual trust to be established. As the newly united party took on its pro-war opponents in the House of Commons it displayed a spirit and purpose not witnessed since the Parnell heyday. However, if the war created a space for the parliamentarians to regroup, it also precipitated the emergence of a new non-clandestine separatist politics with the formation of the Transvaal Committee – the pre-cursor of Sinn Féin – in September 1899. What is important about this development is that, for the first time since the Act of Union, radical Irish nationalists visibly rejected English foreign policy and began to formulate an independent attitude to the South African War. Not only did they support the Boer struggle like their parliamentary counterparts, they went quite a way further by opposing British recruitment in Ireland and the colonial strategies to encourage it. Unhappy that 'as an integral part of the United Kingdom, Ireland was officially at war with the two Boer republics',[5] these nationalists were of the belief that Ireland's destiny lay outside the empire as an independent sovereign nation. The Boer War is generally read as a great unifying moment for Irish nationalism. Such a reading, however, overlooks that fact that the war precipitated the first significant moments of tension between parliamentary home rule and an emerging separatism, when 'attitudes to the empire and the real nature of Irish loyalty and disloyalty'[6] became central issues. In November 1845 John Mitchel's seminal article, 'England's Difficulty Is Ireland's Opportunity', was published in the Young Ireland newspaper, the *Nation*. Now just over fifty years later the first real 'opportunity' presented itself, anticipating the more catastrophic events of the 1914–16 period.

Without a doubt the establishment of the *United Irishman* in March 1899 by Arthur Griffith and William Rooney played a crucial role in generating widespread pro-Boer sympathy in Ireland and advancing a separate foreign policy to the British position. Griffith was intimately acquainted with South African affairs, having worked there from the end of 1896 until 1898. In fact his 'articles on the Transvaal are the most accurate to be found in the Irish press of the time'.[7] Furthermore, the editorial in the first edition of the paper left no doubt as to his views on Irish politics:

> Lest there might be any doubt in any mind we will say that we accept the Nationalism of '98, '48, and '67 as the true nationalism and Grattan's cry 'Live Ireland – Perish the Empire!' as the watchword of patriotism.[8]

It was James Connolly, however, who organized the first pro-Boer street rally. As we have seen, the socialist leader had been involved in street protests before, when he enlisted the help of Maud Gonne and Yeats to demonstrate against Queen Victoria's jubilee celebrations. This first pro-Boer gathering took place in Foster Place on 27 August. The republican socialists held weekly meetings at this location but 'this one was different, firstly because an "abnormally large" crowd turned up to chant "Long live the Boers", and secondly because it received extensive coverage in the national press'.[9]

Pro-Boer activity was given a significant boost with the formation of the Irish Transvaal Committee on 30 September. The committee met in the rooms of the Celtic Literary Society and drew many of its members from that group. The prime movers on the committee were James Connolly, Maud Gonne, Arthur Griffith and John O'Leary and meetings were attended by W. B. Yeats, Michael Davitt and William Rooney, among others. The aim of the new committee was to express sympathy with the Boers in their fight against British injustice, to discourage Irishmen from entering the British army and to deliver an Irish flag to the Irish Brigade. Particularly noteworthy in the operations of the committee was the co-operation between Connolly and Griffith. As Padraic Colum has pointed out, it was 'seldom Arthur Griffith and James Connolly came together: one was out for a worker's republic, the other for a national government of any kind'.[10] Hardly had the Irish public heard of the existence of the Irish Transvaal Committee than they were informed that 'Ireland was at war with the Boers, and that Irish regiments were to be mobilized without delay for imminent despatch to South Africa'.[11]

Over the next three months the Boer conflict rapidly captured the public imagination and generated an unprecedented level of street protest and civil disobedience in Dublin, the likes of which would not be seen again until the 1913 lockout. On 1 October the first major pro-Boer rally was held at Beresford Place. Remarkably, a crowd of up to 20,000 attended the proceedings which was, according to the *United Irishman* report, 'representative of all shades of National opinion and was harmonious and enthusiastic throughout'.[12] The meeting was chaired by John O'Leary, addressed by Michael Davitt and attended by Yeats and Maud Gonne. Davitt empathized with the Boer struggle for independence and condemned the conflict as an unjust war. Gonne notified the crowd of the formation of an Irish Transvaal Brigade by Irishmen in South Africa to advance the Boer cause – her future husband, Major John MacBride, was among its recruits. It was at this event that she began her epic drive to stop British army recruitment in Ireland. Three resolutions were passed by the meeting: the first extending sympathy to the Boers and hoping for a victory 'over the tyrannous armaments of England'; the second supporting the Irish Transvaal Brigade; and the last condemning 'all enlistment of Irishmen in the English army'. During the meeting a *Viekleur* – the Transvaal flag – was unfurled and as the meeting concluded 'the crowd rushed towards the brake and unyoking the horses, proceeded to drag it through the streets'. The people formed behind in processional order and 'a vast impromptu procession swept through the street, cheering for the Boers, the Irishmen of the Transvaal, and Majuba Hill'.[13]

Pro-Boer fever was not an exclusively Dublin phenomenon. With the introduction of local government, nationalist councils had replaced unionist grand juries all over the country. The war provided an ideal opportunity to advance the nationalist agenda by passing pro-Boer resolutions. Limerick borough council passed the most well-known of these on 7 September:

> That we consider it a great sign of National weakness and decay that the various organisations in Ireland have not in a more determined manner expressed their sympathy with the plucky Boer farmers in their fight against the English, and this especially when the Englishmen themselves are protesting against the contemplated slaughter at the instance of Chamberlain and the other English Capitalists, and we express a hope that if a war takes place it may end in another Majuba Hill.[14]

In Westminster the following month a series of dramatic events would inject a new momentum into the Irish pro-Boer movement and accelerate the emergence of a new separatism. In a debate over supplementary funding for the war the veteran radical nationalist, Michael Davitt, vigorously articulated his unwillingness to submit to an unjust colonial agenda in order to secure political gain for Ireland:

> Had I been offered not Home Rule only, but an Irish Republic by Her Majesty's Government on yesterday week in return for one word or one vote in favour of this war to destroy the independence of the Republics of the Transvaal, I would

speak no such word nor record any such vote. Sir, I would not purchase liberty for Ireland at the base price of voting against liberty in South Africa.[15]

Davitt was unequivocal in his view that the ideals of the empire and the ideals of the Irish nation were incompatible. This undoubtedly gave credence to the belief gaining ground that Ireland should pursue a separate foreign policy. But, more dramatically still, Davitt ended his speech by resigning his seat in the British parliament, not just because of his objections to the Boer War, but also because of his loss of faith in the effectiveness of parliamentary agitation at Westminster:

When I go I shall tell my boys, 'I have been some five years in this House, and the conclusion with which I leave it is that no cause, however just, will find support, no wrong, however pressing or apparent, will find redress here, unless backed up by force.' This is the message which I shall take back from this assembly to my sons.[16]

As Davitt was delivering his swan-song to the House of Commons he was also laying the foundations of the Sinn Féin movement. In this moment the Irish strategy of withdrawal from Westminster was born. The lesson was not lost on Davitt's Transvaal Committee colleague, Arthur Griffith, who would soon develop this tactic of parliamentary withdrawal as the cornerstone of Sinn Féin policy. Yeats, who had never before written to a politician, communicated his admiration for the speech to Davitt. It was 'just the kind of speech [sic] we most need to lift our politics to their old nobility & out of the depression of the last four or five ignoble years', Yeats confided.[17]

Throughout October sporadic outbreaks of civil disobedience continued in Dublin and elsewhere. Thousands of anti-enlistment notices were posted, and the Irish Daily Independent arranged 'a magic lantern display from their office window' which showed South African scenes and prominent Boer leaders'.[18] On several occasions disturbances broke out during pro-Boer gatherings in College Green as students from Trinity College 'shouted insults and anti-Boer remarks down from the college's windows'.[19] There were also instances of soldiers being attacked as they walked through the streets of Dublin. Maud Gonne noted in Servant of the Queen that 'fighting soldiers became quite a popular evening entertainment with young men – in which Arthur Griffith and Mary Quinn's brother used to take part, though Griffith I think hated it'.[20] There was also significant pro-Boer activity in Cork. In November Gonne and Griffith 'found half the population of Cork turned out to greet them when they arrived to speak at a meeting'.[21]

It is also important to point out that there was a significant level of support for the war against the Boers, particularly among the ascendancy. Indeed the Trinity College students' magazine of the time took pride in relating the gallant deeds of old Trinity men in South Africa, and honoured those who fell. However, there was not the same need among loyalists to demonstrate openly, since their position was in sympathy with the imperatives of the state. Notwithstanding, there are numerous reports of loyalists, mainly drawn from the student body of TCD, countering pro-Boer demonstrations in Dublin.[22]

One of the most violent confrontations between the police and pro-Boer demonstrators occurred in late December. The British forces had recently suffered defeats at Stormberg, Magersfontein and Colenso, and were beginning to feel the effects of the Transvaal Committee's anti-recruitment drive. At this crucial moment it was announced that Joseph Chamberlain, the colonial secretary, would travel to Dublin on 18 December to be conferred with an honorary degree from Trinity College.[23] Buoyed up by recent Boer victories, the Transvaal Committee set about organizing a protest against Chamberlain's visit. The colonial secretary was distrusted in Irish nationalist circles on two counts. Firstly, it was not forgotten that 'Chamberlain and his followers led to the defeat of the first home rule bill in June 1886 by 343 votes to 313'.[24] Secondly, in the role of colonial secretary he was seen as the architect of the present war.

The protest was planned for Sunday 17 December by Gonne, Griffith and Connolly, but at one o'clock the previous night Gonne was informed by the police that the Beresford Place meeting had been proscribed. 'By eleven o'clock in the morning 330 DMP men were patrolling the streets converging on the Liffey; 130 constables held Beresford Place and the approaches thereto. It was obvious that the authorities were determined that this was to be the occasion to show the Irish Transvaal Committee that they had overstepped the mark and to check the pro-Boer excitement in the country.'[25] Nevertheless, the organizers decided to ignore the ban and by lunchtime a horse and cart containing Gonne, Griffith, O'Leary, Connolly and Pat O'Brien MP,[26] among others, broke through a police cordon to address a cheering crowd at Beresford Place.[27] Several resolutions were read in support of the Boers and in condemnation of Chamberlain.[28] Yeats had sent Gonne a letter of support for the Boers which read:

> I need hardly say that I am with you and the meeting over which you will preside in wishing victory for the just cause of the Boers. I am not English, and owe England no loyalty; but if I were I would still think with Tolstoy that there is no loyalty that should make a man wish anything but victory to a just cause.[29]

From here the large and excited crowd proceeded behind the cart to Trinity College. It was at this point that skirmishes with the police began. The crowd was forced down Dame Street by a series of police baton charges and was met by a large group of mounted police from Dublin Castle as it turned onto Parliament Street. A riot situation developed, with the police on horseback using their sabres to break up the demonstration. Meanwhile the demonstrators used poles, sticks, bars of iron and bare fists to fight back. Sean O'Casey recounts how he himself made use of a flagpole to unseat a policeman before retreating to a nearby pub.[30] James Joyce also made use of this incident in *Ulysses*, as Bloom recalls:

> That horsepoliceman the day Joe Chamberlain was given his degree in Trinity
> he got a run for his money. My word he did! His horse's hoofs clattering after
> us down Abbey Street. Luck I had the presence of mind to dive into Manning's
> or I was souped. He did come a wallop, by George. Must have cracked his skull
> on the cobblestones. I oughtn't have got myself swept along with those med-
> icals. And the Trinity jibs in their mortarboards. Looking for trouble.[31]

This was to be the last of the great pro-Boer demonstrations, but one can see
how in moments of defiance and open disloyalty like this, the separatist policies of Sinn Féin began to crystallize.

If Griffith, Connolly and Gonne were mobilizing popular sentiment in urban
Ireland against the Boer War for the separatist cause, in the rural west, William
O'Brien's United Irish League (UIL) had caught the imagination of the people as
the 'latest instrument for agrarian agitation'[32] and undoubtedly facilitated the
reunion of the Irish Parliamentary Party on 30 January 1900. Although the
politicians had been working hard to find a way of burying the hatchet since the
unity conference the previous April, the advent of the UIL provided a perfect
opportunity for a new beginning. However, if the UIL provided the mechanism
for unity – the league was proclaimed official nationalist organization in the convention of June 1900[33] – the war was the central issue around which the party
cohered as the Irish Party became the most stringent pro-Boer group in the
House of Commons. The reunification of the party was completed on 6 February when John Redmond was unanimously elected as the new leader.

It is one of the ironies of Irish history not often remarked on that, as the
constitutional politicians were drawing together in February 1900, a noticeable gap was defining itself between the newly emerging separatists and the
reunited Irish Parliamentary Party. By uniting around the conservative John
Redmond, it became increasingly apparent that the final goal of the parliamentarians was to be the achievement of home rule within the empire. As
F. S. L. Lyons noted of Redmond:

> . . . he appears always to have been more conscious than any of his Irish col-
> leagues of Britain as the centre of a great empire where, for white men at least,
> self-government was a natural and realisable objective. This vision of a com-
> munity in which Ireland, home rule at last conceded, would have an honoured
> place, was fundamental to his political thinking and was to colour his action at
> the most decisive crisis of his life.[34]

Tension between the new separatists and the parliamentarians had been in the
air since October. In February 1900, the election of John Redmond as leader
of the Irish Party, however, which gave the new separatists an opportunity to
assert themselves as the true standard-bearers of Irish independence. In an editorial written four days after Redmond's election, the *United Irishman* moved
swiftly to draw a clear distinction between its separatist agenda and the imperial priorities of the home rulers:

> The Irish Parliamentary Party has given the seal of its approval to the policy of 'Home Rule *plus* Empire', by electing Mr. John Redmond as its chairman. Mr. Redmond's election renders it impossible for Irishmen who believe in the re-establishment of their country as an independent nation to give support of any kind, in the future, to the party of which he is now the leader. It is only five years ago since Mr. Redmond declared, amid the plaudits of Englishmen, that the separation of Ireland from Great Britain was 'undesirable and impossible', and described Ireland's demand as 'a demand for a federal union, one of the essential constituents of which was the preservation of the unity and integrity of the Empire.[35]

The leader writer was here referring to and quoting from a speech Redmond had given at Cambridge University in February 1895. Redmond's aspirations to an imperial senate or commonwealth were rejected by the editor, who declared unequivocally that British imperialism and Irish nationalism were irreconcilable. The leading article further stated that 'the gulf between Home Ruler and Nationalist [had] been immeasurably widened' by the election of the Irish Party leader.[36] This was not just empty rhetoric: it only took the new separatists a week to act on their words.

A by-election was occasioned in South Mayo by the resignation of Michael Davitt. This was to provide Griffith and Rooney with an ideal opportunity to advance their separatist ideas and precipitate the first electoral contest between the Irish Parliamentary Party and the separatists. On 17 February the *United Irishman* reported that Major John MacBride would be nominated for the by-election and that his supporters did not anticipate any opposition to his candidacy. Griffith was banking on the fact that 'it would obviously be embarrassing for the Parliamentary Party, with the country caught up in pro-Boer fever, to oppose an Irishman fighting for the republicans in South Africa'.[37] An approach was made to the Irish Party asking it not to run a candidate against MacBride, since, if elected, MacBride would be debarred from taking his seat because of his treasonous activities. In such a scenario a new election would be called leaving the way clear for the Irish Party candidate.[38] However, William O'Brien, perhaps feeling the political threat of the new separatism, or perhaps detecting the hand of his arch-rival Tim Healy, refused to withdraw his candidate John O'Donnell.[39] A bitter campaign ensued which copper-fastened the split between the separatists and the Irish Parliamentary Party. In the end victory went to William O'Brien, the UIL and the Irish Parliamentary Party, with O'Donnell polling 2,401 votes to MacBride's 427. However, as McCracken has pointed out, it is significant that 'it was in South Mayo in 1900, and not North Leitrim in 1908, that Griffith first ran an election campaign'.[40] The Davitt by-election, therefore, stands as the first electoral contest between the new separatism and the reunited Parliamentary Party.

The Irish Literary Theatre and the Boer War

If the inaugural productions of the Irish Literary Theatre had provoked a debate on the nature of Irish cultural identity, the plays of the next season were staged at a time of a more radical political questioning as a result of the outbreak of the Boer War. One cannot but be struck by the extent to which the leaders of the theatre movement worked more overtly to align themselves and their artistic output with the concerns of advanced nationalism at this time. This undoubtedly happened because of a residual sense of disappointment that the 1899 programme had not been universally well received in national ist quarters. Out of this came a renewed sense of the importance of this constituency, particularly the Irish language movement, to the success of the Irish Literary Theatre.[41] In response to the stringent criticism of *An Claidheamh Soluis* in the aftermath of *The Countess Cathleen*, the Irish Literary Theatre leaders worked more visibly in support of the language and committed themselves to the staging of Irish plays as an integral part of its activities. Also contributing to the pro-nationalist ethos was the fact that many of the prominent theatre leaders were genuinely exercised by the complex issues of the South African war and openly took part in pro-Boer activity. All three playwrights chosen for the second Irish Literary Theatre programme were either already seriously engaged in advanced nationalist politics or in the process of being converted to that position. Alice Milligan was by far the most committed nationalist among the three, Edward Martyn was beginning a journey that would see a supporter of the union become the first president of Sinn Féin in 1905, while George Moore, rediscovering his Irish roots, was to become a most vehement pro-Boer supporter and opponent of Queen Victoria.[42]

W. B. Yeats is conspicuously absent from the 1900 programme, although he was still very active behind the scenes arranging the February event and publicizing the forthcoming productions. However, he was troubled by the Boer War and made it his business to attend Transvaal Committee meetings and pro-Boer demonstrations. Writing to his sister Lily in November 1899 he observed that the 'spectacle of John Bull amassing 90 or 100 thousand men to fight 20 thousand & slapping his chest the while & calling on the heavens to witness his heroism has not been exhilarating'.[43] Yeats certainly did not have the same inclination towards public protest as Maud Gonne; he was, however, together with Moore and Martyn, to become much more useful to the movement as a skilled propagandist, sending provocative letters and articles to the press and engendering what he considered to be more dignified forms of protest.

Theatre business was not impeded by the war and Yeats announced to the *Irish Literary Society Gazette* that from 19 February the Irish Literary Theatre would be performing the *Last Feast of the Fianna* by Alice Milligan, *Maeve* by Edward Martyn and *The Bending of the Bough* by George Moore. Despite the controversy over *The Countess Cathleen* the previous summer, there was an air of confidence about this notice which contrasts sharply with the tentative tone of his inaugural statement. 'These plays', he wrote, 'are written to expound Irish characters and Irish ideas, and with no thought of any but an Irish public; and whatever be their merit they are written with sincerity, as one writes literature, and not as one writes for the Theatre of Commerce'.[44] There are no long-drawn-out apologies or elaborate manifestos here, just a simple statement that these plays are written for Irish audiences as an alternative to the crassness of the commercial theatres.

We have seen how Yeats's blunder with *The Countess Cathleen* was to put forward a play in which a corrupt materialist peasantry is saved by a spiritual aristocracy as an exemplar of national drama. It was the Boer War, however, and the contrary responses to it in Ireland and England which enabled Yeats to refashion this binary as a struggle between a corrupt, materialist, imperial England and a moral, ideal, nationalist Ireland. His ideas on spirituality and race began to embrace politics as he equated Irish spirituality, a history of political subservience and pro-Boer sympathy. London for him became a dying centre of materialism which would 'not endure a spiritual superiority'. This was in sharp contrast to Ireland, where a 'moral nature [had] been aroused by political sacrifices' and the country's imagination had been awakened 'by a political preoccupation with her own destiny'. As a result, according to Yeats, the country was 'ready to be moved by profound thoughts that are a part of the unfolding of herself'.[45] Undoubtedly these ideas were influenced by the mood of jingoism sweeping Britain at the outbreak of the Boer War. Lady Gregory provides an interesting insight into the poet's state of mind at this time:

> He believes a new period of political activity is coming on in Ireland, but does not think it will be agrarian, because of the strength of the artisans in the towns – His occult ideas make him think there may be a revolution coming on, for Miss Gonne believes that she had been 'sent' to stir up disloyalty, and though he thinks her hopes unreasonable, he thinks a prophet is 'an unreasonable person sent by Providence when it is going to do an unreasonable thing'.[46]

This overlap of the occult and the political produces an early articulation of the Yeatsian notion of apocalyptic revolution, which would become a central concern in his later poetry.

Lady Gregory was also deeply engaged with the war, as her diaries testify. Many of the entries of this period are taken up with war news and provide an interesting insight into the views of the Gregory circle on the Boer question. In general she seems to have taken a pro-Boer position but was less willing to express her opinions openly. On a visit to her close friend Lady Layard in January, Gregory noticed that she was busy making 'fisher caps' for injured soldiers and 'sewing little Union Jacks on to various garments'. The diary records this as an example of the British 'frenzy of rage with the Boers', but Lady Gregory felt that there was no point in saying anything, since 'people think it is because one is Irish and wishing for the downfall of England'.[47]

Enter Alice Milligan: *The Last Feast of the Fianna*

Alice Milligan came to the Irish Literary Theatre with a well-established pedigree as a writer, Irish language enthusiast and advanced nationalist.[48] A Methodist from Omagh in County Tyrone, Milligan attended the inaugural meeting of the Gaelic League in Belfast and quickly became one of its most active members. Her influence in nationalist circles reached its zenith in the late 1890s, when she founded and co-edited the *Shan Van Vocht*, a pivotal nationalist newspaper, with fellow poet Anna Johnson (who wrote under the name Ethna Carbery). The name was taken from the popular song of 1798, the centenary of which was approaching. In terms of its politics, the *Shan Van Vocht* 'went back to a nationalism that had never been Parliamentarian',[49] evoking instead the republican ideals of the United Irishmen. In a poem entitled 'Westminster 1895' published in the *Shan Van Vocht*, Milligan made an unambiguous statement of her separatist views:

> O Irishmen, not here, not here
> Should Freedom's boon be longer sought,
> Nor to our foe's disdainful ear,
> Demands for Nationhood be brought.[50]

Some of the earliest writings of James Connolly first appeared in print in the *Shan Van Vocht*. In important essays such as 'Socialism and Nationalism' and 'Patriotism and Labour', both published by Alice Milligan, Connolly was given the opportunity to communicate his ideas of republican socialism to a wider audience.[51] With the launch of the weekly *United Irishman* in March 1899, however, the monthly *Shan Van Vocht* found itself superfluous to requirements in the burgeoning world of nationalist publications, and as a result 'its work was taken over by a publication with more resources than its own'. Milligan and Johnson reluctantly decided to cease publication and magnanimously 'sent the list of their subscribers to Griffith'.[52]

In many respects, the inclusion of Alice Milligan's play in the 1900 programme was part of a concerted attempt by the Irish Literary Theatre to heal the rift with the Gaelic lobby, which emerged in the wake of the *Countess Cathleen* debate. She was an active member of the Belfast Gaelic League from the start and is noteworthy as a pioneer of Gaelic drama. In a letter to the *Daily Express* in January 1899 she pointed out that the Gaelic League had 'theatrical ambitions' and hoped that this would 'only increase public interest in the National [*sic*] Literary Theatre's dramas'.[53] Indeed she herself had acted in a Gaelic interlude in Letterkenny on 18 November 1898, in Belfast the following March and in Derry in April.[54]

As William J. Feeney has pointed out, *The Last Feast of the Fianna* tends to be ignored in histories and studies of Irish theatre.[55] Yet the play is clearly innovative, in that it marks the first attempt to take Irish legend as the subject of a national drama, a strategy which Yeats and Moore would adopt the following year and that Yeats in particular would draw upon throughout his dramatic career. Milligan's use of such Irish material as the basis of a literary drama was particularly important, coming as it did in the wake of the Mahaffy/Atkinson condemnation of Irish literature as immoral. Indeed the playwright seems to have been aware of her play as a strategic intervention in the debate initiated by the Trinity professors. Explaining the need to supplement her play with explanatory notes published in *Beltaine*, Milligan noted that 'an "educated" Dublin audience will need to be told who these people were; for have not the most cultured and learned men of Trinity College declared that a finished piece of Irish literature does not exist'.[56]

The play itself is somewhat simple and unsophisticated and certainly owes a lot to Milligan's experience of *tableaux vivants*. Taking up the story of the Fianna after the death of Diarmuid and before óisín's departure for Tír-na-nÓg the playwright was inspired by the question of how óisín endured 'to live in the house with Grania as a stepmother after all that had happened'.[57] The result of her musings is a twenty-minute play which attributes óisín's departure to his inconsolable despair on the death of Oscar and his dislike of Grania. During the feasting of the Fianna, exquisite music is heard coming from across the sea, yet the source remains mysterious.[58] Grania, speculating that the music might herald the arrival of kings, begins to preen herself in preparation for the arrival of potential suitors. It is óisín who at last sees the beautiful Niamh riding over the waves on horseback. She is invited in against the wishes of Grania and, having sung three enchanting songs, succeeds in luring the melancholic óisín to follow her to Tír-na-nÓg, marking the end of the great era of the Fianna. The play, then, is a simple enactment of the Celtic preference for a mystical, artistic otherworldly existence over the prosaic drudgeries of earthly life.

In general this opening production of 1900 was fairly well received. There was an awareness of the shortcomings of the play and the production – the long undramatic passages and the inadequacy of the English actors – yet there was a palpable willingness to tolerate the flaws and weaknesses and to recognize the play as a contribution to the development of a national drama. Only the *Irish Times* condemned the play outright for its 'dullness' and lack of wit, dismissing it sardonically as the kind of play which has 'no claim for the slightest toleration on the stage'.[59] Interestingly, the production 'featured the old Fenian John O'Leary as one of Finn's band at the banquet'.[60] The most significant achievement of Milligan's play, however, is that it 'established an aesthetic tension between grassroots Irish and avant-garde European modernist aesthetics, pointing toward a dramaturgy simultaneously endogenously Irish and modernist, a theater that validated the viability of Irish culture in the contemporary world'.[61]

Edward Martyn's *Maeve*

In 1900 Edward Martyn took his first steps towards the presidency of Sinn Féin, to which he would be elected five years later. Once again the Boer War stands out as a pivotal moment in the evolution of his political consciousness. In February of that year Martyn carried out his first significant political act. Disgusted with the Boer War he resigned his offices as JP and deputy-lieutenant for his county, thus formally relinquishing his involvement in colonial administration.[62] One can trace his emerging separatist ideas in his essay 'A Comparison Between Irish and English Theatrical Audiences', published in *Beltaine* the previous February. Here Martyn mounted a scathing attack on what he perceived as a decadent England consumed by arrogance and jingoism during the Boer War. In his view England had reached a cultural nadir by making 'such a writer as Kipling her mouthpiece'. On the other hand he had perceived 'a great intellectual awakening in Ireland'.[63] Significantly at a time when the Transvaal Committee was working to articulate a separate Irish foreign policy, Martyn concluded his essay with a passionate statement of Irish cultural autonomy. 'The best thing that could happen to the intellect of Ireland would be if England were blotted out of Ireland's sphere', he argued. 'English influence can be nothing but bad. No two countries, as no two languages, blend worse than these.'[64]

The second production on the opening night of the 1900 season was Martyn's *Maeve*. Like *The Heather Field* his second play operates on many levels, overlaying realism with the folklore of the old woman Peg Inerny and the myth of Queen Maeve. Just as Milligan's play works consciously against the Mahaffy/Atkinson idea that Irish literature was immoral, so too does *Maeve* by drawing on legend and folklore. The play is set 'during the present time about and at O'Heynes Castle among the Burren Mountains of County Clare'.[65] Colman O'Heynes, prince of the Burren, lives in a crumbling castle without the means of living according to his station. As the play begins, this state of affairs looks like changing, with the news that his daughter Maeve is to marry a wealthy Englishman, Hugh Fitz Walter. Maeve is a prototypical revivalist: having read books on Irish history and folklore she has discovered the 'unreal beauty' of the Celt. As the wedding day approaches Maeve seems to have doubts about the impending marriage and at the same time becomes more and more mesmerized by the stories and lore of the old woman Peg Inerny. Peg tells her of Queen Maeve, Tír na nÓg – 'the Celtic dream-land of ideal beauty' (p. 32) – and the land of faery. Maeve in turn recounts a vision she has had in which the old woman was transformed into Queen Maeve. Later she witnesses a more elaborate Celtic pageant, again featuring Queen Maeve, boy pages, ancient Irish harpers, chieftains and warriors. During this display the ancient Irish Queen proclaims that 'the empire of the Gail is Tír-na nÓgue [sic]' (p. 34). The following morning Fitz Walter arrives to visit his bride-to-be only to find her dead at her open window.

In truth there is little of lasting value to recommend *Maeve*. The realist setting sits uncomfortably with the mythic and folkloric elements, Arnoldian Celticism abounds without the lyricism of a Yeats and the language is very much at odds with the subject matter:

MAEVE: Last Princess of Eire, thou art a lonely dweller among strange peoples; but I the great Queen Maeve have watched thee from thy birth, for thou wert to be the vestal of our country's last beauty. Behold who in thy love hath called to life. Mark him well, for already his hour of dissolution has come. (p. 31)

What is interesting is the manner in which the Celticism is politicized by Martyn into an allegory of Irish separatist nationalism. Obviously drawing on the Gaelic Aisling tradition the central character, Maeve, becomes a symbol of Ireland and the relationship with Fitz Walter evokes the Act of Union. The central concern of the play is with the true identity of Maeve, which is defined by her attitude to the marriage. She agrees to enter into the union in order to restore her father materially, but at a huge cost of wilful alienation from her true self. However, as she reacquaints herself with Irish history and folklore she finds it impossible to go through with the marriage and opts instead for her own spiritual integrity. The political message is clear: Irish separatism must be pursued even if this is materially detrimental to the nation. Within the rhetoric of the play the separatist aspiration is linked with anti-material-ism, and Irishness is seen to be best expressed in a flight from the modern world.

Although the play was produced 'before one of the best houses ever seen in the Gaiety Theatre',[66] critical reaction to it was mixed. The *Freeman's Jour-nal* critic was delighted by 'the way in which the audience . . . followed the allegory in Mr. Martyn's play'; the *Irish Times* reporter, however, was not as impressed. Unmoved by the political allegory of the play the reviewer slated it as a 'complete and unadulterated failure'.[67] Not surprisingly the most favourable review of all came from the *United Irishman*, which saw the play as a symbol of 'the rising of our people from all English influence'.[68] Interestingly, although *Maeve* was perhaps more obviously 'Celtic' than *The Countess Cath-leen*, there was no manifestation of antipathy towards the 'fraudulent Celtic note' that greeted Yeats's play the previous year. The political impact of the play can be gauged from Lady Gregory's recollection that 'Lady Mayo who was at a performance reported to the castle that they had better boycott it, which they have done'.[69]

'A Splendid and Intricate Gospel of Nationality':
The Bending of the Bough

The third and most significant production of the 1900 season was George Moore's *The Bending of the Bough*, which was performed on 20 February. Of the three authors Moore had to overcome the most hostility to his work. In Ire-land he was notorious as the author of *Parnell and His Island*, in which he dis-played 'his active prejudice against folk and peasants'.[70] Moore, however, was to change his views radically as the Irish revival gathered pace and Martyn and Yeats succeeded in convincing him that Ireland was once again establishing itself as a centre of cultural excellence. By the end of the run Lady Gregory could record in her diary that 'G. Moore has been received back as a prodigal with gr amiability & is delighted with his reception' but that 'he is I think a little puzzled by his present political position'.[71] Indeed the extent of his change in attitude to his native country was bound to be puzzling, yet few could have anticipated such a staunch commitment to advanced nationalism. By early 1900 he had become virulently pro-Boer, a convert to the Irish language cause, a critic of parliamentary politics and a supporter of self-help. His commitment to advanced nationalism was short-lived though and he was to row back on many of these beliefs afterwards as testified in his famous memoir *Hail and Farewell*. The following examination of *The Bending of the Bough*, however, will be less concerned with the consistency, integrity or strategic nature of Moore's politics than with the significance of his intervention in the Irish politico-cultural matrix at this important historical moment.

Most critical commentary on *The Bending of the Bough* concerns itself with the process by which Edward Martyn's play *The Tale of a Town* was found lacking by Yeats and Moore, and was rewritten and renamed by the latter with the help of the former. The entire episode is summarized neatly by Lady Gregory:

> Some unpleasantness about E. Martyn's 'Tale of a Town' – Moore & Yeats having pronounced against it in the state he left it, he gave it over to them to alter – They did this at Tillyra, & made too much mystery over it, & vexed him till he 'hated the sight' of them both – & then Moore stayed in Dublin, still re-writing & showing it to [T P] Gill & [George] Russell each day.[72]

Significantly the play was rewritten between November 1899 and January 1900 during a period which, as we have seen, witnessed the rise of pro-Boer sentiment, episodes of civil disobedience and Davitt's withdrawal from Westminster – events which were to find resonances in Moore's play.[73]

With the outbreak of the Boer War, Moore's disenchantment with England 'suddenly flared into a violence totally out of proportion to his usual response to such issues'.[74] The playwright had decided to forsake his hired rooms at the Shelbourne Hotel and to return to London in order to complete the rewriting of *The Bending of the Bough*. On his arrival England struck him as a place of 'shameful and vulgar materialism',[75] and he experienced what he describes as a 'spiritual transformation'.[76] As he recoiled from the imperialism and jingoism he witnessed all around him, he found that 'the Englishman that was in [him] (he that wrote *Esther Waters*) had been overtaken and captured by the Irishman'.[77] It was this transformation which led to his staunchly pro-Boer stance. Indeed he spent much of his time 'insulting old friends who disagreed with him, making scenes in public places, and writing inflammatory letters to the newspapers'.[78] Appropriately enough it was in a state of twilight reverie that he heard the words, 'Go to Ireland! Go to Ireland',[79] which finally convinced him to move to Dublin permanently.

The preface to *The Bending of the Bough*, however, provides the fullest explanation of Moore's relocation:

> So I take advantage of the publication of my play, *The Bending of the Bough*, to explain why Mr. Martyn, Mr. Yeats and myself prefer to have our plays produced in Dublin rather than London . . . Well, it is because we believe London to be too large, too old, and too wealthy to permit of any new artistic movement, and this belief rests upon knowledge of the art history of the world, and some experience of London theatrical conditions.[80]

This very public withdrawal from the London stage was announced shortly after Davitt's parallel withdrawal from Westminster, and at a time when the Transvaal Committee was working to articulate an independent foreign policy for Ireland. If there was a rising mood of separatism, Moore's preface worked to signal not just a cultural integrity and distinctiveness but also a growing awareness of Irish cultural sovereignty as he left behind the London theatres for those of Dublin. Moore, then, bought into the Yeats–Martyn binary of material England/spiritual Ireland, which was vital to the resuscitation of Irish cultural activity. But this was rhetorically at odds with the actual work of the Irish self-help movements eager for material advancement, an endeavour which Moore himself supported. This tension between the propensity to represent a notional spiritual Ireland and the actuality of a materially advancing Ireland is everywhere present in *The Bending of the Bough*. In fact the play can be seen to offer a contradictory representation of the nation, in so far as it simultaneously portrays an Ireland of 'spiritual values' that is also keen to agitate for material advancement. Yet in another way Moore's play can be interpreted as a perfect embodiment of the revival's strategy of modernization on Irish terms in its rhetorical embrace of the mystique of Celtic Ireland on the one hand, and its advocacy of material development on the other.

The play was, to a large extent, inspired by the report of the Childers Commission on the financial relations between Great Britain and Ireland. This document disclosed the fact that since the early nineteenth century Ireland had been overtaxed to the extent of £2,700,000. Almost immediately a nationwide campaign to readjust the financial relations between the two countries was started. Initially this drew the support of all shades of Irish opinion, including the various nationalist factions and the unionists. 'Mass meetings, at which men who ordinarily despised each other stood arm-in-arm, were held in Dublin, Kingstown, Belfast, Limerick and Cork, in support of Ireland's financial claims.'[81] After six years of division in Irish politics it looked as if the nation was finally uniting on this issue. Reflecting the general sense of optimism of the time, Standish O'Grady wrote:

> There is much coming to light in Ireland, much beginning to stir here other than this national demand for our millions 'lost, stolen, or strayed'. Something is struggling to birth now, to-day in Ireland, whose gestation needed two thousand years

> of historic time. If this be not the birth of that mighty one foretold of yore by the
> prophets of our race, it is the first leap of the infant in the womb. Greater things
> than millions are concerned in this new Irish movement.[82]

One of the leading figures of this new movement was Lord Castletown of
Upper Ossory. 'At a rally in Cork, on 16 December 1896, the audience cheered
his ominous comparison between the Boston Tea-Party of 1773 and the current Irish protest.'[83] In the end, despite the formation of the Irish Financial
Reform League, the campaign failed, due to squabbling over how the financial
grievance should be addressed. With the breakdown of this latest attempt to
unite Protestant, Catholic and Dissenter, the venomous infighting of Irish
politicians resumed with renewed vigour. Moore's play makes use of this
episode to highlight the folly and inadequacy of Irish parliamentary politics
and to advance the cause of self-help.

Like *Maeve*, *The Bending of the Bough* is allegorical, but whereas Martyn's
play explores the mythical possibilities of a spiritual Ireland *The Bending* deals
with the *realpolitik* of Irish parliamentarianism, scrutinizing the commitment
of the Irish politicians to represent the interests of the Irish nation. The plot
centres on a dispute between two fictional towns, Northhaven (Ireland) and
Southhaven (England). The northern town is in dispute with Southhaven over
the fact that its steamship lines (parliament) have been cut off by the larger
town, to its advantage and to the cost of Northhaven. The aldermen of the corporation cannot agree on what course of action to take to remedy the situation and there is a general feeling that any attempt at redress would lead to an
unfavourable disruption of relations with the neighbouring town. Alderman
Lawrence sums up this deferential attitude when he declares that 'All fashion,
all society, all culture comes from Southhaven' (p. 31). However, in a rousing
speech the young alderman, Jasper Dean, inspired by his mentor, Kirwin, succeeds in reuniting the disrupted forces of the Northhaven Corporation with his
proposal that action should be taken for the recovery of their claim.

> We must cast to the winds the deference to Southhaven that makes us weak . .
> . I for one do solemnly declare that I am prepared to advocate the buying of
> new vessels and to run them in defiance of all existing agreements. (pp. 34–5)

Strong words, which seem to endorse the unilateral withdrawal from Westminster – as Davitt had recently done – and the establishment of an Irish parliament – as Griffith would soon advocate.

In the second act, however, Jasper's political ideals are compromised by
his relationship with fiancée Millicent Fell, niece of George Hardman, Mayor
of Southhaven. Concerned by Dean's radical political stance she alerts her
uncle to the imminent danger to the interests of Southhaven. It emerges that
Millicent has a significant investment in the Southhaven line and Jasper is put
in the position of having to choose between his political ideals and his personal interests. Meanwhile the united front of the Corporation is shattered by

the double-dealing of Lawrence, who diffuses the resolve of the Corporation by diluting their demands with the promise of a tramway-line and other minor concessions for Northhaven and is rewarded with a lucrative position in Southhaven by the mayor of that town. In the final act a huge crowd of activists gathers outside in the streets in the expectation that the new leader, Dean, will address them.[84] After much agonizing, Dean, lacking the courage to follow his convictions, declines to speak. In the end the meeting degenerates into a riot, with 'the mob chasing the corporation up the street' (p. 82). Alderman Foley sums up the political mores of the Corporation with his declaration that:

> . . . the state is founded on such happy lives as Jasper's and Miss Fell's will be, that our private interests are the foundation of the state, and that he who does the best for himself does the best for the state in the long run. (p. 84)

It would be very difficult to make a case for the inclusion of *The Bending of the Bough* in any canon of Irish drama. It is tedious, long-winded and overly complex in plot. In fact Yeats described it retrospectively in *Autobiographies* as badly constructed and diffuse in ideas.[85] However, what is interesting about the play is that there is no indication that it was written with any high aesthetic ideals in mind, despite the Irish Literary Theatre's loudly vaunted commitment to aesthetic excellence. Certainly the conditions under which the final text was produced were not conducive to producing a literary masterpiece. Wrested reluctantly from Edward Martyn, it was hastily rewritten by Moore with some help from Yeats[86] during the outbreak of a war and at a time when the author was undergoing a radical change in his aesthetic and political thinking. In fact all the indications are that the play was produced to make the maximum political impact.[87] Writing to George Russell in November 1899 Yeats predicted that the play would 'make an immense sensation, & our theatre a national power'.[88] In a letter to Lady Gregory shortly after he elaborated on this:

> Moore has worked a lot on 'The Tale of a Town', & I have a little, since you saw it & it is now extraordinary [sic] fine & he has done a fine preface too. It is now a splendid & intricate gospel of nationality & may be almost epoch making in Ireland. A chief part of what I have done in it is that I have rewritten Dean's speech in the first act. My anxiety at the moment is how to get at the Dublin press as I shall not be there some weeks before hand as I was last year; & I am afraid Martyn has been abusing Moores [sic] play to people there.[89]

This 'splendid and intricate gospel of nationality', as we have seen, amounted to a scathing attack on Irish parliamentary politics and expressed the growing belief, encapsulated in Davitt's withdrawal from parliament, that the interests of the Irish nation could never be represented in Westminster. In fact, by identifying the politicians as self-interested materialists who openly disregarded the wishes of the people, the play associated them with the worst evils of imperial England, out of tune with the 'spiritual' impulses of Ireland. Ironically Moore's play was performed a little over two weeks after the Irish Parliamentary Party had reunited under Redmond. Yet Yeats could dismiss this development with a nonchalant expression of regret that the Irish Party had had 'the inconsiderateness to unite before "The Bending of the Bough" came out'.[90]

There may be some truth in Lionel Pilkington's contention that *The Bending of the Bough*, in its concern with financial relations, had its origins in the dilemmas of ascendancy Ireland trying to redefine its power in the rapidly changing conditions of post-Parnell Ireland.[91] Clearly, though, it also spoke to the newly forming energies of separatism. In the context of the Boer War the play came to exemplify the deferential attitudes of Redmond and the newly reunited Parliamentary Party to the imperial agenda. It also brought the Transvaal Committee into relief as the undisputed vanguard of advanced nationalism. The *Freeman's Journal* saw it as 'a powerful, biting and unsparing political sabre directed against the influences that have destroyed the Irish gentry's sense of patriotism and reduced them to the position of social dependants upon an alien society and country'.[92] Likewise the *Irish Daily Independent* saw it as satirizing the 'fawning submission of time-serving weaklings amidst the class in subjection, to the flattery or bribes of the "predominant partner"'.[93] The most fulsome praise came from the *United Irishman*:

> The play is undoubtedly a work of genius, and the biting sarcasm of the dialogue places our modern political methods in such a light that the educational influence should be very considerable. The ambitious politician, the place-hunting lawyer, the political weather-cock, the 'respectable' element, and every other influence which disturbs the peace and disorganises the National forces, are admirably depicted.[94]

At last the Irish Literary Theatre had succeeded in producing the kind of play the *United Irishman* had called for at the beginning – politically engaged if aesthetically unchallenging. Not surprisingly the *Irish Times*, obviously out of sympathy with the political sentiments expressed in the play, honed in on the dramatic inadequacies. 'Story none, dialogue dull, action weak', was its terse evaluation.[95]

As well as functioning as a critique of parliamentary politics, the play also worked to criticize the paternalistic policies of conciliation adopted by the British government[96] and to endorse the efforts of the self-help revivalists through the character of Ralf Kirwin. In the play Lawrence describes him as 'a compound of literature, patriotism, and belief in what he calls the spiritual inheritance of the race' (p. 65). Loosely based on Standish O'Grady, or perhaps Horace Plunkett, Kirwin is the conscience of the play constantly hovering in the background. Like Peg Inerny in *Maeve* he inspires Dean to commit himself to the genuine needs of the nation. Echoing Douglas Hyde's ideas on de-Anglicization, he contends that 'we have exchanged our arts, our language and our native aristocracy for shoddy imitation' (p. 31). He is the tragic hero of the play, who is dedicated to his ideals of cultural nationalism, but lacks the political acumen to make the nation a political reality. It is through his character that Moore articulates the central paradox which was emerging within the self-help movements: that the revival depended on the rhetoric of a spiritual Ireland to proclaim the distinctiveness of the nation culturally, and yet also demanded a material transformation to legitimize the nation politically. These contradictory imperatives are articulated by Kirwin when he remarks:

> Behind this money is something more, far more precious than the material prosperity that the money will bring; the material prosperity we want, and sorely, for we want to liberate the mind, and we can only do that through the body. This money will be the liberation of many ideas which poverty holds in slavery, and the ideas thus liberated will urge the race to its appointed destiny. (p. 41)

Essentially, then, we are left with the apparently contradictory idea that a degree of *material* prosperity is needed to nudge the Irish people towards their *spiritual* destiny. Yet, looked at another way, this 'contradiction' can be reconciled in an interpretation which sees *The Bending of the Bough* as a dramatization of the alternative modernization strategy which was at the heart of the Irish revival.

The Bending of the Knee

In contrast to the 1899 season, the post-1900 production debate witnessed a *rapprochement* between the Gaelic League and the Irish Literary Theatre. The inclusion of Alice Milligan's play was clearly a conciliatory gesture and was perceived by the League's president as such. At the celebration dinner at the Gresham hotel Douglas Hyde moved to bridge the gap that had appeared between the theatre movement and the Gaelic League the previous year. Hyde commended the work of the Irish Literary Theatre but reminded the audience that the theatre movement was 'one, an important one, but still only one of the many agencies which were at this present moment at work in trying to create a new Ireland, proceeding on national lines'.[97] In so doing he recast the Irish Literary Theatre and the Gaelic League as allies rather than antagonists. George Moore reciprocated by announcing that a Gaelic play would be performed the following year and that the production of Gaelic drama was central to the vision:

> The performance of plays in our language is part and parcel of the idea which led up to the founding of the Irish Literary Theatre. The Irish Literary Theatre has been founded to create a new centre for Irish enthusiasm, a new outlet for the national spirit and energy . . . I would not be understood to mean that the Irish play to be given next year is to stand as a mere sign of our project; it will do this, it is true, but it will do a little more than this – it will serve as a flag to lead to the restoration of our language as the literary and political language of this country.[98]

It was at this point that Moore launched into his by now infamous apologia for the Irish language. This speech is well known for his over-enthusiastic pledge to have his brother's children taught Irish by a nurse from the Aran Islands.[99] However, what is perhaps more worthy of note is Moore's criticism of John Redmond's attitude to Irish:

> My fellow countrymen, the moment has come – Ireland is becoming united and the language should be made the bond of union . . . I notice with regret that Mr. Redmond has not a word to say for the language. He speaks of a new University, but a University without our language would be like a stable without a horse.[100]

Picking up on Moore's cue, Yeats in his speech stated that 'the vital question of the moment was the Irish language'.[101] Remarking that a new education system was about to be introduced to Ireland he argued that 'all Irishmen should insist upon their representatives in Parliament opposing a denationalising system of education'.[102] Yeats concluded with an attack on the provincialism of Trinity College. Again one cannot but be struck by the extent to which the proceedings were dominated by wider politico-cultural matters rather than the aesthetics of theatrical performance. *An Claidheamh Soluis*, an antagonist of the Irish Literary Theatre up to this point, was clearly delighted by these pronouncements:

> It would be simply impossible to exaggerate the significance of the pronouncements that have been made or of the incidents that have occurred in connection with the Irish language movement within the last fortnight. Some of them have been described as sensational . . . Mr. Moore and Mr. Yeats have publicly given their adhesion to the movement. Both spoke strongly, fearlessly and sympathetically in favour of the language. Their adhesion to the cause at such a juncture must have a good effect. The announcement, too, that the first steps towards building up a Literary Theatre in the national Language have been taken will send a thrill of hope through the heart of every worker in the cause. Truly we are approaching the dawn.[103]

The Irish Literary Theatre would deliver on this stated commitment to the Irish language with the production of Douglas Hyde's *Casadh an tSúgáin* the following year.

In a climate of growing tension between the Irish Parliamentary Party and an emerging non-clandestine separatism, the Irish Literary Theatre clearly aligned itself with the latter. The overall message of the 1900 season was that Ireland was culturally distinctive and that the 'toadying' politicians of Westminster were working against the best interests of the nation. Moreover, during the next three months the gap between the separatists and the parliamentarians would become more clearly defined, thanks to the continued efforts of the Transvaal Committee and the strategic intervention of such prominent intellectuals as George Moore, Maud Gonne, W. B. Yeats, Lady Gregory and Edward Martyn. As the British authorities worked to mobilize Irish

energies to fight their imperial war, advanced nationalists responded by deny-
ing British jurisdiction over Ireland. Significantly, this battle for the hearts and
minds of the Irish people involved the staging of elaborately choreographed
politico-cultural events and counter-events.

Little over two weeks after the Irish Literary Theatre's productions a dramatic announcement marked a shift in British policy towards an increasingly
recalcitrant Ireland. Clearly worried by the success of Maud Gonne's anti-
recruitment campaign, the British government announced that Queen Victoria would visit Ireland ostensibly for non-political reasons but in reality to
counter the propaganda of the Transvaal Committee.[104] Furthermore, a new
Irish regiment – the Royal Irish Guards – was to be founded, and all ranks in
Her Majesty's Irish regiments were to be allowed the concession of wearing a
sprig of shamrock in their head-dress on St Patrick's day.[105] Thus, rather than
suppress all manifestations of Irish nationality, British policy now was to harness 'safe' expressions of nationalist sentiment for imperial ends. This development marks a watershed, which served to articulate and clarify the
difference in attitudes to the empire between the parliamentarians and the separatists. Responding to the announcement in the House of Commons, Redmond stated that:

> . . . the Irish people will receive with gratification the announcement that Her
> Majesty has directed that for the future the shamrock shall be worn by all Irish
> regiments on Ireland's national festival. The Irish people will welcome this
> graceful recognition of the valour of their race – whatever the field upon which
> that valour has latest been exhibited – and our people will, moreover, treat with
> respect the visit which the venerable Sovereign proposes to make to their shores,
> well knowing that on this occasion no attempt will be made to give that visit a
> party significance, and that their chivalrous hospitality will be taken in no quar-
> ter to mean any abatement of their demand for their national rights, which they
> will continue to press until they are conceded.[106]

Redmond's enthusiasm for the Queen's visit caused uproar, and for the next
two months the separatists made much capital out of what they perceived as
the sycophancy of the Irish Party leader – the very quality which Moore had
satirized in *The Bending of the Bough*.

Redmond's Jasper Dean-like gesture of welcome for the Queen's visit, in
fact, precipitated a series of events uncannily similar to the scenario depicted
by Moore on stage some weeks previously. Picking up on Redmond's lead, the
Lord Mayor of Dublin and the members of the Corporation 'voted in favour of
presenting an address to the Queen and calling on the Nationalists of the various wards to repudiate their conduct'.[107] In response to this a meeting of
15,000 people at Beresford place proclaimed that they repudiated 'with scorn
and loathing the action of the slaves and scoundrels of the Dublin Corporation'.[108] The following day, St Patrick's day, in a virtual re-enactment of the closing scenes of Moore's play, the Lord Mayor's inaugural procession was seriously

disrupted by a sizeable group of nationalists angered that their views were not being clearly represented by the Corporation.[109]

In a letter to the *United Irishman* published on the day, George Moore was stringent in his contradiction of Redmond's opinion that the Queen's visit was not politically motivated. Quoting the list of losses in Natal among General Buller's forces, he pointed out that fatalities among the Irish Regiments were substantially higher and concluded that the Queen's visit undoubtedly had a political purpose:

> . . . but the reason of the Queen's visit is clearly political; she comes to do the business which her recruiting sergeants have failed to do; she comes with the 'shilling' between her forefinger and thumb and a bag of shillings at her girdle . . . The wearing of the shamrock, the creation of a regiment of guards, above all the presence of the Queen in Ireland are undoubtedly bribes to Ireland to abandon the National for the Imperialistic idea . . . She needs soldiers to fill up the gaps that Boer bullets have made in Irish regiments.[110]

The editorial in the same edition took a similar line but teased out more clearly the political ramifications of the different reactions to the Queen's visit. The leader writer condemned 'the Irish slaves in the British House of Commons who cheered Mr. John Redmond's calumny on the Irish people last week', but was also careful to clearly delineate the new gap opening up in Irish politics:

> The Queen of England's visit will be made the occasion of an attempt to entrap Irish nationalists into support of the United Irish League and the new Parliamentarianism. They will be asked to lend their aid in stamping out whiggery. The cry 'organise' will be raised and the United Irish League will open its arms to embrace its victims. Let the Nationalists of Ireland freely and fully lend their aid in crushing out the toadying vermin who disgrace humanity as much as they do Ireland; but at the same time let all believers in our country's nationhood stand on their guard against an attempt to seduce them from their allegiance to the cause of national independence.[111]

Lady Gregory also had strong feelings on the queen's visit, although, characteristically, she refrained from expressing them publicly. 'If I were in politics', she confided to her diary, 'I wd certainly show no welcome either to the head of the English state, or to a woman who has been callous to the failings & the famines in Ireland during a long reign'.[112] In London on St Patrick's day she refused to wear the royally approved shamrock 'for fear of being mistaken for a Cockney'[113] and chose to adorn her attire with an ivy leaf instead, in memory of Parnell. It was also around this time that she wrote 'The Felons of our Land'. This article ranks as one of the most overtly nationalist of her writings, celebrating as it does 'the heroes of Irish rebellions since 1798 in a discursive study of the ballads written about them'.[114]

If the hope of the British authorities was that the pomp and ceremony surrounding the Queen's visit would bolster loyalism and increase recruitment, advanced nationalists saw an opportunity for a show of defiance. However, after the unruly events of St Patrick's day, there was a real danger that nationalist disenchantment would lead to riot. To avoid this outcome Yeats was called upon to stage-manage nationalist outrage and transform it into a dignified form of protest. Having been involved in the jubilee riots of 1897 he was anxious that 'mob rule' would not be the order of the day. Taking up George Moore's suggestion that the Queen should be received with 'a chill politeness',[115] Yeats argued in a letter to the *Freeman's Journal* that nationalists should 'protest with as much courtesy as is compatible with vigour'.[116] Noting that the Queen's visit coincided with the centenary of the Act of Union he proposed a mass meeting in the Rotunda 'to dissociate Ireland from any welcome that the Unionist or the time-server may offer to the official head of that Empire in whose name liberty is being suppressed in South Africa as it was suppressed in Ireland a hundred years ago'.[117] In a reference clearly aimed at the mainstream politicians he drew attention to the fact that violence was more likely to break out when the politicians failed to represent the wishes of people, as *The Bending of the Bough* had dramatized and as manifested by the events of St Patrick's day. A further letter to the *Freeman's Journal* quoted the French revolutionary, Mirabeau, and his famous maxim that 'the silence of a people is the lesson of kings',[118] which reiterated Yeats's call for a peaceful protest to the visit. James Joyce may have had this in mind when, recalling the moment some years later, he wrote that 'the queen of England entered the capital of Ireland in the midst of a silent people'.[119]

The peaceful protest which Yeats hoped for on 4 April, though not proscribed by Dublin Castle, was prevented by a force of 200 policemen who cordoned off Lower Abbey Street where the gathering was to take place (outside the Transvaal Committee rooms). As the committee meeting concluded, fifty men bearing lighted torches walked into the street from the committee rooms but were quickly charged down by the police. According to a report, 'the torchbearers were knocked down, kicked and in two instances batoned on the ground. Messrs. [James] Connolly and [Francis] Dorr were felled by the police and Messrs. [O'Leary] Curtis and [Arthur] Griffith struck.'[120]

Further controversy was generated three days later when the publication of Maud Gonne's famous essay 'The Famine Queen' led to the seizure of the *United Irishman* by order of Lord Cadogan, which instantly achieved the notoriety for the article that the authorities wished to avoid.[121] Joining the chorus in condemnation of 'our servile Irish members', Gonne reminded her readers that 'Every eviction during sixty-three years ha[d] been carried out in Victoria's name.'[122] As the propaganda war intensified, the loyalist society journal *Figaro* published an article which claimed that Gonne was 'in the pay of the British government because her father's army pension was supposedly paid into her estate'.[123] This article so annoyed Griffith that he horsewhipped the editor, Colles, with a *sjambok* he had taken with him from South Africa, which resulted in a spell in gaol for the nationalist leader. This incident is in fact most

revealing. It illustrates the extent of his 'deep devotion' to Maud Gonne pro-
voking an 'uncharacteristic act in defence of her reputation'.[124] It also provides
an interesting insight into Griffith's patriarchal propensity to defend the honour and reputation of women, which would become a central issue in the
Shadow of the Glen controversy.

Maud Gonne, however, tiring of patriarchal sanction and anxious to facil-
itate the more active involvement of women in the nationalist struggle, was in
the process of founding another self-help movement – Inghinidhe na h-Éireann – which held its inaugural meeting on Easter Sunday 1900. She recalls
gathering together friends who, 'like myself resented being excluded, as
women, from National Organisations'.[125] The aim of the group was to work
for Irish independence, encourage Irish culture and discourage the influence
of English culture in Ireland.[126] Angered by the mileage which loyalists were
making out of a free treat for 15,000 children staged in the Phoenix Park during Victoria's visit, Inghinidhe na h-Éireann organized a counter-event the following July.[127] The Patriotic Children's Treat Committee drew on nationalist
goodwill to organize 'the largest peaceful demonstration that anyone could
remember'.[128] Clonturk Park in north Dublin was the venue in which 25,000
children assembled to enjoy the oranges, sweets and buns provided. In her
autobiography Gonne recalled how the 'Patriotic Children's treat became leg-
endary in Dublin' and that, even in middle-age, 'men and women come up to
me in the streets and say: "I was one of the patriotic children at your party
when Queen Victoria was over"'.[129] Clearly such an event was to have a profound effect on the formation of the political consciousness of a generation
who would come of age a decade later.

. . . Ireland's Opportunity

The Boer War was certainly an important factor in the uniting of the Irish Parliamentary Party in 1900, but it also served to bring to birth a new type of separatist nationalism, not secretive like the Fenian movement, but overt in its
articulation of an independent foreign policy for the Irish nation. By opposing
recruitment the new separatists challenged British jurisdiction over Ireland
and developed the use of organized demonstrations and staged publicity
stunts as an important nationalist tactic to provoke confrontation with the
authorities and subvert the imperial agenda. Parallel to this, one can detect
among the separatists a growing disillusionment with the Irish politicians at
Westminster, who were viewed, increasingly, as a toadying coterie interested
in serving their own needs rather than the interests of the nation. In a climate
of tension between the Irish Parliamentary Party and the emerging separatism,
the Irish Literary Theatre clearly aligned itself with the latter. In keeping with
the pro-Boer and anti-parliamentarian opinions of the theatre leaders and playwrights, the plays of the 1900 season, especially *The Bending of the Bough*, made
a significant contribution to the rich ferment of advanced nationalist thought

in this period on the eve of the emergence of Sinn Féin. In fact Moore's drama played an important role in critiquing the policies of the Irish Parliamentary Party and articulating the emerging gap between the home rulers and the separatists. Furthermore, the Irish Literary Theatre personnel made a significant contribution to the wider theatre of anti-royal protest, generating debate in the newspapers and stage-managing demonstrations. The withdrawal of support for the theatre venture by Trinity historian. W. E. H. Lecky was a consequence of this radical nationalist stance. Yeats, however, was not upset by the loss of his support and was consoled by the fact that 'our present politics will have done more good than harm'.[130] Whether or not the politics of the theatre activists were strategic and motivated by a desire to increase their audience by tapping into popular sentiment is difficult to prove conclusively and, in the end, irrelevant to the wider political effects they caused. What is noteworthy is that they were centrally involved themselves in generating a level of popular awareness and activity that was crucial to the crystallization of the nascent Sinn Féin movement.

A BATTLE OF TWO CIVILIZATIONS?

Self-Help and Cumann na nGaedheal

Although Yeats and Moore would eschew any literary comparison, their writings served to legitimize the activities of the Irish Transvaal Committee at a time when Kipling's 'Absent-Minded Beggar' provided a major source of propaganda for British involvement in the South African war.[1] The year 1900 saw closer co-operation between leading writers and separatist politicians around the nucleus of the Irish Transvaal Committee, and that link was to be copper-fastened later that year by the foundation of Cumann na nGaedheal – a federation of self-help movements. This new alignment allowed a connection to develop between the Irish Literary Theatre and the Fay brothers – a relationship which would give birth to the first Irish company of professional actors dedicated to the performance of Irish plays. Moreover, Cumann na nGaedheal would become a patron of the theatre movement and stage plays under its auspices during its annual Samhain festival.[2]

The formal launch of Cumann na nGaedheal took place at a convention on 25 November 1900, although preliminary arrangements were being made as early as March of that year.[3] Essentially, this new organization grew out of the head of steam that had been built up by the Transvaal Committee; when formal meetings began they took place at the offices of the Celtic Literary Society in Abbey Street, as did the meetings of the Transvaal Committee. The main movers behind the new initiative were Arthur Griffith, Maud Gonne and William Rooney. Padraic Colum has recorded that Griffith 'had discussed its formation in John O'Leary's rooms and in Maud Gonne's little house in Rathgar with William Butler Yeats sometimes present', marking the involvement of major cultural and political figures from the start.[4] The scope of the new organization was outlined by Griffith in an article published in the *United Irishman* on 15 March. Realizing that an impressive number of disparate self-help groups all working in various ways for the betterment of the Irish nation were flourishing all over the country, Griffith felt that it was time to draw together and co-ordinate them. Not wanting to stifle the individuality of any self-help movement, he envisaged a loose federation that would:

> . . . require all groups or individuals associated with it to aid the diffusion of knowledge on all matters Irish, to undertake the education of the people in the history, literature, and language of their country, to teach them to appreciate

> Irish art, and to induce them to study the resources of Ireland – military as well
> as economic, and to revive throughout the land the spirit of brotherhood which
> animated the United Irishmen.[5]

Outlined here was a very clear cultural programme: the revival and practice of the Irish language, music, dancing and sports and 'the discountenancing of English ideas, manners, and customs', not because they were foreign but because they were detrimental to national distinctiveness. There was also a clear political message: 'that Home Ruler and Nationalist mean wholly opposite and irreconcilable things'.[6] Cumann na nGaedheal, therefore, would function to develop the strategy begun by the Transvaal Committee of undermining the Irish Parliamentary Party while providing an outlet for those Gaelic League members with strong separatist views to engage in language and cultural activities outside the neutral zone of the League. But perhaps the most important development of the Cumann na nGaedheal initiative was the realistic acknowledgement of 'the present inability to lead Ireland to victory against the armed might of her enemy'. The concentration, therefore, would be on the intellectual front – 'the disciplining of the mind and the training of the forces of the nation'[7] – a process which Yeats had initiated with the foundation of the literary societies in Dublin and London almost nine years previously.

At the first annual convention in November 1900 Rooney presided over proceedings, John O'Leary was elected President and Robert Johnston (the old Fenian) and John MacBride became vice-presidents. As Padraic Colum noted, the profile of the personnel attracted by Cumann na nGaedheal was revealing. The gatherings were 'of men [and women] of thirty and under, earnest, but with no training in affairs. They were intelligent; they wanted to have a part in the regeneration of their country and they looked for direction.'[8] During the inaugural meeting the aims of the organization were formally outlined. These included: the cultivation of a fraternal spirit among Irishmen; support for Irish industries; the teaching of Irish history, literature, language music and art; the cultivation of Irish games and pastimes; the discouragement of Anglicization; the development of an Irish foreign policy; and the nationalizing of public boards.[9] In this respect its foundation built on the work of the pioneering coalition of the Gaelic League, the Irish Literary Theatre and the IAOS. As well as functioning as a co-ordinating body, Cumann na nGaedheal was also active in initiatives on both the cultural and political fronts. For example, it continued the anti-recruitment work begun by the Transvaal Committee sending lecturers to towns and villages frequented by recruiting sergeants, it organized cultural events during its Beltaine and Samhain festivals, and it brought Irish drama to its London branches.[10]

Ethnic vs Civic Nationalism:
D. P. Moran and William Rooney

One of the most enduring orthodoxies of the Irish Revival holds that the period can be usefully seen as a battle of two civilizations, between the rival cultural groupings of 'Irish Ireland' and 'Anglo-Ireland'. The most famous statement of this position is contained in F. S. L. Lyons's *Culture and Anarchy*, where he argued that:

> . . . the great interest of the first decade of the new century is to see how fusion [of culture] was first resisted, and then destroyed by hostile forces. Essentially, they were the forces of resurgent nationalism, allied with a still powerful and articulate Catholicism.[11]

This analysis has been variously restated and elaborated from a broad range of ideological perspectives and by cultural analysts as diverse as Conor Cruise O'Brien, John Hutchinson, Harry White, Roy Foster, Deirdre Toomey and Stephen Regan, among others.[12] In her seminal rebuttal of Lyons's argument Margaret O'Callaghan pointed out the extent to which this image of Irish cultural dynamics in the early twentieth century had become fixed in historical accounts of the period. The 'shabby reality of a burgeoning, philistine, Catholic-Gaelic power', she argued, is held responsible for the demise of 'a dignified, gracious and urbane Anglo-Irish ethos'.[13] One does not have to look too deeply to find evidence to challenge this configuration of the socio-political landscape at the turning of the century. Analysis of the Mahaffy/Atkinson affair clearly shows that this episode was not a clear-cut 'ethnic contest' but rather a conflict between those who believed in the cultural worth of the Irish language and its literature and others intent on wiping it out in the name of imperial cosmopolitanism. In this memorable cultural row, significant Anglo-Irish figures such as Douglas Hyde, W. B. Yeats and George Russell were numbered among the most vocal critics of Mahaffy and Atkinson. At a more overtly political level, James Connolly's socialist republicanism, notwithstanding his interest in Irish culture, was influenced by Marxist ideas of class struggle and was, clearly, informed by a deep scepticism of bourgeois ethnic nationalism. Much of his writing challenged the very notion of such stable ethnic categories by drawing attention to the ubiquitous presence of capitalist domination across cultural boundaries.[14] It may well be pertinent, at a century's remove from the period, to further interrogate this 'battle of two civilizations' thesis – which is usually configured as a titanic struggle between the Anglo-Irish W. B. Yeats and D. P. Moran, 'the principal architect of the influential Irish Ireland ideology'[15] – by drawing attention to the work of a largely forgotten republican figure, William Rooney. Rooney was as formidable an opponent of D. P. Moran as Yeats, yet his civic nationalist challenge to Moran has been almost entirely forgotten.

On 1 September 1900 D. P. Moran launched the first edition of the *Leader*. This weekly newspaper was to become the forum for Moran to popularize the kinds of ideas he had been working on in a series of articles published in the *New Ireland Review*.[16] Although there were many overlaps and points of contact between the interests of Moran and the leadership of Cumann na nGaedheal, their respective analyses of the Irish question were fundamentally divergent. In fact the differences were so pronounced that one cannot easily use the much abused epithet 'Irish Ireland movement' as a term to describe the main preoccupations of Irish nationalism at this time without gross oversimplification.

D. P. Moran was very much of the belief that nationalist politics, rather than working to benefit the nation, were in reality sapping the energy of the nation. Clearly influenced by Hyde's de-Anglicizing ideas, Moran highlighted the contradiction he saw in a country which was expending so much energy agitating for national independence on the one hand, while it gave up its own distinctive cultural practices and imitated those of its professed 'enemy' on the other. Political nationalism could only lead to a dead-end, according to Moran:

> While everyone has been quarrelling about political party cries, the essentials of national life have been overlooked. From whom can one get any rational expression of that nationality about which all talk so loudly? The '98 processions are a grand intoxication, and no more. What, after all, was the great Wolfe Tone demonstration significant of? Violent, undefined passions of love and hate probably filled most of the great mass who took I don't know how many hours to pass a given point. How many of them had any seriously considered views, reasonable or unreasonable, as to the building up of national life? What was it all but a mere parade of men being dragged further and further after the British chariot, or rather not being dragged, but going open-eyed that way, the while they cried out to deceive themselves and the world: – 'We are not English!' If not, what are they? let [sic] me ask again. They have discarded their language, and they know nothing of their literature.[17]

As a pragmatist Moran conceded that a political or military victory was beyond the capabilities of Irish nationalists and that it would be much wiser to channel energy into the preservation of Irish cultural distinctiveness.[18] This could be done, he argued, by isolating Ireland from English influences and encouraging native cultural initiatives like the Gaelic League.

Moran, however, was not an anti-modern nativist. He shared with Cumann na nGaedheal the belief that 'economic tendencies rule the world'[19] and that the regeneration of the Irish economy could only happen through the development of indigenous industry. But, most importantly, such industrial development could only take place, he felt, on the back of Irish cultural regeneration. He saw a strong connection between 'the development of a native civilization having its roots in the native language, and the production of economic wealth'.[20] Moran also placed great emphasis on education and human resources, realizing that the mere possession of land did not guarantee economic success:

> We have come now to see that land, though indispensable, is by no means the main source, of modern economic wealth. Human skill in all its manifold manifestations has taken the premier place, and conditions precedent to the production of that skill, are that existence of initiative, self-dependence. If you have to begin with a self-distrusting people who are afraid to rely on their own judgement, who have learnt by a long and reluctant effort to imitate a rich and highly developed people foreign to their genius, to conceive a mean and cringing opinion of themselves, you will never get much economic initiative out of them.[21]

One can clearly detect the strong influence of Horace Plunkett and his ideas on self-help here. Plunkett, as we have seen, was a practical social philosopher as well as a self-help pioneer who designed and put into effect 'a comprehensive scheme for the regeneration of country life based upon the twin pillars of co-operation and education'.[22]

Like Plunkett, Moran was largely indifferent to constitutional issues, but he further believed that 'a separation of national personality, the keeping distinct and clear cut as many things as possible that may mark us off from our neighbours' was the best strategy for preserving Irish nationality.[23] Indeed, he drew an interesting comparison between the cultural vitality of Wales, where political union was not questioned, with the stagnation of Irish culture which had been accompanied by centuries of political agitation.[24] In a challenge directed squarely at political nationalists he asked:

> Will a few soldiers dressed in green, and a republic, absolutely foreign to the genius of the Irish people, the humiliation of England, a hundred thousand English corpses with Irish bullets or pike wounds through them satisfy the instinct within us that says: – 'Thou shalt be Irish?' These things we probably can never see, though we may try to drown our national conscience by dreaming of them. But were they possible they were vain; for a distinct nation is a distinct civilization.

One of Moran's central beliefs, therefore, was that Ireland's battle needed to be won on a cultural rather than a political front. Furthermore, Moran's cultural nationalism did not in any way embody a critique of the principle of imperialism. In fact he endorsed the empire by arguing that Ireland should play its part in empire building but only to spread the virtues of the Irish language and culture. 'If the rebel sentiment against serving the Empire were removed', he argued, 'hundreds of Irish boys, out of the National Christian Brothers' schools, would rise to the front ranks of Empire-makers, and load their pockets with riches'.[25] He further stated that, given the opportunity, he 'would attempt to spread by legitimate means the Irish language, Irish civilization and Irish sway over as much of the world as possible'.[26]

Although Moran laid an emphasis on culture and directed many of his criticisms against political nationalism – particularly the republican variety – his own ideas, as they formed in the opening decade of the twentieth century, were anything but apolitical. In fact one can place him firmly within the O'Connellite utilitarian tradition. Although he disagreed with O'Connell's stance on the Irish language he believed that the best alternative for Ireland was to prosper within the existing political system. By opening up participation in the British parliament to Irish Catholics, O'Connell established the pattern for Moran. Much of Moran's crusading journalism was driven by a 'resentment at the way the business community and upper reaches of the civil service were dominated by Protestants, who maintained their position through patronage networks such as the Freemasons'.[27] He saw it as his task to expose Protestant over-representation in the civil service and in the ranks of the large employers such as the banks and railways with the hope of opening these bastions to the Catholic population. The more the Catholic middle class took over these positions the more they would be able to 'confer social distinction' on national character.[28] Essentially, then, Moran, who is often wrongly supposed to represent the vanguard of separatism, was in favour of replacing an Anglo-Irish élite with a 'Gaelic' Catholic one and was content to leave matters constitutional unchanged. Moreover, he was even prepared to court the favour of the British monarch to achieve his aims. 'We accept the King', he was to declare in 1903, 'but want fair play in our own country; we want our share of the law-making power and the positions'.[29] Notwithstanding his support for the Irish language, therefore, he was politically closer to the Irish Parliamentary Party than to the embryonic Sinn Féin organization.[30]

It was Moran's view that the Anglo-Irish ascendancy constituted the greatest stumbling-block to the growth and development of Irish character by constantly taking a cultural lead from England. He was very much aware of the disabling and alienating impact of a colonial education system, on the one hand, and the widespread availability of cheap English popular literature in the absence of indigenous equivalents, on the other. 'A literature steeped in the history, traditions, and genius of one nation', he argued, 'is at the best only an imperfect tutor to the people of another nation'. Commenting on the fact that the Irish nation in the nineteenth century had 'been brought up on English literature', he expressed concern that the people 'were driven to look at literature as a thing not understandable and above them', and that this had had an adverse effect on intellectual self-dependence.[31]

Moran's insight here can be read as an early post-colonial critique of the debilitating effects of an imperial cultural superstructure on a colonized people. However, his espousal of the primacy of cultural distinctiveness led him to take a steadfastly essentialist view of Irish identity. To his mind Irish culture and Gaelic Catholic experience were simply coterminous. This led him to denounce vehemently the possibility of an Irish literature in the English language and to pour scorn on Yeats and his fellow revivalists, who were striving to make just such an Irish literature in English possible.[32] Moran failed to appreciate the extent to which Yeats and his cohorts had alienated themselves from ascendancy interests and had spearheaded an intellectual revival for the regeneration of Ireland. In fact, he did not see any distinction between the younger generation of Anglo-Irish revivalists and die-hard ascendancy colonials like Atkinson and Mahaffy. He had no qualms in dismissing the 'Celtic note' as 'one of the most glaring frauds that the credulous Irish people ever swallowed'.[33] Moran went further, pouring scorn on the literature of the Young Irelanders that was so sacred to Irish nationalism. Whereas the poetry of Yeats was too difficult ('Practically no one in Ireland understands Mr. Yeats or his school'), the poetry of Thomas Davis was too simple ('Thought was necessarily absent from all this literature'[34]). The bottom line as far as Moran was concerned was that there was 'no essential difference between first-class literary work executed by an English-speaking man born in Ireland and that executed by an English-speaking man born in England'.[35] These essentialist views circumscribed Irish identity within the narrow confines of Gaelic Catholic experience and left no room for any expression of a Protestant Irishness. Furthermore, his analysis disregarded the cultural choices made by the Irish people in giving up the language, and thus denied their autonomy as cultural agents. Although he was alive to the disabling influence of colonial education, the equally disabling effect of forcing Gaelic on a largely English-speaking population did not register with him.

The tendency among Irish historians and cultural analysts to focus attention on D. P. Moran as the principal theorist of the influential Irish Ireland movement has been noted. Yet much of the analysis has occluded the extent to which Moran was at odds with the main thrust of Irish political separatism in 1900. As Brian Maye has recently pointed out, 'There were many clashes between Griffith and his rivals. The liveliest was with D. P. Moran.'[36] Although there was broad agreement about the importance of self-help, Griffith had no sympathy with Moran's racial nationalism and attacked him for trying to 'arouse the suspicions and antipathy of the Irishmen of fifty generations against the Irish men of five'.[37] However, by far the most trenchant and engaging critique of Moran's ideas was levelled by William Rooney.

Rooney is now a largely forgotten figure of Irish history but, until his untimely death on 6 May 1901, he 'held a unique position of authority and trust'[38] within separatist nationalism, with Griffith playing second fiddle to him. In fact it was only after the death of Rooney that Griffith reluctantly stepped into his shoes to become the leader of the movement.[39] Griffith, indeed, recorded how he came to build his 'hopes for Ireland on him, and to regard him as the destined regenerator of his people'.[40] After his death the *United Irishman* editor conjectured that, had he lived, he 'would have become, perhaps, the greatest leader Ireland has known' and had no difficulty in describing him as 'the Thomas Davis of the 1890s'.[41] Rooney came from a Dublin Catholic working-class background, was educated by the Strand Street

Christian Brothers and was one of the earliest members of the Fireside Club, where he received his first lessons in the Irish language and learned his trade as a public speaker.[42] Some of his most important work was carried out under the auspices of the Celtic Literary Society, which was formed at a meeting in his house on 3 February 1893, nearly six months before the founding of the Gaelic League, 'to study Irish language, literature, history and music'.[43] One of the reasons for the success of the Celtic Literary Society was its co-operation with the Young Ireland League, which included John O'Leary and Yeats as active members. Rooney has been credited as an important contributor to the heightened profile of the Irish language movement in country districts in the late 1890s, having spent many weekends in rural Ireland addressing meetings in Irish. Indeed it was he who was selected to speak in Irish at the great '98 demonstration in Dublin on 15 August 1898. Writing under at least eleven pseudonyms,[44] Rooney was undoubtedly the most prolific writer for the *United Irishman* until illness struck him down in March 1901. In his articles for the paper he wrote of the Young Ireland writers, the need for an Irish republic and the importance of material, as well as cultural regeneration, the need for indigenous industry and the importance of the self-help ethos.[45]

Given the importance of Rooney to the emergence of non-clandestine separatism it is regrettable that his writing and influence have been overshadowed by a sustained concentration on the work of D. P. Moran, who has been canonized as the singular voice of 'Irish Ireland'. There is no doubt that both men shared much in common in relation to the Irish language, cultural revival and self-help, but quite clearly Rooney stands out in this period as the voice of civic-minded republicanism, very much at odds with the racial ideas of bourgeois cultural nationalism espoused by Moran and, to a large degree, with the Hungarian policy later to be outlined by Griffith.

Moran was of the opinion that nationalist politics were sapping the energy of the nation, yet Rooney believed that this was because a genuinely radical politics had not emerged in post-Parnell Ireland. Broadly speaking, although firmly committed to the revival of Irish culture, he was an advocate of a civic politics of individual rights rather than a collective ethnic nationalism. Although he had much in common with James Connolly he did not share his socialist views and adhered more firmly to the Irish republican tradition. He did, however, share Connolly's distrust of the Irish Parliamentary Party.[46] In sentiments echoing those expressed by Moore in *The Bending of the Bough*, Rooney drew attention to the self-serving antics of the parliamentarians, who, he felt, had abdicated their responsibility to the Irish people:

> 'Advanced' nationalism is in truth, no petty, compromising propaganda, which talks of healing the wounds of centuries, or guarantees the aid of Irish arms for Imperial buccaneering, 'if our rights are conceded.' It is indeed no convenient creed which would toast a foreign queen or flaunt the Union Jack on College Green for the privilege of being allowed to concoct a drainage scheme, or pass

an authority for a railway cutting through Cork or Connemara. It is no tempo-
rising, time-serving, half-hearted sentiment which fears the future, but likes to
take advantage of the present, trusting to the forgetfulness of the popular memory to overlook any vacillation from the right road. It is a spirit which takes
something more than an antiquary's interest in the struggles and beliefs of the
past, which does not talk of the superior advantages of our fathers to excuse
inaction or indifference today. It is in fine, the spirit of Irish Nationality, which
recognises nothing short of supreme and entire independence as the limit of
Irish hopes and aspirations.[47]

Both Moran and Rooney agreed on the inefficacy of mainstream politics; however, Rooney's solution was to rediscover the radical impulse within Irish politics whereas Moran, as we have seen, preferred to channel energy away from
politics altogether.

Rooney's blueprint for an independent Irish republic was forcefully articulated in an important lecture, 'The Development of the Nation Ideal', delivered to the Celtic Literary Society in January 1900. This in many ways can be
read as a rejoinder to Moran's 'Irish Ireland' articles that were circulating at this
time. Here Rooney surveyed 700 years of Irish history, outlining what he called
'The National Ideal' – 'an Irish State governed by Irishmen for the benefit of
the Irish people'.[48] Among his idealists can be found Swift, who 'united all the
elements of Irish society for the first time in centuries', and his great exemplar
Wolfe Tone. Drawing from Tone's inspiration Rooney outlined his ideal:

> An Irish State self-supporting, self-defending, her flag respected in every port,
> her shores and her sympathy for the oppressed of every race and colour. Her
> voice in the councils of the nations; her language, her laws, and her achieve-
> ments the pride of all her people. Such is a national ideal and to Tone do we
> owe the fact that any of its most militant features still recommend themselves
> to the vast bulk of our countrymen.[49]

Such an emphasis on radical politics with a heightened civic consciousness
was anathema to the thinking of Moran, who felt that republicanism was
'absolutely foreign to the genius of the Irish people'[50] and who was content to
accept the existing constitutional arrangements as long as a Gaelic Catholic
élite was to become the dominant force.

Moran's endorsement of O'Connellite utilitarianism also marks a point of
fundamental disagreement between the *Leader* editor and Rooney. Although
conscious of the achievements of O'Connell, Rooney was of the opinion that the
Liberator had made a fundamental mistake in confusing religious freedom with
national liberty. It was just such a conflation of ideals that underpinned Moran's
thinking. O'Connell's loyalty to the British crown, his hostility towards the
United Irishmen and his fear of revolution blotted his reputation in Rooney's
eyes. Catholic Emancipation, argued Rooney, by opening up positions to Irishmen in the English service, diverted energy and talent away from the republican

cause. 'By throwing over their Gaeldom, and accepting the service of Britain under the terms of the Emancipation Act', he argued, 'they enslaved still further, instead of enfranchising, their co-religionists'.[51] It was the shambles of parliamentarianism, however, which most raised Rooney's ire. He had nothing but contempt for the home rule strategy and believed that its achievements would only dull Irish resistance. His rejection of these ideas also carried an unequivocal anti-colonial message. Home rule, he argued, would only be achieved at the cost of enormous compromise on the part of Irish republicanism. The pay-off from Britain would take the form of the 'portion of plunder our masters did not need, and their gracious permission to rob the nations of the East and South under the protection of the British flag'.[52] Such sentiments again provide a striking contrast to the imperialist aspirations of Moran.

If Moran's great rallying cry was the need to channel political energy into cultural regeneration, Rooney took the opposite view. As far as the republican was concerned mainstream cultural movements, particularly the Gaelic League, were not overtly political enough. In his opinion the term 'non-political' was being too narrowly adhered to by the League. He believed that the League, by refusing to take part in the commemoration of the anniversary of '98, 'took up a position occupied by every anti-Irish and West British individual in the country':

> . . . with most of us politics has begun and ended with Parliamentarianism, but it surely needs but little thought to see that 'politics,' even in Ireland, is broader than its supposed synonym – yet the projectors of the language movement refuse to allow the branches of their organisation to take part in any public Nationalist propaganda.[53]

One of the great innovations of Rooney's thinking was his realization of the extent to which culture and politics are inextricably bound up. He saw that, in a colonial context like Ireland's, culture had long been a site of colonial advance and that it had an important role to play in anti-colonial resistance. If one were to draw a distinction between Moran and Rooney on this issue, then, it is clear that Moran wanted to mask the politics of culture, while Rooney was motivated to lay them bare.

Rooney and Moran were also poles apart in their attitudes to Irish literature. It is generally assumed that Moran directed his venom exclusively at Yeats and his Anglo-Irish confrères. In fact, as we have seen, Moran was equally disparaging of the Thomas Davis tradition, which counted Rooney as its chief contemporary exponent. In 'The Future of the Irish Nation' he lambasted Rooney's literary project without naming him. Clearly, though, any informed reader could not have failed to recognize Moran's target:

> One of the most common flourishes of the minor leader is the one about 'the Isle of Destiny,' and what vague things it is going to do in a manner never explained, as the gallery don't want explanations. Then the minor leader knows

that a Sarsfield flourish will always bring down the house; and a reference to Owen Roe, in a language which that chieftain would not have insulted his throat by attempting to speak, stamps him as a man deeply versed in his country's historic lore.[54]

Even Moran's dismissal of 'the Celtic note' had resonances beyond the towering figure of Yeats, calling into question as it did the work of the Celtic Literary Society, which numbered Rooney and Griffith as prominent members. Such a critique, therefore, was not aimed exclusively at writers with an Anglo-Irish background.

Its seems likely that it was Moran's 'Irish Ireland' articles which provoked Rooney to challenge his essentialist views of Irish culture. In an important and largely forgotten essay, 'Is there an Anglo-Irish Literature?', Rooney argued convincingly for the necessity of an Irish literature in the English language:

> Surely no one is insane enough to imagine that we can de-anglicise Ireland by teaching the people to regard as non-Irish the writings of Davis, Mitchel, Mangan, *and their confrères and followers* [emphasis added] . . . Are we to ask the young men and women who are so unfortunate as to never have heard Irish spoken to give up reading until they are able to satisfy themselves with the literature of Gaelic Ireland? I am not by any means to be taken as making an *ad misericordiam* appeal for the creators of an Irish literature in English. They have a raison d'être, and the popularity that their works have won, and still find, amongst the most Irish of Irishmen, is a proof of their truth to Ireland, and their service to their cause.[55]

What is noteworthy here is not only Rooney's appraisal of the Davisian tradition as an integral part of the Irish literary inheritance, but also the importance he attached to contemporary Anglo-Irish literature, which counted Yeats as its chief exponent.[56] The evidence that Yeats in turn held Rooney in high regard is borne out by the fact that he was to dedicate the first edition of *Kathleen ni Houlihan* to his memory in 1902.[57] What also distinguishes Rooney among Irish language activists was his common-sense realization that a profound language shift had taken place in Ireland and that Irish could not 'be brought back into general use by a miracle'.[58] This was a sensible antidote to Moran's unpragmatic notion of a spontaneous Gaelic revival. For Rooney, then, the importance of Anglo-Irish literature lay in the 'fact that the history of Ireland, a whole host of her traditions, legends, performances, hopes and sacrifices, are enshrined in it'.[59] He was shrewd enough to realize that the access to cultural memory enabled, however awkwardly, by Anglo-Irish literature was vital at a time when Irish continued to decline as a vernacular.

Rooney, however, was not alone in making a case for an Irish literature in the English language and was joined by the able apologist, W. B. Yeats. Significantly, one of Yeats's earliest defences of Anglo-Irish literature was published in the first edition of the *Leader*:[60]

> Side by side with the spread of the Irish language, and with much writing in the Irish language, must go on much expression of Irish emotion and Irish thought, much writing about Irish things and people, in the English language, for no man can write well except in the language he has been born and bred to, and no man, as I think, becomes perfectly cultivated except through the influence of that language; and this writing must for a long time to come be the chief influence in shaping the opinions and the emotions of the leisured classes in Ireland in so far as they are concerned with Irish things.[61]

Like Rooney, Yeats was sensitive to the linguistic shift which had taken place in Ireland and was pragmatic about the necessity of a vigorous Anglo-Irish literature to the full imaginative expression of the Irish people, notwithstanding his vested interest as the leading Irish writer in the English language and his concern for 'the leisured classes'. He neatly summed up the flaw in Moran's analysis by noting that 'The Leader's weakness is that it tries to convince people that a nation can drop a century & half [sic] out of its life as if Irish history ceased to be Irish history when the men that made it spoke English.'[62]

Clearly then, William Rooney stands out as a very influential civic nationalist of this period, bridging the gap between nineteenth-century fenianism and a newer generation of republican radicals. In many respects his dialogue with Moran signals the opening up of a gap between a conservative bourgeois cultural nationalism and a more radical republicanism within Irish cultural politics that would reach a crescendo during the Civil War. The fact that Rooney was himself an enthusiastic Irish language activist who, with Yeats, championed the cause of an Irish literature in English significantly disrupts the orthodox interpretation of this period as a clear-cut battle between Anglo-Ireland and Irish Ireland. Rooney's position was, in many ways, analogous to Yeats's championing of Irish in the wake of Mahaffy and Atkinson. By promoting the right to artistic expression in both English and Irish, Rooney and Yeats worked to enlarge the possibilities of Irish national identity beyond the narrow ethnic demands of Moran. They were not alone in this endeavour – in fact they formed part of a significant cadre which promoted a national literature in both languages but whose impact has been neglected due to the prolonged emphasis on the 'battle of two civilizations' in accounts of the period, from D. P. Moran to the present.

Irish Voices in English: Lady Gregory and Frank Fay

Rooney and Yeats could see, at a time when English had quite clearly taken over as the vernacular, that a vigorous Irish literature in English was essential for the intellectual and imaginative development of the nation. If there was to be a meaningful engagement with the Gaelic cultural inheritance it would have to happen, for the most part, via the English language as long as Irish continued to decline and until a time when Irish would rival it as a vernacular.

Rooney had no difficulty acknowledging that 'the history of Ireland, a whole host of her traditions, legends, performances, hopes and sacrifices'[63] were enshrined and would continue to be enshrined in Irish writing in English. Likewise Yeats was frank in his belief that 'no man can write well except in the language he has been born and bred to'.[64] Their negotiation of linguistic realities provided a sharp contrast to the attitude of D. P. Moran, who longed for a spontaneous Gaelic revival but could offer no practical suggestion as to how this might be brought about.

At the same time as Rooney and Yeats were providing the apologia for an Irish literature in English, other leading figures were experimenting with new cultural forms which would transcend the Anglo-Irish/Irish Ireland binary promoted by D. P. Moran and ascendancy intellectuals like Mahaffy and Atkinson from different cultural perspectives. It was Lady Gregory who would emerge as an early literary innovator with her work on the Cuchulain cycle, begun a matter of weeks after Rooney's untimely death in May 1901.[65] With her knowledge of the Irish language and its literature Lady Gregory was perfectly placed to render these stories into English at a time when there was 'very little of the history of Cuchulain and his friends left in the memory of the people'.[66] *Cuchulain of Muirthemne* functioned as an act of cultural retrieval, but it served as more than just a literal translation. Just as Hyde's translations of the songs of Connacht took on a literary life of their own, so too did Gregory's stories of ancient Ireland – but not without initial difficulties. She had planned for quite a while to put together the Irish legends into 'a sort of Morte d'Arthur'[67] but was having considerable stylistic difficulties in finding an authentic voice to articulate these ancient stories. The problem of faithful translation from original Irish sources began to be felt from the end of the eighteenth century. In an early articulation of this cultural crux William Carleton recalled the difficulties his mother experienced while singing English words to Irish songs. 'The Irish melts into the tune', she remarked, 'but the English doesn't', highlighting the vital connection between form and language.[68] In the same way, Lady Gregory's greatest fear was 'of being influenced, in spite of herself, by the French, German, and bad English translations'.[69] It was out of this dilemma that she came up with the truly innovative idea of adopting the dialect of the Kiltartan peasantry to overcome her difficulties. The most distinguishing feature of this dialect was the degree to which it was nuanced by idiomatic translations from Irish which did not conform to the grammatical and syntactical rules of standard English. Yeats was quick to realize the significance of this moment, in which Lady Gregory 'became the founder of modern Irish dialect literature'.[70] In the preface to the collection he signalled the magnitude of her achievement by way of a personal recollection:

> Some years ago I wrote some stories of mediaeval Irish life, and as I wrote I was sometimes made wretched by the thought that I knew of no kind of English that fitted them . . . I knew of no language to write about Ireland in but raw

> modern English; but now Lady Gregory has discovered a speech . . . and a liv-
> ing speech into the bargain. As she moved about among her people she learned
> to love the beautiful speech of those who think in Irish, and to understand that
> it is as true a dialect of English as the dialect that Burns wrote in.[71]

Lady Gregory later interpreted Yeats's changing perception of her literary ability as an important moment in her career. In *Seventy Years* she recalled that 'it
was only when I had read him one day in London my chapter the "Death of
Cuchulain" that he came to look on me as a fellow writer'.[72]

Clearly *Cuchulain of Muirthemne* was conceived to strengthen the case of
those in favour of an Irish literature in English, but it also worked to fulfil
another purpose – to argue for the integrity, beauty and moral value of the
Gaelic inheritance. It is not difficult to see that at the heart of *Cuchulain of
Muirthemne* lies another concerted attempt to refute the allegations that
Mahaffy and Atkinson had levelled against the Irish language and its literature
in 1899.[73] To counter their negative views of Irish literature, Alfred Nutt suggested that a retelling of the principal Irish sagas should be undertaken. Lady
Gregory duly obliged by producing *Cuchulain of Muirthemne*. In her dedication
to the people of Kiltartan she made a thinly veiled reference to the Trinity College Irish language controversy by noting that 'if there was more respect for
Irish things among the learned men that live in the college at Dublin, where
so many of these old writings are stored, this work would not have been left
to a woman of the house'.[74] In her anxiety not to verify the claims that Irish
literature was indecent, Lady Gregory took the liberty of 'sanitizing' material
that may have been offensive to the Victorian sensibilities of Mahaffy and
Atkinson. In the book's dedication she admitted that she 'left out a good deal
I thought you would not care about for one reason or another'.[75] She was, of
course, also mindful of the scruples of the Catholic Church, which was playing an important role in the idealization of the Irish-speaking peasantry at the
time. As the analysis of the *Countess Cathleen* affair has shown, the Church was
dogged by an anxiety that 'native' culture should not appear to conform to the
expectations of the colonials. Gregory's 'improvements' generally took the form
of downplaying material of a sexual nature. In a well-known incident in the
Táin, for example, Cuchulain is exposed to 150 naked women. In Lady Gregory's account, however, they are described as coming to meet him with 'their
breasts uncovered'.[76]

In some respects then, Lady Gregory can be accused of internalizing the
colonial critiques of Mahaffy and Atkinson. However, if the ever-expedient
Gregory did in any way surrender to middle-class Victorian values in *Cuchulain of Muirthemne*, it may have been out of the hope that her collection 'might
be made a school reading book'. It was for this reason that she professed to be
'particularly careful about the Boy Deeds'.[77] Yeats was alarmed by her willingness to pander to the puritans – both colonial and nationalist – and urged her
not to 'bowdlerize' her text.[78] Notwithstanding Lady Gregory's editorial

scruples, however, *Cuchulain of Muirthemne* endures as an important pioneering attempt to render the Gaelic literary inheritance into Hiberno-English dialect. It stands at once as a significant text of Gaelic cultural retrieval and a landmark in the development of Irish literature in English which inspired other writers, among them J. M. Synge.

At the same time as Lady Gregory was breaking new ground writing *Cuchulain of Muirthemne* an important figure emerged to call for a 'new voice' for Irish drama in a similar attempt to move cultural thinking beyond an ethnic contest between Anglo-Ireland and Irish Ireland. As the drama critic for the *United Irishman*, Frank Fay campaigned relentlessly for the employment of Irish actors in Irish Literary Theatre productions.[79] Just as Yeats had difficulties with the use of 'raw modern English' to translate stories from Irish, so did Fay have problems with the incongruity of English accents in Irish plays. This had been a feature of the early productions of the Irish Literary Theatre, in which professional actors from the London stage were used because of a perceived lack of local acting talent. In his article 'Mr. Yeats and the Stage', Fay put it up to the poet, arguing that 'plays dealing with Ireland should be played by Irish actors; they are available if sought for'.[80] Like Rooney, Fay was an enthusiastic member of the Gaelic League, committed to the restoration of the Irish language, but he also believed in the necessity for an Irish drama in English. He was a vocal supporter of Yeats as a dramatist and had no difficulty admitting that 'English will have to be heard on our stage' despite his aspiration to see an Irish theatre 'express itself solely in the Irish language'.[81] Again, unlike Moran, Fay was aware of the difficulties facing drama in Irish. He was very anxious to see plays in Irish acted but was conscious that:

> . . . there are not sufficient people in Dublin at present able to follow with ease
> and enjoyment dialogue in Irish to beget that sympathy between the actors and
> the audience which is so vital to a play's success.[82]

In the meantime, he argued, Irish rather than English voices should be heard on stage at the Irish Literary Theatre. In the coming years Frank Fay and his brother William would become central figures in the founding of the Abbey Theatre and the main innovators in the evolution of an Irish acting style. It was largely due to the Fays that English actors were soon replaced by home-grown talent, marking another significant advance for Irish self-help.

The 1901 Productions: *Casadh an tSúgáin* and *Diarmuid and Grania*

While Rooney, Yeats, Gregory and Fay defended the necessity of an Irish literature in English, there was, simultaneously, a growing feeling within the Irish Literary Theatre that drama in Irish should become an integral part of the programme. Having joined Lady Gregory, W. B. Yeats and Edward Martyn in supporting the Irish language the previous year, George Moore continued his assault on Mahaffy throughout the summer of 1901.[83] He was vocal in his support for a Gaelic drama and helped in the production of *Casadh an tSúgáin*, which was performed in October 1901.[84] Yeats, too, was eager for the development of Gaelic drama. Addressing the Árd-Chraobh of the Gaelic League in 1900 he advised Gaelic playwrights to keep their plays short and simple and to focus on 'the treasures of the Irish language'.[85] Significantly, Yeats has a claim to the co-authorship of *Casadh an tSúgáin*, given the fact that he provided Hyde with the original scenario of the play.[86] Once again what is striking among the major figures here is their support for the development of a national literature in *both* Irish and English.

Preparations for the third season of the Irish Literary Theatre during the summer of 1901 illustrate the high level of co-operation that existed between the Gaelic League and the theatre movement at this time. It is also clear that the theatre people were eager to be part of the self-help effort promoted by Cumann na nGaedheal. In a letter to Lady Gregory, Yeats stated his belief that the journal *Samhain* (as the former *Beltaine* was now called) 'should be a Gaelic propaganda paper this time' and it was agreed that any profits accruing from its publication should go to the Gaelic League.[87] Lady Gregory, who was concerned that the reputations of both Moore and Yeats would damage the prospect of success for the 1901 season, was keen that the theatre movement be seen to participate in the self-help effort:

> As to *Beltaine* I am very strongly of the opinion it should be printed and published in Ireland. We must take advantage of every wind that blows, and the home industry people would be put in good humour . . . And we want all the aids to popularity we can get for the theatre, having your enemies and Moore's enemies and the Castle in general against us.[88]

Like *Cuchulain of Muirthemne* the plays selected for production on 21 October 1901 can also be read as a rejoinder to the criticisms of Atkinson and Mahaffy. The success of the Hyde/Yeats collaboration, *Casadh an tSúgáin*, provided proof that a dramatic literature was indeed possible in the Irish language. Stephen Gwynn provided one of the best accounts of the audience's reaction to the play:

> I never was in an audience so amusing to be among; there was magnetism in the air. In the entractes [sic], a man up in the gallery with a fine voice, sang song after song in Irish, the gallery joining in the chorus, and an attentive house applauding at the end. One began to realise what the Gaelic League was doing – and one felt a good deal out in the cold because one had to rely on the translation.[89]

The inclusion of the play in the Irish Literary Theatre programme conferred institutional sanction on the Irish language at a time it badly needed it. Performed by members of the Keating branch of the Gaelic League, the production also lent weight to Frank Fay's belief in the potential of Irish actors to perform well on the national stage. Likewise, the decision by Moore and Yeats to dramatize the story of Diarmuid and Grania was an illustration of their conviction that the substance of ancient Irish literature was not 'silly or indecent' but rich in literary and dramatic possibilities. It is significant that they chose to dramatize the very story that Atkinson singled out for special mention because of its immorality. No human being could read through *Tóraíocht Dhiarmada agus Gráinne*, he argued, 'without feeling that he had been absolutely degraded by contact with it'. Notwithstanding their choice of material, *Diarmuid and Grania* was to embroil Moore and Yeats in controversy yet again.

Despite the difficult conception of *Diarmuid and Grania*, its obvious flaws as a play and the shortcomings of the original production, it remains of interest for the responses it generated on its opening production, and for its anticipation of the Synge controversies.[90] Dogged by disagreement and infighting, this Moore/Yeats collaboration attempted to achieve for Irish drama what *Cuchulain of Muirthemne* had achieved for Irish prose – a successful transformation of Gaelic legend into an Irish drama in English. The two playwrights, however, had difficulties in rendering an authentic 'Irish voice' to the extent that Lady Gregory had succeeded in her collection. This was both a fault of the play and of the production. The play is marred by dialogue which is stilted and incongruous, while the production was ruined for many by the foreign accents of the F. R. Benson Company, who had difficulty pronouncing the names of the characters they were playing.[91] Interestingly, the play was criticized for its 'fraudulent Celticism' by that champion of aristocratic values, Standish O'Grady, as well as by the stalwart of Irish Ireland, D. P. Moran. Both of these critics found themselves in an unholy alliance to undermine the Moore/Yeats collaboration, even if their motives were unrelated.

The Moore/Yeats treatment of the Diarmuid and Grania story flew in the face of O'Grady's work on Irish legends. Widely regarded as the authority on this subject, O'Grady was enthralled by the heroics of the Irish sagas and believed that the ruling class of his own time 'were the heirs of that order and the destined inheritors of its virtues'.[92] He did, however, retain a Victorian distrust of the pre-Christian mores of these stories and was disgusted by the 'ignoble' elements of the stories which detailed sexual liaisons that were anathema to his Victorian sensibility. Such incidents were often omitted or 'improved upon' by O'Grady. In his book *Finn and His Companions*, he left out the Diarmuid and Grania story entirely, not only because of its frank investigation of human sexual desire but because it 'depicted Gráinne as being unfaithful to the memory of Diarmaid'.[93]

Although O'Grady saw in the legends an allegory for the aristocratic ideal, Moore and Yeats recognized that hidden in these ancient stories of Ireland lay many subversive possibilities. In their collaboration the story was transformed 'from a narrative of event to a drama of character'. There was also a more sustained concentration on the character of Grania than had been the case in the sources.[94] The play, therefore, while drawing on the ancient story, is unrestrained in its expression of female desire and autonomy in a way that echoes Ibsen and prefigures Synge. As Anthony Farrow has remarked, Grania is very much a 'Celtic Hedda Gabler' as she oscillates between her love for the young virile Diarmuid and a fascination with the ageing Finn. There is no trace of a distressed Sean Bhean Bhocht or a Kathleen ni Houlihan in need of rescue here. Instead the emphasis is on the active role of Grania, who remains the agent of her own destiny throughout.

By tapping into, rather than suppressing, the pre-Christian elements of ancient Ireland with its more liberal conception of female desire and agency, Moore and Yeats uncovered new possibilities for a critique of the mores of Victorian Ireland endorsed by colonials like Mahaffy and Atkinson and aristocrats like Standish O'Grady and aped by conservative nationalists like D. P. Moran, eager to display their own respectability. Rather than look to the past to escape 'the facts of life', as John Eglinton feared, they cleverly used the past to reflect allegorically on their contemporary moment.[95] The true innovation of the play lies in this clever reconciliation of tradition and modernity. If Grania is indeed a 'Celtic Hedda Gabler', the radical message is not delivered via a relentless modern realism but by means of the most ancient of Irish stories – *Diarmuid and Grania*.

Standish O'Grady did not even wait to see the play before condemning it. In a move reminiscent of Cardinal Logue in the *Countess Cathleen* affair he lambasted Moore and Yeats for writing on this subject at all. He could not countenance the fact that Moore and Yeats had chosen to dramatize an ancient Irish tale 'in which the fame of the hero and prophet is sullied and his character aspersed'.[96] D. P. Moran's *Leader* did send a critic to the play but followed the lead of O'Grady. The ensuing review accused the playwrights of twisting the play beyond recognition and of changing Diarmuid from 'a fenian chief to a modern degenerate'. The character of Grania, it was felt, had been turned into 'one of these kind of creatures that have been so prominent in the degenerate London drama'.[97] Another article in the same edition, which bears traces of Moran's distinctive style, attributed the deficiencies of the play to:

> A want of real understanding of the Irish mind and character, a want of sympathy with Irish thought; also very largely to ignorance of the legend and of the manners and customs of the time to which it belongs.[98]

Ironically, then, the playwrights' refusal to portray the characters as paragons of Victorian virtue was taken as a measure of their lack of sympathy with 'Irish thought'. This provides an interesting insight into Moran's bourgeois nationalist thinking at this time: at the heart of his cultural programme was a conception of national identity which dressed Victorian values in Irish apparel. One of the few critics to champion the play unequivocally was the *United Irishman*'s Frank Fay. In a rejoinder to Standish O'Grady he stated:

> I cannot say that I am displeased that the authors have humanised the heroic
> and made Diarmuid a man and Grania a woman of flesh and blood like our-
> selves; our hearts go out to them more readily than if they were merely beauti-
> ful statues.[99]

But if the play was to be praised, Fay could not speak too scathingly about the
'execrable' acting of the Benson Company from London, and used the occasion to call again for the use of Irish actors.[100] Despite his misgivings he was
not behind the door in censuring critics like D. P. Moran, whose hostility to
the play stemmed from the fact that it was written in English. To him it was
ridiculous that Gaelic League members should dismiss plays in English until
an audience existed that was 'able to follow our Irish-speaking actors'.[101]

'A.E.I.O.U.': James Joyce and the Revival

Several weeks after the 1901 productions a precocious nineteen-year-old
James Joyce published his evaluation of the year's dramatic offerings. 'The Day
of the Rabblement', however, was written ten days before the opening of the
plays. Joyce, like O'Grady, therefore, offered an evaluation of plays he had not
seen. For the young writer the news that the Irish Literary Theatre would present a play in Irish and a play based on Irish legend was cause enough for com-
plaint. It was his view that 'a nation which never advanced so far as a miracle
play' could offer 'no literary model to the artist' and that, as a result, 'he must
look abroad'. For Joyce, the decision to stage two Irish plays represented a surrender of artistic principles to appease 'the most belated race in Europe'. He
seemed to be particularly motivated by hostility to the language movement.
'Until he has freed himself from the mean influences about him', the young
writer argued, 'no man is an artist at all'.[102] Joyce's contention that the Irish Literary Theatre had 'surrendered to the trolls' did not go unchallenged. It was
Frank Fay again who pointed out that neither the Irish Literary Theatre nor
the language movement were 'popular'. 'Surely', he wrote, 'they both represent the fight of the minority against the "damned compact majority"'.[103] This
view could only be compounded by the level of hostility directed at *Diarmuid
and Grania* in the wake of its production. One wonders, had Joyce seen the
Moore/Yeats play would he have been taken with the manner in which they
used ancient myth to reflect on their contemporary moment – a technique not
unlike his own method in *Ulysses*.

   'The Day of the Rabblement' is often quoted to support one of the most
enduring orthodoxies of Joycean criticism – that the writer's *oeuvre* was fashioned in contradistinction to the demands of Irish cultural nationalism and
that it can be read as an antidote to the traditionalist nostalgia of the revival.
In such a manoeuvre Joyce's work is regularly analysed as a category apart
from, or antithetical to, the Irish revival project in such a way as to occlude
the possibility of consensus between his artistic priorities and those of the

major revivalist thinkers and writers.[104] Notwithstanding Joyce's scepticism about certain elements of the revival, the idea that he may have been in sympathy with aspects of revivalist thought, is rarely countenanced.

The young Joyce, of course, would gain first-hand experience of the key Revival groupings – the Gaelic League, the co-operative movement and the Irish Literary Theatre in the early years of the twentieth century. His involvement with these three nascent organizations, however brief, provided him with much raw material for his own fictions but also serves as another neat illustration of their appeal and interconnectedness as the new century dawned. If Patrick Pearse's Gaelic League classes failed to inspire Joyce,[105] he in turn failed to make an impact on the Irish Literary Theatre. During the summer of 1901 he translated two plays by Gerhart Hauptmann, *Before Sunrise* and *Michael Kramer*,[106] more than likely anticipating (as Yeats had promised in *Samhain*) that the theatre movement was about to begin producing European drama. Yeats returned Joyce's version of *Before Sunrise* with the comment that the young writer 'was not a very good German scholar' and that it was 'very unlikely that we can make any use of them for the theatre'.[107] The vitriol directed at the theatre movement in 'The Day of the Rabblement', therefore, may have had its origins in this blunt rejection of the budding writer's talents. In that essay Joyce memorably blamed 'Mr. Yeats's treacherous instinct of adaptability' for his 'recent association with a platform from which even self-respect should have urged him to refrain'.[108] Yet Joyce himself was to display a similar facility for clever adaptability in his dealings with the co-operative movement by accepting an invitation to publish his early short stories in that most unlikely literary repository – the *Irish Homestead*.

On the face of it the *Homestead* would seem an unlikely place for Joyce to publish his first stories. It has been claimed that he used the pseudonym of Stephen Daedalus because he was ashamed of publishing in 'the pigs' paper'.[109] In *Ulysses* Stephen imagines Mulligan heaping on him a new insult – 'bullockbefriending bard' – because of his efforts to have Mr Deasy's letter published in the *Homestead* (p. 29). Yet in his fiction and occasional journalism, Joyce displayed more than a passing interest in the agrarian issues which exercised the *Homestead* readership. One thinks, for example, of foot-and-mouth disease, which forms a motif in *Ulysses* and which became the subject of an article he later published in the *Freeman's Journal*.[110] Also of significance is the fact that in *Ulysses* Joyce's Dublin, for the most part wearing the mask of the Irish metropolis, at times appears more like a large rural market town, as the intruding rhythms of the countryside upset the pulse of city life. The dignified urbanity of Paddy Dignam's funeral cortège is, in spite of everything, halted by the bucolic chaos of herds of cattle and sheep being driven to the slaughterhouse. This provides an occasion for Bloom to meditate on the peculiarities of the meat trade and to suggest an alternative mode of transportation for the animals by way of 'a tramline from the parkgate to the quays'.[111] Earlier in the novel Stephen listens 'in scornful silence' (p. 16) to the rustic simplicity of the milk woman who had crouched 'by a patient cow at day-break in the lush field' (p. 15). Yet such primitive methods of dispensing milk as she uses were, at that time, being revolutionized by the scientific methods of the IAOS creameries. It may be tempting to read the aged woman as a parody of a typical revivalist image of 'old Ireland' but it must also be pointed out that other revivalist energies were mobilizing scientific farming methods to make her kind extinct.

Joyce's interest in matters agrarian was reciprocated by the *Homestead*'s commitment to cultural ideas. Plunkett, after all, employed the services of George Russell, who would exercise an important influence on Joyce's early writing career. Joyce pokes fun in *Ulysses* by referring to him as 'AE the master mystic' (p. 178) and as a 'high figure in homespun, beard and bicycle' (p. 210). But he also took the trouble to enshrine in his Dublin epic Russell's essentially democratic vision of social transformation. In the National Library the Russell character comments that 'the movements which work revolutions in the world are born out of the dreams and visions in a peasant's heart on the hillside' (p. 238). Once again, it is easy to read this as Joycean lampoon, yet one should bear in mind that it also works as an apt maxim to describe the *modus operandi* of the co-operative movement.

Early in 1904 work began on a text dedicated to the examination of the Irish character which would place particular emphasis on the moral timidity of Catholic Ireland and on the urgent need to cure the paralysis endemic in all sections of Irish life. 'Initial reaction was favourable and the author was pleased and surprised with comments on his literary accomplishment.'[112] Within weeks of publication, however, the piece was attacked by the *Freeman's Journal* as 'one prolonged libel on the Irish people'[113] and calls were heard for it to be banned. The text in question was not 'The Sisters' by James Joyce but rather *Ireland in the New Century* by Horace Plunkett. Yet again opinion in Ireland seemed to divide predictably according to cultural lines, with Plunkett being denounced as an Anglo-Irish bigot by senior Catholic figures.[114] Some months later, in August 1904, 'The Sisters' was published in Plunkett's newspaper, marking the beginning of Joyce's chapter of the moral history of his country. This story was commissioned by George Russell, who famously asked for something 'simple?, rural?, livemaking?, [pathetic]'. 'It is easy earned money', wrote Russell, 'if you don't mind playing to the common understanding'.[115] Much could be made of Joyce's ostensible lack of regard for Russell's editorial directives, yet the finished story turned out to be a fictional reworking of Plunkett's central thesis in *Ireland in the New Century* and a cryptic parable of self-help revivalism.

'The Sisters' certainly endorsed Plunkett's controversial view that Catholic Ireland 'required the exercise of strengthening influences on [its] moral fibre'.[116] As the first story of the collection that would become *Dubliners*, it established the theme of moral weakness as the keynote of that book. Associated with this, Joyce was keen to highlight the lack of independent thought that he saw as characteristic of Irish Catholic society. This is most obviously illustrated in the story by the provisional and tentative nature of the opinions offered by old Cotter and Eliza, who, through the deployment of ellipsis and strategies of obfuscation, avoid the naming of Fr Flynn's condition. 'I have my own theory about it', says old Cotter, 'I think it was one of those . . . peculiar cases . . . But it's hard to say . . .'[117] What we witness repeatedly through the story is a community lacking the moral courage and the intellectual wherewithal to confront, define or articulate its own problems. Instead the characteristic response is to evade and circumvent the malaise by using vocabularies of vagueness and mystery. Paralysis and moral weakness, therefore, do not reside entirely in the malign influence of the dying priest but are also very much in evidence in the secular world of those who seek and fail to make sense of his condition.

Just as Plunkett turned his attention to both the cultural and material realms in *Ireland in the New Century*, so too Joyce concerns himself with an investigation of the secular and the sacred in 'The Sisters'. Here the characters of old Cotter and Fr Flynn are offered as alternative exemplars for the boy-narrator as he hovers on the cusp of adolescence and attempts to fashion his own perspective on life. The ageing priest represents the sacred world of mystery, while Cotter is emblematic of the hard-nosed pragmatic world. Connecting both is the centrality of alcohol to their professions. Cotter's expertise in the 'faints and worms' of the distillation process has been learned from years in the distillery, while Fr Flynn's use of the chalice in the act of transubstantiation is central to the delineation of his character.

As the story begins, one senses that the narrator has recently given up one 'mentor' for the other. He has grown tired of old Cotter, who seems to be a regular visitor to his uncle's house. The 'tiresome old red-nosed imbecile' and 'his endless stories about the distillery' no longer interest him. Cotter has been replaced by Fr Flynn, whom the maturing boy has sought out himself – in effect he has exchanged the acquaintance of his uncle for that of his aunt. She tacitly endorses the boy's visits to the priest by furnishing him with High Toast snuff to present to the ageing cleric. This gendering is significant: Cotter and the boy's uncle embody Victorian ideals of utilitarian manhood which are deeply sceptical of the intellect, the mystical and the aesthetic. Noticing the boy's developing interest in matters contemplative, they comment:

> —What I mean is, said old Cotter, it's bad for children.
>
> My idea is: let a young lad run about and play with young lads of his own age and not be . . . Am I right, Jack?
>
> —That's my principle, too, said my uncle. Let him learn to box his corner. That's what I'm always saying to that Rosicrucian there: take exercise. Why, when I was a nipper every morning of my life I had a cold bath, winter and summer. And that's what stands to me now. Education is all very fine and large . . . (p. 2)

This is classic social Darwinism with a lower-class inflection, an ethos of survival of the fittest, which champions male competitiveness and physical strength and applauds individual material success. Empiricism is the dominant mode here. Against this we get a deep scepticism of the world of contemplation and idealism, symbolized by Cotter spitting rudely into the fire and the uncle's use of the term 'Rosicrucian' to suggest a dark, medieval mysticism. Yet the boy is clearly trying to wrest himself from Cotter's patronizing influence. He is angry with the old man for alluding to him as 'a child' and will not acknowledge him, though he can 'feel that his little beady black eyes' are examining him.

Turning in distaste from Cotter's Victorian utilitarianism, the boy gravitates towards the contemplative world that Fr Flynn represents. From him he gains intellectual stimulation: he learns to pronounce Latin properly, hears about the catacombs and the deeds of Napoleon. He also gains an insight into the mysteries of the church – like 'the duties of the priest towards the Eucharist' and 'the secrecy of the confessional'. Yet, as we find out, Fr Flynn defiles both these sacraments by dropping the chalice and by his demented outburst of laughter in the confessional. He is not, therefore, a redeeming counter-exemplar to the crass Cotter. In fact he is associated with, and becomes emblematic of, an oppressive mystical tradition which, in the vanity of its dotage, has degenerated into a corrupt and demented esotericism. The use of the term 'Rosicrucian' suggests an extreme, intoxicated, almost gothic Catholicism which has disengaged from the realities of modern life. This is far removed from the liberation of the spirit that the narrator hungers for. And yet in the course of the story there is a clear sense in which the boy has already outgrown the priest's influence. As he ruminates on Fr Flynn's death, we are told, he 'walked away slowly along the sunny side of the street, reading all the theatrical advertisements in the shopwindows' and at the same time 'enjoying a sensation of freedom'. This, perhaps, anticipates a turn to the aesthetic by the narrator, who might eventually reconcile the real and the ideal through art.

What we find in this story, therefore, is a critique of Cotter's extreme utilitarian materialism on the one hand and Fr Flynn's oppressively corrupt and senile mysticism on the other. Both of these positions are eschewed for a more balanced accommodation of the material in the spiritual, which, as we have seen, was the hallmark of Plunkett's analysis and social programme as much as it was a blueprint for Joyce's own aesthetic. As the narrator of this story begins the task of finding his own voice and his own place in society we can see in him an analogue for wider Irish society. In this story of nascent self-definition can be heard echoes of Plunkett's ideas on the importance of independent thought and self-reliance. In the critique of Cotter's Victorian individualism one could, perhaps, make connections with the notions of collective self-help and co-operation which Plunkett posited as an alternative to the rampant exploitation of naked capitalism. Furthermore, in his portrayal of Fr Flynn's corrupt and senile Catholic mysticism Joyce recalled Plunkett's critique of aspects of Irish Catholicism in *Ireland in the New Century*. Notwithstanding the offence these texts may have generated within conservative Catholic circles, one can detect in these writings of Plunkett and Joyce a plea for a more *engagé* and socially committed Catholic sensibility, as well as a yearning for a more vigorous civic dimension to Irish social and cultural life. Both Plunkett and Joyce highlighted the great lacuna that existed in the intellectual life of Ireland as the nation entered the new century. This lacuna was caused by the dominance of a Church that was too mystically aloof from the real world and a secular nationalist politics that was physically courageous but morally and intellectually timid. Yet, even as these texts were being written, this gap was being filled by Cumman na nGaedheal and the various self-help movements who had pledged to move the nationalist struggle beyond physical force, concentrating instead on the intellectual front and the building up of a civic dimension to Irish life.

Beyond Two Civilizations

Just as the reunion of the Irish Parliamentary Party occurred at a time when new divisions were opening up between home rulers and separatists, Cumann na nGaedheal was founded at a moment when tensions were beginning to develop between those who emphasized the ethnic nature of Irish nationalism and those who adhered to the republican tradition of civic nationalism. Within the broad church of civic nationalism, leading figures included William Rooney and W. B. Yeats, who sought to transcend the Anglo-Ireland/Irish Ireland divide by lending their support both to the Irish language and to the development of an Irish literature in English. Such a position did not in any way signal an abandonment of the Gaelic inheritance or the Irish language but a pragmatic realization that Irish would not be restored overnight and that a literature in English was essential to the imaginative and political development of the Irish people. D. P. Moran, on the other hand, was vocal in his hostility to Anglo-Irish culture and influence, and in his emphasis on a Gaelic Catholic Irishness. Moran's ideas, however, were directly and vigorously challenged from within the ranks of nationalism by the secular republican writings of William Rooney, a key figure in the emergence of Sinn Féin as a political force before his sudden death in 1901.

As well as Rooney and Yeats, Lady Gregory and Frank Fay were to the forefront in enlarging Irish cultural possibility at this time. The innovations of these leading figures at once challenged Mahaffy and Atkinson's dismissal of the value of Gaelic literature and hard-line Gaelic League antipathy to a national literature in English. The choice of plays for the 1901 theatre season reflected very well the priorities of this new civic thinking. *Casadh an tSúgáin*, a short play in Irish, was presented to an audience of learners, and its inclusion in the programme helped to lend institutional gravitas to a language rediscovering its literary potential. Meanwhile, *Diarmuid and Grania*, like *Cuchulain of Muirthemne*, legitimized the value of Gaelic Ireland as a literary source and simultaneously helped the development of a fledgling Irish literature in the English language.

James Joyce was scathingly critical of these plays in 'The Day of the Rabble-ment', yet his relationship to the revival was not always one of straightforward hostility as is often portrayed. One could argue that, despite Joyce's avowed criticism and scepticism of certain aspects of Irish revivalism, he was also clearly in sympathy with, and indebted to, a great deal of revivalist thought, art and politics. Reading 'The Sisters' in relation to *Ireland in the New Century* reveals the significant degree of common ground that Joyce shared with Plunkett. Although committed primarily to the material development of the nation, Plunkett was also a clear-sighted maverick who displayed an unswerving concern for Ireland's civic advancement and spiritual liberation in ways that invite comparison with Joyce's artistic project. Although Joyce would follow an aesthetic path of his own making that was radically at odds with the revival *zeitgeist*, his diagnosis of Irish ills was, in many ways, remarkably similar to that of the leading revivalist thinkers. Significantly, it was in the pages of the *Irish Homestead* that his seminal portrait of Irish cultural paralysis first appeared.

SINN FÉIN, THE ABBEY THEATRE
AND *THE SHADOW OF THE GLEN*

Griffith, Yeats and Synge

After the sudden death of William Rooney in 1901, Arthur Griffith took over at the helm of the separatist movement. Despite his avowed debt to the legacy of Rooney, Griffith did not feel bound to uphold the fastidious republicanism of his predecessor. He quickly put his own stamp on the movement with the formulation of his 'Hungarian policy', which was published in the *United Irishman* in 1904 and laid the groundwork for the foundation of Sinn Féin in 1905. Almost concurrently, W. B. Yeats was attempting to gain control of the Irish theatre movement. In an essay, 'The Reform of the Theatre', published in *Samhain* in late 1903 he argued for a theatre of 'intellectual excitement' that was not compromised 'in the seeming service of a cause'.[1] A little over a year later, thanks to the financial support of Annie Horniman, the movement was to find a permanent home in the Abbey Theatre. The founding of these two institutions formalized the acrimonious sundering of Cumann na nGaedheal into a 'political wing' and a 'cultural wing' as a consequence of a developing antagonism between Yeats and Griffith. Their fundamental disagreement was exacerabated by the fact that Griffith was a consummate politician with more than a passing interest in literature, while Yeats was a poet-playwright with more than a passing interest in politics. The rivalry that was to erupt between them would have its origins in a fierce battle over what the priorities of a national theatre should be, and who had the right to sanction them.

As a chain of events which led Griffith to found Sinn Féin and Yeats to establish the Abbey theatre unfolded, a theatre production, once again, was to play a significant role in defining the vital points of divergence between two leaders. In this case it was the inaugural staging of J. M. Synge's *The Shadow of the Glen* on the 8 October 1903.[2] Synge, himself, was a hugely important figure who distinguished himself as an astute social critic as well as a creative artist during the revival. Like Lady Gregory, he could see the profound changes taking place in Irish life as they happened. Indeed he had much to contribute to important revival debates about self-help, the co-operative movement and the language revival.

Politico-cultural Tensions 1902–5:
The Emergence of Sinn Féin and the Abbey Theatre

With the ending of the Boer War in late May 1902, a certain unity of purpose was lost as the leaders of advanced nationalism began to diverge in their strategies to forward the nationalist cause. Coupled with this, key changes in personnel among the protagonists precipitated a series of personality clashes which would lead to a breakdown in close co-operation between them. The winding down of the three-year Irish Literary Theatre experiment in 1901 did not end the theatre movement's co-operation with Cumann na nGaedheal; if anything, it allowed a greater *rapprochement*. In the summer of that year Frank Fay petitioned Yeats to 'give us a play in verse or prose that will rouse this sleeping land'.[3] By January the following year Yeats had entrusted *Kathleen ni Houlihan*, co-authored with Lady Gregory, to the Fays' company, which operated under the auspices of, and drew its actors from, the ranks of Cumann na nGaedheal and Inghinidhe na h-Éireann.[4] Ironically the success of *Kathleen ni Houlihan* was to mark the beginning of the end of close relations between Yeats's theatre movement and Griffith's Cumann na nGaedheal.

Richard Davis has pointed out that in the beginning Arthur Griffith was very much a reluctant leader of separatist politics. With the death of William Rooney in May 1901 he 'had leadership thrust upon him', even though he 'would have preferred to act as *eminence grise* for a more popular chief'.[5] Rooney's death, as we have seen, was a great blow. Yeats recorded how this sudden tragedy had 'plunged everybody into gloom' and how Griffith 'had to go to hospital for a week, so much did it effect him'.[6] Yet he recovered to become, in time, the undisputed leader of advanced nationalism. At this stage, of course, 'John O'Leary was a veteran and the other men of Griffith's generation did not equal Griffith in ability'.[7]

It did not take Griffith long, however, to stamp his authority on the movement. At the third convention of Cumann na nGaedheal in October 1902 he gave his first public utterance to a policy which would endure as his most lasting contribution to separatist politics but would lead the movement down a different road than that envisaged by William Rooney and supporters of the republican tradition. The decisive moment occurred when:

> . . . the Cork Celtic Literary Society, an affiliated body [of Cumann na nGaedheal] proposed a motion condemning the Irish Parliamentary Party for betraying the Irish republican tradition. Griffith, holding that 'sovereign independence' was a more suitable aim than a republic, proposed an amendment calling for an end to the 'useless, degrading and demoralising policy' of Irish attendance at Westminster and the substitution of the policy of the Hungarian deputies of 1861. He called on the Irish Parliamentary Party to refuse to attend Westminster or recognise its right to legislate for Ireland but instead to remain at home 'to help in promoting Ireland's interests and aid in guarding its national rights'. This was his first public advocacy of what came to be known as 'the Hungarian policy'.[8]

The Hungarian analogy, which Griffith would expound on in a series of twenty-seven articles in the *United Irishman* between 21 January and 2 July 1904, was to become the bedrock of Sinn Féin policy. The kernel of the strategy was to restore the constitution of 1782 which gave rise to Grattan's parliament. By evoking the Renunciation Act (passed by the English parliament in 1783) which held that for all time Ireland could only be bound by laws enacted by the King and parliament of Ireland, Griffith argued that the Act of Union of 1800 was illegal and that the 1782 constitution was still legally binding.[9] The way was clear, argued Griffith, for elected Irish representatives in Westminster to withdraw and set up a national parliament in Ireland.

Although Griffith's 'King, Lords and Commons' policy attempted to 'tread a middle road between parliamentarianism and republicanism',[10] it marked a considerable shift to the right of Rooney's republican aspirations. 'For our part', wrote Griffith, 'we care little whether our government be republican or monarchical so long as it be Irish, independent and just'.[11] Such a desire to seize national sovereignty at all costs betrayed Griffith's preference for a bourgeois nationalism to take over the reins of power from the colonial administration rather than for a radical republicanism that would totally refashion an Irish polity. This was anathema to the thinking of Rooney. In his prose writings Rooney unequivocally discounted the restoration of Grattan's parliament under an English monarch as a desirable solution to Ireland's problems. Such a move, Rooney suggested, would only dull Irish resistance and lead to complicity with imperial agendas.[12] His rigorous anti-imperialism, therefore, was not a concept that Griffith felt obliged to uphold at all costs. Yet Griffith's 'King, Lords and Commons' policy did not go unchallenged within the nascent Sinn Féin movement.[13] One of the most vocal republican critics of Griffith's policy was Bulmer Hobson, a senior figure in the IRB-dominated Dungannon Clubs. Hobson dates 'the beginning of an estrangement' between Griffith and himself to Griffith's Hungary policy. Griffith, he recalls, 'had ceased to be a member of [the IRB] some time before and was not on good terms with the men who controlled it'.[14] He had also 'abandoned the republicanism of the early *United Irishman* days' and was now 'definitely attempting to make the restoration of the last Irish Parliament the aim to be achieved'.[15] In contrast, Hobson's Dungannon Clubs adhered to Rooney-style republicanism. 'We set as our aim an independent Irish republic', wrote Hobson, 'because we did not see how complete independence could take any other form in Ireland'.[16] Clearly, then, as Arthur Griffith took over the reins of leadership from William Rooney a significant shift in his own political thinking began. By late 1902 he had become an advocate of parliamentary autonomy for Ireland. In so doing he placed himself at odds with a republican tradition working towards a complete break with Britain and new Irish political formations.[17]

If Griffith's 'King, Lords and Commons' policy was not fully articulated until the publication of his Hungarian articles under the title *The Resurrection of*

Hungary in November 1904, he was clearly beginning to formulate these ideas as early as 1902.[18] Interestingly, at the very moment his politics began to shift to the right, Griffith also started to take a greater interest in the theatre. After the successful collaboration between the Fays and the Irish Literary Theatre movement under the auspices of Cumann na nGaedheal in April 1902 when *Kathleen ni Houlihan* was staged to great acclaim, and again during the Samhain festival in October,[19] Griffith began to eye the renewed theatre project as an important vehicle for his political programme. The success of the 1902 Samhain season was deemed important enough to merit an editorial in the *United Irishman*. Here Griffith outlined his vision of an Irish national theatre:

> We look to the Irish National Theatre primarily as a means of regenerating the country. The theatre is a powerful agent in the building up of a nation. When it is in foreign hands and hostile hands, it is a deadly danger to the country. When it is controlled by native and friendly hands it is a bulwark and a protection. We have been cursed in Ireland with a horde of dishonest politicians, a stupid or a venal Press, and a degraded and anti-National Theatre. We are getting rid of all these.[20]

On the face of it, these were sentiments not unlike those expressed by Yeats in the run-up to the launch of the Irish Literary Theatre in 1899, yet it would not be long before Griffith would insist on a national theatre dedicated to the obedient service of his own political agenda.

Yeats, however, had other ideas. With the drawing to a close of the Boer War he dusted off his old hobby-horse and argued that the time had come for the leaders of the Irish revival to work towards fostering a spirit of independence in the national mind rather than promoting a slavish devotion to, and uncritical acceptance of, Irish nationalist propaganda. In an interview published on St Patrick's day 1903, he reflected on what he thought should be the priority of Irish nationalism.

> The greatest need is more love for thoughts for their own sake. We want a vigorous movement of ideas. We have now plenty of propaganda and I would not see less. For now the agrarian movement seems coming to a close the national movement must learn to found itself, like the national movement of Norway, upon language and history. But if we are to have an able nation, a nation that will be able to take up to itself the best thought of the world, we must have more love of beauty merely because it is beauty, of truth merely because it is truth. At present if a man make us a song, or tell us a story, or give us a thought, we do not ask 'Is it a good song, or a good story, or a true thought?' but 'Will it help this or that propaganda?'[21]

Yeats, therefore, conceded the need for propaganda in the nationalist movement but went further to insist that every effort should be made to liberate the national mind as well as the national territory, to create the conditions in which 'Ireland will be able to take up to itself the best thought of the world'.

This, after all was one of the main reasons why Cumann na nGaedheal was set up in the first place. This was no belletristic retreat from politics or haughty embrace of art-for-art's-sake, but rather a trenchant statement of Yeats's view that a genuine national art must aspire to the highest standards, challenge the public mind and generate public debate – a view he had held since the founding of the National Literary Society in 1892.[22]

Yeats was not the only one growing uncomfortable with the expectations of Cumann na nGaedheal for a national theatre. Frank Fay, who had earlier challenged him to write a play that would 'send men away filled with the desire for deeds',[23] now began to distance himself from a conception of national drama that was purely politically motivated. In fact Fay was to adopt a much more doctrinaire position on the subject than Yeats. Commenting on the fact that Fay wanted to 'get out of playing political plays' altogether, Yeats was clear that he would 'differ from him on the point'.[24]

It was in early 1903 that simmering tensions over the future of the Irish theatre came to a head over the question of whether Padraic Colum's *Saxon Shillin'* and James Cousin's *Sold* should be performed. At this time it was becoming obvious that a great deal of confusion existed over what the foundation of the National Dramatic Society was all about.[25] Maud Gonne felt that, by shedding the aristocratic guarantors of the Irish Literary Theatre, the way had been cleared for an overtly nationalist drama. She was the main supporter of Colum's play. Written to promote the anti-recruitment campaign (a cause close to her heart), Gonne felt that it was 'good from [a] national point of view & would please Cumann na [n]Gaedheal so much as it won the prize competition'.[26] Willie Fay, however, believing the ending to be weak from a theatrical point of view, changed it. This annoyed Griffith who had published the play in the *United Irishman*. As far as he was concerned Fay had spoiled the play 'from an artistic point of view' and had really changed it because he feared to 'vex the respectable' – a charge which Fay denied.[27] In the end the play was dropped from rehearsal.[28] Yeats, it seems, did not take great exception to the play and had no trouble describing it as 'a powerful little play' in the 1903 edition of *Samhain*.[29] However, he did block Cousin's play *Sold*. Again this play was endorsed by Griffith, who published it in the *United Irishman* and described it as 'the first real comedy of Irish life'.[30] To Yeats it was 'rubbish [and] vulgar rubbish'. He was particularly annoyed that Griffith had published the play with a statement that it was to be performed before Yeats had even received a copy of it.[31] What was at stake in these minor tussles over the sanction of new plays was, of course, a much larger struggle for the authority to endorse national drama. In regard to the battle between Griffith and Yeats, it was ultimately a struggle for the intellectual leadership of the advanced nationalist movement.[32]

Griffith was not the kind of person who could easily forgive such an obvious disregard for his literary judgement and for what he considered to be the true aims of the movement. As Padraic Colum recalled, Griffith had a tendency to judge people 'by their willingness to work impersonally for Irish independence; as soon as one who he thought had such a dedication faltered, Griffith was no longer cordial to him or her'. Not surprisingly, 'he tended to have about him men of unchanging views, men whose minds were not enterprising, men with party minds'.[33] However, as Yeats had shown before in his joust with Gavan Duffy, a 'party mind' could work to enslave rather than liberate the nation.

These 'literary' squabblings soon gave way to the more 'political' issue of the visit of Edward VII to Ireland in July 1903. Notwithstanding Yeats's fears about a propaganda-driven theatre, he once again stepped forward to lead the intellectual argument against the visit of the English monarch. In so doing he showed as much eagerness to engage in *realpolitik* as Griffith did to control matters theatrical. He wrote three letters to the national press outlining his objections and was co-signatory of at least one more.[34] He also suggested the founding of a 'National Council' to co-ordinate agitation against the king.[35] His public statements on these matters are very revealing and cast new light on his earlier pronouncements against Irish nationalist propaganda:

> Like Edward Martyn I see nothing good in this Royal visit. If the King is well received in this country, his reception will be used by the English Unionist papers as an argument against the Irish Nationalist movement. I remember that the 'Times' and the 'Spectator' used our supposed enthusiastic reception of the late Queen in this way, and yet I have no doubt that they will join with the other papers in telling us that the King is above politics. But it matters very little to us what the English papers say. What does matter is that Royal visits, with their pageantry, their false rumours of concessions, their appeal to all that is superficial and trivial in society, are part of the hypnotic illusion by which England seeks to take captive the imagination of this country, and it does this not by argument nor by any appeal to the intellect, but by an appeal to what are chiefly money interests. The shopkeeper must hang out a flag, not because he wants to, but because he will lose rich customers if he does not; the workman must pretend loyalty or he will be dismissed by his rich employer; the children of the poor must stand in troops and cheer under supervision, because their schools are afraid to offend rich patrons. A Royal visit has always been both a threat and a bribe, and even the Nationalist who considers what is called the 'link of the crown' inevitable, should offer but the welcome that a man gives to a threat or a bribe.[36]

This was entirely consistent with his already stated views on Irish nationalist propaganda. For clearly Yeats was distrustful of *all* forms of coercive nationalist propaganda at their most crassly expedient, and here categorized the royal visit and its inevitable pageantry as a base expression of *British* nationalism all the more invidious for its attempt 'to take captive the imagination of this country'. Yeats's crusade against the forces promoting popular nationalism in Ireland, therefore, can be seen as a warning against the tendency of conservative nationalists, like Griffith, to replicate in local terms the very evils and oppressions they professed to undo.[37] Although Yeats used the royal visit to subtly warn against the shortcomings of popular nationalism, he also made some important political points of his own. Reacting to rumours that the king had personally sanctioned the Wyndham Land Act, he again felt compelled to write to the press to disabuse the public of this notion. 'Whenever Royalty had come to Ireland', wrote Yeats, 'rumours of this kind have been spread and spread with an object. 'The Land Bill has not been given to us by English Royalty', he argued, 'but won by the long labours of our own people'.[38] Yeats, therefore, was entirely consistent in countering what he saw as obfuscating propaganda, whatever its political hue.

In contrast to Yeats, who was forthright in his critique and unequivocal in his unmasking of the politics behind the royal visit, D. P. Moran advocated an expedient loyalism as a way of gaining concessions for the 'mere Irish'.

> The King . . . has talked of cherishing national characteristics and ideals, and by that one phrase not to go further, he put all the anti-national bigots . . . who hate Ireland and her language and customs, into rebellion against his wishes . . . As Home Rulers we have no quarrel with the King as the King of Ireland; we have anything but a quarrel with him since he threw over the wicked foreign garrison that has bred such trouble in this land, and told the Parochial University to adapt itself to modern needs.[39]

Once again Moran showed that his main aim was to undermine the Anglo-Irish élite and replace it with a Gaelic Catholic one, rather than work towards any radical political change. Interestingly, then, it was Yeats rather than Moran who took the more 'republican' line on the royal visit and kept the spirit of William Rooney alive. He was also critical of the Catholic hierarchy's fawning shows of loyalty on the occasion of the king's visit to Maynooth. In a letter to the *United Irishman* he mocked with relish the hosts' decision to decorate the king's room in his familiar racing colours. 'Hitherto the priest has been almost the only man in Ireland who did not bet', noted Yeats, 'but that is to be changed, so powerful are the smiles of Royalty'.[40]

By 17 May the Yeats-inspired National Council (also known as the People's Protection Committee) was set up by Edward Martyn, Maud Gonne and Arthur Griffith to co-ordinate opposition to the king's visit. This was, in many respects, another incarnation of the Transvaal Committee. Yeats, who was in London at the time, sent a letter requesting that his name be added to the committee.[41] In the same way as the Transvaal Committee worked to drive a gap between the advanced nationalists and the Irish Parliamentary Party, so too did the National Council work towards the same end. A public meeting organized by John Redmond and the Lord Mayor of Dublin, Tim Harrington, was interrupted by a deputation of the National Council led by Martyn and Gonne. Their aim was to petition the Lord Mayor not to present a loyal address to Edward VII. A fracas broke out and several people were slightly injured during what became known as 'the Rotunda Riot'. Significantly, the corporation subsequently decided against presenting a loyal address, not wishing, perhaps, to engender the level of opposition which was visible during Victoria's visit.[42]

Although Yeats masterminded the anti-royalist activities in Dublin, he did not actually take part in them, as he had travelled to London with the Irish National Theatre Society (INTS) in early May on their first visit to London, which was organized by Stephen Gwynn, the secretary of the Irish Literary Society in London. This tour would prove to be an important step for the INTS towards securing a permanent home in Abbey Street and was the cause of further antagonism between Yeats and Griffith. Yeats's *Hour Glass*, *Kathleen ni Houlihan* and *The Pot of Broth*, Lady Gregory's *Twenty Five* and Fred Ryan's *The Laying of the Foundations* made up the programme performed at the Queen's Gate Hall. These performances were an overwhelming success with the INTS receiving favourable reviews in all the London daily and evening papers, and an enthusiastic notice from Arthur Walkley in the *Times Literary Supplement*. Annie Horniman was also enthusiastic about the performances, which, no doubt, influenced the decision she would make in October 1903 to fund the Abbey Theatre the following year.[43] Griffith, not surprisingly, took a contrary view of the London enterprise. Wrestling with Yeats for the authority to sanction national drama, Griffith sought to discredit him by portraying the poet as a turncoat craving the attention of the London critics. The Irish National Theatre Society 'made a false step', wrote Griffith, 'when it went last year to play in London'.[44] That Yeats reprinted the favourable *Times Literary Supplement* review in *Samhain* added insult to Griffith's injury.[45]

Yet the London performances and Walkley's review did represent an important watershed in Irish cultural history. Here a distinctive and self-styled Irish national drama written by Irish playwrights for Irish audiences was favourably received by London audiences and critics. This brought to an end a situation in which expatriate writers had no choice but to go to London, and initiated a tradition of the export of Irish plays rather than Irish playwrights to the great stages of the world. By breaking the monopoly of the London stage on Irish playwrights the Irish National Theatre Society achieved at a cultural level what Griffith's Sinn Féin would not achieve at a political level for another fifteen years. Griffith, who had railed against the import of popular London entertainments, was noticeably silent about the fact that the Irish national theatre had gone one further and reversed the direction of cultural influence. If Walkley's review betrayed a fixation with the exotic in Irish drama, it did clearly mark a profound shift in the perception of Irish character on the English stage and in particular in the Irish use of language.

> If the peculiarities of Irish thought and feeling can be brought home to us through drama we shall all be the better for the knowledge; and the art of drama, too, cannot but gain by a change of air, a new outlook, a fresh current of ideas . . . we had never realised the unusual possibilities of our language until we had heard these Irish people speak it.[46]

By condemning the London visit Arthur Griffith seriously misread the situation, seeing it as a capitulation to English taste rather than as an important recognition of the work of the Irish theatre on its own terms. It is conceivable that Yeats's high-level political interventions, especially in relation to the visit of Edward VII, were threatening to Griffith as he worked to reshape separatism according to the principles of his Hungarian policy. In his scepticism of bourgeois nationalism and in his spirited opposition to the royal visit, Yeats advanced a political line more in tune with the ideas of William Rooney than Arthur Griffith. It was the performance of Synge's *The Shadow of the Glen*, however, that was to bring the simmering battle between Yeats and Griffith to a conclusive head.

The Dreamer Leans Out to Reality: Synge and Self-Help

Some time in 1908 John Millington Synge wrote the following in his personal notebook:

> . . . what is highest in poetry is always reached where the dreamer is leaning out to reality, or where the man of real life is lifted out of it, and in all the poets the greatest have both these elements, that is they are supremely engrossed with life, and yet with the wildness of their fancy they are always passing out of what is simple and plain.[47]

If this gives us an insight into Synge's aesthetic, it also demonstrates the respect he held for those men and women of affairs who could straddle both the realm of the spiritual and the realm of the material. This ability to bestride the worlds of the real and the ideal was a talent shared by many of the important figures of the Irish revival: W. B. Yeats was a self-help pioneer and poet; AE organized co-operatives and dedicated a considerable amount of energy to literature, painting and Celtic mysticism; Lady Gregory was a cultural activist and playwright; William Rooney wrote poetry as well as being a political agitator. Indeed Synge's epigram can usefully be applied to his own involvement in the Irish revival. He was not only a key participant in the revival but also an astute interpreter of it. Apart from his obvious impact as a dramatist, Synge made an important contribution to the revival through his travel writing, which focused on the material conditions of the Irish peasantry at the turn of the century. In his sojourns in Wicklow, West Kerry, Galway, Mayo and Aran he developed a rapport with the marginalized of Irish society that was quite unusual for one of his ascendancy background. Of these experiences he writes with the keen eye of a sociologist or social anthropologist and displays a Swiftian capacity for diagnosing the ills of Irish society, yet with a sympathy and understanding of ancient cultural practices beyond a mere nostalgia for their quaintness.

Like many of the leading Anglo-Irish revivalists, Synge separated himself from the norms and privileges of his own background at an early age. A 'rift between him and the rest of his family' developed over his religious crisis, which was precipitated by his reading of Darwin.[48] His disavowal of conventional religion was the first of a series of conscientious decisions which would widen the gulf between him and the rest of his family over the years. At the age of fourteen Synge caused further friction by condemning his own brother for carrying out evictions in Cavan, Mayo and Wicklow and by arguing for the rights of the tenants.[49] Later he was to witness one of the last evictions in the Aran Islands and remark pointedly that the 'mechanical police' and the 'commonplace agents and sheriffs and the rabble they had hired represented aptly enough the civilization for which the homes of the island were to be desecrated' – a damning indictment of his own social background.[50]

Synge recorded in his autobiographical writings that, shortly after he had 'relinquished the kingdom of God', he began 'to take a real interest in the kingdom of Ireland'. This resulted in a change in his politics 'from a vigorous and unreasoning loyalty to a temperate Nationalism'.[51] Such a change of heart led him to furtively read the poetry of the Young Irelanders anthologized in the *Spirit of the Nation* and to take a greater interest in the Irish language, which he chose as a subject of study on his entrance to Trinity College in 1888. Although 'the Chair of Irish had been established in 1840 in order to prepare clergymen for the Irish-speaking ministry',[52] Synge was to develop a deep love of Irish far beyond the expediencies of evangelical Protestantism.[53] Yet, if his devotion to the Irish language flourished, his commitment to the revolutionary politics of Thomas Davis did not.[54] Having joined Maud Gonne's Young Ireland society – *Association Irlandaise* – while living in Paris, the ever-conscientious Synge explained his reasons for resigning shortly afterwards. 'I wish to work in my own way for the cause of Ireland', he wrote, 'and I shall never be able to do so if I get mixed up with a revolutionary and semi-military movement'.[55] Like many other leaders of the revival, therefore, he preferred to operate outside the realm of conventional politics for the regeneration of Ireland.

One of the greatest acts Synge performed in the service of the revival was to interpret and mediate developments in Ireland to a wider European audience. In an important article published in *L'Européen* in May 1902, he highlighted the various self-help movements as the most important agents of change in post-Parnell Ireland:

> However, in a certain sense this period has been fertile, perhaps the most fertile of the last century since it has seen the birth or at least the blossoming of three movements of the utmost significance; The Gaelic League (an association for the preservation of the Irish language), a movement for the development of agriculture and animal husbandry,[56] and finally, a new intellectual activity which is even now creating a new literature for us.[57]

As the title of the essay suggests, Synge saw the Gaelic League, the literary movement and the co-operative associations as inextricably linked in a wider movement for Ireland's revival. 'These three movements', noted Synge, 'are intimately linked; it is rare to find someone who is interested or active in one of the three movements who is not also concerned with the others'.[58] It was the self-help front, therefore, rather than the newly reunited Irish Parliamentary Party which Synge pointed to as the most progressive force for change in Irish society.

'The Groggy-Patriot-Publican-General-Shop-Man': Synge and the Co-operative Movement

It is not surprising that Synge should empathize with the work of Horace Plunkett. Indeed much of his travel writing reveals the extent to which the dramatist concurred with Plunkett's diagnosis of Irish problems. Plunkett was among the first to express disquiet with the operations of the Congested Districts Board (CDB) towards the end of the century. The CDB owed its origins to Balfourian amelioration policy, which sought to diffuse political dissent by improving the dire social and economic problems of the congested districts of the west of Ireland. The role of the Board was to purchase and amalgamate the smallest holdings, import stock, organize relief works and establish fisheries.[59] Despite being a one-time member of the CDB, Plunkett 'was never happy with its undisguised paternalism'.[60] In the end the policies of the CDB were discredited, because of its proclivity to generate an ethos of dependency in the congested districts and also because of its role in creating a new farming class at the expense of small tenants who were given no choice but emigration. It was to counter such a culture of dependency that Plunkett began his self-help co-operative campaign as an alternative to the centralist colonial policies of the CDB.

Synge got to study the effects of the CDB at first hand after a commission by the *Manchester Guardian* to write a series of articles on the congested districts in the summer of 1905. One of the recurring themes to emerge from these essays is the extent to which paternalistic schemes like those of the CDB turned the locals into dependent provincials, stifling rather than fostering a spirit of innovation and creating an atmosphere of dejection. Having come upon a relief works scheme beyond Carraroe, Synge described the scene as follows:

> As we drove quickly by we could see that every man and woman was working with a sort of hang-dog dejection that would be enough to make any casual passer mistake them for a band of convicts. The wages given on these works are usually a shilling a day, and, as a rule, one person only, generally the head of the family, is taken from each house. Sometimes the best worker in a family is thus forced away from his ordinary work of farming, or fishing, or kelp-making for this wretched remuneration at a time when his private industry is most needed. If this system of relief has some things in its favour, it is far from satisfactory in other ways, and is not always economical.[61]

This state of affairs stands in pointed contrast to the buoyancy of a team of kelp-makers he encounters in the village of Trawbaun. Here the melancholy of the relief workers gives way to the 'merry songs in Gaelic' that the seaweed gatherers sing as they go about their work 'as light-hearted[ly] as a party of schoolboys'.[62] If this seems like a romantic flight of Syngean fancy it is, in fact, grounded in a sound socio-economic observation outlined at the beginning of the essay. 'Some of those who have undertaken to reform the congested districts', argued Synge, 'have shown an unfortunate tendency to give great attention to a few canonised industries, such as horse-breeding and fishing, or even bee-keeping, while they neglect local industries that have been practised with success for a great number of years'.[63] The point is clear: people are more likely to thrive by developing pre-existing native industries than throwing them over for new economic practices of which they have little or no experience or expertise. This was, in many ways, little more than Synge's application of Douglas Hyde's central thesis in 'The Necessity for De-Anglicising Ireland' to the realm of rural economics. We must 'show the folly of neglecting what is Irish', wrote Hyde, 'and hastening to adopt pell-mell, and indiscriminately, everything that is English, simply because it is English'.[64] Any genuine economic revival, according to Synge, would have to give due attention to the mobilization of local expertise and innovation, and could not be built on an unquestioning deference to imposed solutions. To this end, Synge, time and time again, drew attention to 'the business intelligence of the smallest tenant farmers'[65] and lamented the widespread 'contempt for the local views of the people which seems rooted in nearly all the official workers one meets with through the country.'[66]

Even in instances where the CDB did succeed in promoting sustainable economic development, it often encouraged rather than stemmed the tide of emigration. Synge encountered this paradox in the Carraroe district of County Galway, where local girls earned 'a good sum' in the nearby lace schools only to save it up to pay their passage to America. The problem in this case was the sheer lack of an appreciable cultural life to entice the emerging generations to stay. According to a local witness who spoke to Synge it was seldom that the people were treated to any form of entertainment, 'though in the old times it's many a piper would be moving around through the houses for a whole quarter together, playing his pipes and drinking poteen and the people dancing round him; but now there is no dancing or singing in this place at all, and most of the young people is growing up and going to America'.[67] Like Synge, Horace Plunkett also realized that cultural regeneration should be a necessary concomitant of economic development if the problem of emigration was to be solved. It was for this reason that he launched his campaign for 'the brightening of rural life in Ireland'. In November 1901 the *Irish Homestead* launched a competition to encourage co-operative societies to promote 'the revival of national sports and Gaelic past-times', 'the establishment of classes for Gaelic, Irish literature and poetry', 'the organisation of village libraries', 'the revival of ceilidhs', 'encouragement of Irish music and song by local concerts or classes' and 'the formation of village choirs', among other initiatives.[68] If the emigration problem was to be solved, therefore, it was as important to reactivate rural cultural life as it was to create economic opportunities.

One of the most significant points of contact between Synge and Plunkett was their attitude to the gombeen class of publican-shopkeepers so prevalent in Ireland. Such a class, in the ascendant at the turn of the century, often exerted as malign an influence on the peasantry as the colonial administration, prospering, as it did, on the misfortune of the worst-off. Synge despised what he called 'the groggy-patriot-publican-general-shop-man who is married to the priest's half-sister and is second cousin once-removed of the dispensary doctor'.[69] He could see that it was within the cosy alliance of commerce, parliamentary politics, religion and the professions that the mean-spirited sectional interests of middle Ireland were being promoted. It disgusted him that the very people who were orchestrating the anti-grazier campaigns of the United Irish League were also 'swindling the people themselves in a dozen ways'.[70] Ironically the CDB's conciliatory policies often worked to consolidate the position of the emerging élite by buying land from the smallest tenants and selling it to more solvent neighbours.[71] This was a phenomenon which also outraged Synge. While travelling in Mayo he noticed that:

> In the last few months a certain number of men have sold out the tenant-right of their holdings – usually to the local shopkeeper, to whom they are always in debt – and shipped themselves and their whole families to America with what remained of the money. This is probably the worst kind of emigration, and one fears the suffering of these families, who are suddenly moved to such different surroundings, must be great.[72]

This drew attention to the way in which land reforms, rather than precipitating radical redistribution of land, often concentrated it in the hands of the better off. At a time of rising economic prosperity in Ireland, Synge was careful to articulate the plight of the most marginalized sections of Irish society.

Synge also highlighted the fact that the shopkeeper in most congested districts was not only the main supplier of consumer items but also the only buyer of many home-produced goods, placing him in a position of unrivalled economic dominance.[73] It was out of an attempt to break this paralysing stranglehold over the peasantry that Plunkett was motivated to found his co-operative movement. Indeed one of the objectives of the IAOS was to provide an alternative to the usurious practices of the local shopkeeper by consolidating the purchasing power of smaller farmers within the co-operative structures. Likewise, co-operatives allowed small farmers access to a corporate marketing system in which profits could be shared equally. Such radical ideas were deeply troubling to the emerging gombeen class, which spared no effort to discredit the ideas of Plunkett and the work of the IAOS. For years the main organs of parliamentarianism, the *Irish Daily Independent* and the *Freeman's*

Journal, tried to discredit the co-operative project by casting aspersions on the movement, at times on the basis of Plunkett's ascendancy background and at other times by charging that it was responsible for the spread of alien socialist ideas in Ireland.[74] Despite such propaganda the *Irish Homestead* remained steadfast that the farmers had 'every right to co-operate for the purchase of agricultural requirements', and that it was possible to 'effect enormous saving thereby'.[75] Such a scheme met the approval of Synge, who railed not infrequently against the 'rampant, double-chinned vulgarity'[76] of the shopkeeper class, whose cultural sterility he equated with their upward mobility.

Synge and the Language Revival

As Declan Kiberd's study has shown, Synge's scholarly knowledge of the Irish language and its literature, together with his first-hand knowledge of Gaeltacht life and the Dublin cultural milieu at the turn of the century, gave him a profound insight into the dilemmas, difficulties and paradoxes of the language revival movement. Unlike Synge, however, 'few [Gaelic League] learners ever became fluent speakers of Irish, although thousands were members of the organisation'.[77] This ambivalent relationship of many Irish people to the native tongue escaped the attention of most of the leaders of the language revival who remained firm in their belief that the removal of institutional biases against the teaching of Irish would be enough to ignite the spark of revival in English-speaking Ireland. As early as 1901, though, Synge was beginning to appreciate the complexities of reviving a language whose intellectual traditions had withered towards the end of the seventeenth century with the dissipation of the cultural infrastructure of Gaelic Ireland, yet whose very existence justified the Irish claim to nationhood.[78] Ironically, it was at a performance of Hyde's *Casadh an tSúgáin* – the first ever professional production of a play in Irish – that he glimpsed these troubling contradictions. Reflecting on what happened in the theatre that night, Synge wrote:

> Despite the importance of [the Gaelic League] (and as it happens so often in movements which are of their nature, popular) there is an element of the ridiculous apparent in its public events, side by side with which are feelings of infinite depth. Thus, at the beginning of the first night it was hard to keep a straight face at the sight of the beautiful Irish ladies of the Gaelic League all around the theatre talking non-stop in the most woeful Irish with their young clerks and workingmen who were quite pale with enthusiasm. But, it happened that during an interval in Diarmuid and Gráinne, according to local custom, the people in the galleries started to sing. They sang old, well-known songs. Until that moment those melodies had never been heard sung in unison by so many voices with the ancient Irish words. A shiver went through the auditorium. In the lingering notes there was an incomparable melancholy, like the death rattle of a nation. One after another, faces could be seen leaning into their programmes. We wept.[79]

Synge was one of the first commentators to highlight the contradiction between the Gaelic Leaguers' deep enthusiasm for Irish and their lack of proficiency in it.[80] In this scenario he captured Ireland's postcolonial linguistic dilemma. Like William Rooney he was acutely aware of the impossibility of a now largely English-speaking population regaining a pre-colonial fluency in Irish. Yet he was also alive to the huge symbolic importance of reclaiming and celebrating the ancient tongue and was himself profoundly moved by the communal celebration of Irish that the singing of the songs in the theatre embodied.

This seeming paradox of an intense devotion to the language accompanied by a lack of competency in it was a widespread phenomenon within the Gaelic League during the early years of the revival. This has been partly explained by the fact that membership of the Gaelic League was attractive to those motivated more by a desire to enhance their own career prospects on the back of nationalist advance than by a sincere commitment to the Irish language. As Sean O'Casey famously put it, 'there's a lot of fretful popinjays lisping Irish wrongly'. In his view they had associated 'the fight for Irish' with the 'fight for collars and ties'.[81] D. P. Moran would seem to fit into this category without too much difficulty. He stands out as a figure whose public crusade on behalf of the Irish language was utterly disproportionate to his competence in it and his less than earnest attempt to learn it. As Patrick Maume has pointed out, 'Moran set about learning Irish, though he habitually disrupted classes with practical jokes and smart remarks'.[82] The *United Irishman* took great delight in pointing out that he was 'as ignorant of the Irish language as any of his saxon contributors'.[83] To Moran, therefore, one can attribute the origins of a lasting tradition of tokenism in relation to the Irish language which would become such a salient feature of the new Irish state.

It is important to point out, however, that the ambivalent attitude towards the Irish language was not simply an example of mass cultural hypocrisy motivated by expedient careerism. Rather, the disparity between the growing support for the language and manifest competency in it was a consequence of the painful linguistic transformation which went hand in hand with colonial attempts to assimilate Ireland into the British cultural mainstream. In this regard the mass support for the Gaelic League can be interpreted as a genuine gesture of affirmation in the validity of Irish cultural forms. Support for the League, therefore, provided a means to defy the state imperative of cultural assimilation and to oppose state repugnance of the language. Yet the harsh reality was that such a project to resuscitate what had become a marginalized, regional language and restore it to the status of a national language after more than two centuries of decline, and in the absence of a surviving Gaelic intellectual life of vigour, would prove to be fraught with difficulties and paradoxes. The special challenges of reviving Irish would impede the progress of even those most willing to learn it. Many of the problems derived from the fact, as Synge well knew, that the Gaelic League's two main aims – standardizing and nationalizing the language on the one hand and encouraging its use among native speakers on the other – would prove to be at odds with each other.

By the time Synge began writing, the Irish language had long since ceased to function as a national language and survived only in dialect form in pockets of Munster, Connacht and Ulster. But Synge well knew that Irish had enjoyed a pre-colonial period of relative standardization when it had functioned as a national language.[84] He was fully aware that:

> By the end of the twelfth century a new type of learned layman had arisen who found his economic support in selling poems of praise to the aristocracy, and for over four hundred years (1200–1650) this class maintained the standard language which we call Early Modern (or Classical) Irish. After the battle of Kinsale in 1601, the Irish aristocracy was ruined and with it the scholars who had maintained the standard language; from that point onwards the Classical language begins to decay, and the dialects of the people to take its place.[85]

Indeed, until the end of the sixteenth century, the accepted mode of exchange for the educated classes was 'a rich and flexible literary language with centuries of cultivation behind it'.[86] Until this point Irish 'had a range fully comparable to that of English or French, and contained far fewer loanwords than either of these'.[87]

The strange and complicated fate to which the Irish language was condemned in the centuries after the battle of Kinsale in 1601 was readily appreciated by Synge. 'When towards the end of the seventeenth century the Irish language ceased to be used as a literary tongue', he admitted, 'all the intellectual traditions of the country were lost'.[88] Synge may have exaggerated the decline of literary Irish,[89] nevertheless in his writings he was careful to draw attention to the rich scholarly traditions of Gaelic Ireland.[90] In so doing he performed a vital decolonizing role by drawing attention to the fact that scholarly and literary activity did not begin in Ireland with the arrival of the English language and that Ireland had well-developed intellectual traditions of its own.

If the breakdown of classical standard Irish into numerous regional dialects from the seventeenth century onwards was occasioned by the collapse of the cultural infrastructure of Gaelic Ireland, it was also due to the fact that Irish as a submerged language of the colonized periphery was never modernized and standardized by the process of print-capitalism, as the metropolitan languages of power were. The increasing capacity for the dissemination of printed material, made possible by the dynamics of capitalism and the development of print technology, had the effect of 'fixing' vernaculars and transforming them into standard national languages. In the case of Irish, the lack of engagement with the processes of print-capitalism meant that the language continued its steady 'decline' into dialects over time and space, and continued to lose ground to an English language rigorously standardized and readily available in print. By 1891 census figures revealed that, out of a population of over four million, the number of Gaelic monoglots had declined to just 38,192.[91] In such a situation 'the threat of uncontrolled 'béarlachas' (anglicisms) overwhelming the minority language in a radically asymmetrical situation was real'.[92]

As the Gaelic League began its project of revival, therefore, it did so against a background in which an agreed standard had not existed for the Irish language for nearly 300 years, only a tiny number of Gaelic monoglots survived and all but a handful of native Irish speakers remained illiterate in Irish, even if they could read some English. Such disabling obstacles would prove deeply challenging to the most enthusiastic and gifted learners and insurmountable to many. As Michael Cronin has noted, 'the extraordinary difficulties faced by those wishing to learn Irish or to write in the language prior to the emergence of broadly accepted orthographical and grammatical standards are too easily forgotten'.[93] The response of the Gaelic League to this state of affairs was to 'artificially regularise the Irish language through a process of accelerated interventionism, that is concealed by the more gradual and long-term changes in major languages'.[94] Much of the work of the League was an attempt to 'fast-forward' the Irish language into the era of print-capitalism by publishing newspapers and encouraging literature, particularly fiction, in Irish.[95] The Gaelic League made it a cultural project to provide the Irish language with the necessary linguistic infrastructure to enable it to become an adequate language of 'modern' culture. It established an entire institutional network of book and newspaper publishing, language classes and literary activity (including the Oireachtas),[96] outside the purview of the state – which rewarded those who conformed to the stated aspirations of the League. By means of this network of cultural sanction the Gaelic League single-handedly initiated the debate on the modern standardization of the Irish language which culminated in the publication of *An Caighdeán Oifigiúil* (the official standard) in 1958.

The process of standardizing Irish did not proceed without difficulty. Indeed, many controversies raged over what form the new standard should take, what was the most suitable script and what modification should be made to spelling. 'A few traditionalists pleaded for the resurrection of the classical language',[97] exemplified by the works of Geoffrey Keating. However, as all contact had been lost with the classical norm, this suggestion proved unworkable.[98] The answer as to what a standardized Irish language could be based on was provided by An t-Athair Peadar Ua Laoghaire. He was vocal in his rejection of the standard classical Irish of the seventeenth century, believing that a revival based on it would require antiquarian knowledge far beyond the ken of most learners. His solution was to advocate 'caint na ndaoine' – literally, the language of the people – which, he felt, could form the basis of a vigorous literature. To make his point, Ua Laoghaire wrote a novel in the dialect of his native Munster, which was serialized in the *Gaelic Journal* between 1894 and 1897. *Séadna* was to have a profound influence on the evolution of a modern standard Irish.[99] Several years before Lady Gregory and Synge turned to dialect to found a new Irish literature in English, Ua Laoghaire anticipated them to inaugurate a contemporary literature in Irish.

The relentless drive to standardize Irish, although enormously helpful to learners, was not always in the best interests of native speakers. In fact attempts to introduce a written standard into the Gaeltacht often had the effect of promoting 'the idea among Gaeltacht speakers that their Irish [was] substandard and best forgotten'.[100] Again Ua Laoghaire was to the fore in defending the literary efforts of native speakers against the over-zealousness of Gaelic League grammarians:

> Men who know the language from the very cradle have from time to time written articles for the Irish papers These articles were written with care and a great deal of thought and study . . . The articles went up to Dublin and were 'corrected' in such a manner that the writers could not recognise them! And the writers were cuffed on account of their spelling!! Not a writer of them ever of course wrote a second article, and the whole field was left to people who did not know a word of correct Irish . . . Anyhow we must not allow any man to put *ceangal na gcúig gcaol* upon us or our poor uneducated speakers of Irish.[101]

In many respects this state of affairs arose out of the cruel paradox that the language revival was led, for the most part, by non-native speakers whose dependence on rigid rules of standard grammar often mystified and discouraged the most fluent native speakers, who were largely unschooled in written Irish

But if a condescending attitude towards native speakers was taking hold of the Gaelic League, Ua Laoghaire was not long in tackling it by reversing the direction of the critique. In a series of articles on Irish prose composition published in the *Leader* between 5 May 1901 and 22 February 1902, Ua Laoghaire took it upon himself to criticize the bad translations of non-native Irish speakers. As far as he was concerned, 'the danger lay in misguided amateurism, enthusiasm being a poor substitute for competence'.[102] This danger surfaced particularly when writers or translators produced texts that 'were syntactically and idiomatically beholden to English'.[103]

> But do not torture us with your translations. They are by far the most deadly element in the disease which is killing our language. They effectually disgust and repel the most courageous of native Irish speakers.[104]

Ua Laoghaire admitted a reluctance to be so forthright in his criticisms 'while our learners were making their first attempts', but he considered that 'it would be unfair, even to them to keep silent longer'.[105] As a native speaker and an established writer, therefore, Ua Laoghaire occupied a moderate position within the language movement. He recognized that the project to standardize and modernize the Irish language, although necessary, should not take place without an appreciation of the distinctiveness and integrity of the spoken language, particularly in view of the asymmetrical relationship between Irish and English.

To return to Synge's reflections on the opening night of *Casadh an tSúgáin*, it would seem that, in articulating a concern about the gap between competency and enthusiasm for the Irish language, he was merely engaging in a debate brought to the fore by Peadar Ua Laoghaire. Indeed, both men had a grasp of the subtleties and complexities of the revival project which often evaded the most enthusiastic Gaelic Leaguers. Like Ua Laoghaire, Synge realized early on that the dynamics of language revival for native and non-native speakers were utterly different and, at times, clashing.

While on Aran, Synge noticed that the Gaelic League was having some success among a younger generation of islanders in restoring a reverence for the Irish language. This contrasted starkly with the attitude of an older generation which did not seem to retain any particular affection for the language. 'Whenever they [the elders] are able', recorded Synge, 'they speak English to their children, to render them more capable of making their way in life'.[106] Yet the paradox of younger native speakers struggling to read and write their own language according to the rules of Gaelic League grammarians struck him forcefully. He could not but empathize with the young women of the island who were 'willing to spend their one afternoon of freedom in laborious studies of orthography for no other reason but a vague reverence for the Gaelic'.[107] However, the ironies of the language revival are most forcefully illustrated by Synge's account of the difficulties experienced by an Aran youth whom he had engaged to read Irish stories aloud:

> In most of the stories we read, where the English and Irish are printed side by side, I see him looking across to the English in passages that are a little obscure, though he is indignant if I say that he knows English better than Irish. Probably he knows the local Irish better than English, and printed English better than printed Irish, as the latter has frequent dialectic forms he does not know.[108]

In many respects this scenario represents in microcosm the confusing linguistic flux which occurred throughout the nineteenth century. The boy, educated in the national school system, is much more competent in standard written English than he is in the newly forming standard Irish, but he speaks better Irish than English. One could not find a better illustration of the extreme difficulties faced by those wishing to resuscitate Irish as the national language.[109] It was this insight that was to vitally inform Synge's dramatic art.

Synge agreed with Ua Laoghaire that the attempts to standardize Irish were having a negative impact on the Gaeltacht and followed the Irish scholar in criticizing the bookish Irish of the Gaelic League. Some months after Ua Laoghaire's series of newspaper articles attacking the poor standards of translation endemic in the League had drawn to a close, Synge was to express his own forthright views on the topic. This act of criticism not only pointed out the shortcomings of the movement's literary project but also served as an apologia for his own decision to commit to an Irish literature in the English language. In an early draft of 'The Old and New in Ireland', Synge betrayed his frustration with what he perceived as the low literary standards of the Gaelic League:

> Mr. W. B. Yeats is the first writer who has written in an Irish spirit with a full appreciation of English rhythms . . . [he] has been attacked over and over by the Gaelic enthusiasts because he writes in English. The Gaelic enthusiasts when they write in Gaelic would certainly be attacked by Mr. Yeats, if he could read them. Most of us have a certain satisfaction when we read the productions of the Gaelic League that these writers use a language that is not intelligible outside their club-room doors.[110]

This was certainly a tenable critique in 1902. Apart from the writings of Douglas Hyde and Peadar Ua Laoghaire, the Gaelic movement had not produced much by way of quality literary output by this time. This would all change a few years later when Patrick Pearse and Pádraic Ó Conaire would move Irish fiction away from the folktale to embrace the European model of realist fiction.[111] It was just such an incorporation of European modes into the Irish tradition that Synge had singled out for special mention in his review of Keating's *Foras Feasa Ar Eirinn*. Keating's exchanges 'with men who had been in touch with the first scholarship in Europe', wrote Synge, '[were] of great use in correcting the narrowing influence of a simply Irish tradition'.[112]

Synge was equally rigorous in his critique of the shortcomings of the Anglo-Irish literature of the nineteenth century. Much of Irish culture had, he felt, been 'pitifully interpreted' by this literature of 'Irish humours'.[113] Yet it was bad translation of Gaelic poetry that most offended him. In a scathing review of A. H. Leahy's *Heroic Romances of Ireland*, he gave a clear explanation of his theory of translation. Having given an example of what he considers abysmal translation from the *Book of Leinster*, he writes:

> This kind of facile parody has been written very frequently by writers who have set out to translate Gaelic poetry, and their verse has shown to an extraordinary extent the provinciality which – at least till quite lately – has distinguished a good deal of Anglo-Irish taste. It is hardly too much to say that, while a great part of Gaelic poetry itself is filled with the most curious individuality and charm, there is probably no mass of tawdry commonplace jingle so worthless as the verse translations that have been made from it in Ireland during the last century.[114]

Clearly it was Leahy's slavish adherence to English poetic conventions in his translations of Gaelic poetry which most offended Synge. One can detect here a concern for the nuances of translation as rigorous as that shown by Peadar Ua Laoghaire. But, if Ua Laoghaire railed against the import of anglicisms into Irish, Synge positively encouraged the importation of 'gaelicisms' into English translations of Irish texts. Indeed, in his own early translations, his method was to render the finished product 'as near the Irish as I am able to make it'.[115] As Michael Cronin has put it:

> [Synge] saw that the challenge was to convey the excitement and beauty of the source language in the target language. To do this, he would have to abandon

the artifice of fluency and allow the target language, the language of the coloniser, to be colonised in its turn by the language of the colonised.[116]

By choosing to infuse English with the idioms and syntax of Irish, Synge invented a new literary method which allowed him to bypass the uncertainties and the squabbling over the standardization of the Irish language, and to avoid the provincialism of an Anglo-Irish literature which could only mimic the strategies of an English poetic tradition. This pivotal decision to base his dramatic art on the importance of dialect was due in no short measure to his realization that 'the linguistic atmosphere of Ireland has become definitely English enough, for the first time, to allow work to be done in English that is perfectly Irish in its essence, yet has sureness and purity of form'.[117]

Synge was quick to pay compliment to Lady Gregory's innovations in the same direction in *Cuchulain of Muirthemne*. But, while he praised her 'wonderfully simple and powerful language', he gently rebuked her for omitting 'certain barbarous features, such as the descriptions of the fury of Cuchulain' from her text.[118] Unlike Lady Gregory, Synge did not feel the imperative to suppress either the dark or carnivalesque energies of peasant Ireland. In fact he grew quite weary of the Dublin intelligentsia's relentless attempts to idealize the peasantry in the wake of the Mahaffy/Atkinson affair.

The Shadow of the Glen

One of Synge's core beliefs about the social and economic modernization of Ireland was that every effort should be made to encourage and rekindle local expertise and to avoid an unquestioning deference to imposed solutions. Such a blend of local and imported knowledge could, he felt, provide an alternative Irish model of modernization that would be sensitive to Irish initiative and distinctiveness but open to outside innovation. Thus, contrary to colonial practices, material advance did not have to be accompanied by contempt for local views and customs. It is not surprising, then, that he should draw on these same principles in his thinking about an Irish national drama. In his first stage play, *The Shadow of the Glen*, performed in October 1903, he draws on the Irish folktale tradition to warn against the physical, economic and imaginative oppression of women. In a manner similar to the Yeats/Moore *Diarmuid and Grania*, his moral is not delivered in the form of a self-consciously 'modern' problem play, but out of the wisdom of the Irish folk tradition. Although Synge alters the original folktale upon which the play is based, he manages to transform a residual Irish folk culture into the basis for a modern national drama.[119]

Significantly, in changing the ending of the folktale, he did so in a manner not incompatible with the values of Gaelic literary and folk culture. At first glance, though, it may appear that Synge 'corrected' a brutish folk story to make it serve the interests of an exotic avant-garde modernist concern for the position of women in society. In Pat Dirane's folktale of 'the unfaithful wife', as retold by Synge in *The Aran Islands*, the lover of the woman is brutally punished with a beating from the aggrieved husband and the narrator:

> Then the dead man got up, and he took one stick, and he gave the other to myself. We went in and we saw them lying together with her head on his arm.
>   The dead man hit him a blow with the stick so that the blood out of him leapt up and hit the gallery.[120]

But, in Synge's play, Dan Burke, the slighted husband, never gets to beat his interloper with the stick. In fact his wrath is reserved for his wife Nora, whom he banishes from the house for ever. She causes the greatest shock, however, by choosing to escape with the visiting tramp. Nora's radical gesture of departure triggered Arthur Griffith's vehement opposition to the play, which he dismissed as 'unIrish':

> The play has an Irish name, but it is no more Irish than the Decameron. It is a staging of a corrupt version of the old-world libel on womankind – the 'widow of Ephesus', which was made current in Ireland by the hedge-schoolmaster.[121]

Yet Griffith, who had no Irish, minimum knowledge of Irish literature outside the Davis tradition and little contact with Irish folk culture, was blind to the fact that Synge had indeed discovered many instances of strong defiant women in his reading of Gaelic literature and in his travels in rural Ireland. In his review of *Cuchulain of Muirthemne*, one of the things that struck him about these ancient stories was the strength and autonomy of the female characters. Comparing the stories to Homeric literature, he remarked that 'few features, such as the imperiousness and freedom of the women, seem to imply an intellectual advance beyond the period of Ulysses'.[122] Declan Kiberd has argued that Brian Merriman's *Cúirt an Mheán Oíche* provided a more obvious exemplar for Synge's unrestrained Nora. Throughout that poem an assembled group of women 'complain of enforced marriages to spent old dotards very much as Nora Burke complains in *The Shadow*'.[123] Synge also had the dramatic exemplar of Moore and Yeats's *Diarmuid and Grania* to draw on. Here, once again, in this most ancient of Irish stories, the tragedy of a young girl betrothed to an older man and her spirited attempt to give free rein to her passion is a central concern.

Synge's experiences of forthright female sexuality in Ireland were not purely literary. In fact *The Aran Islands* is peppered with displays of female desire outside the conventions of a narrow Victorian morality.[124] Synge's analysis of this 'liberal' behaviour is worth considering. 'The women of this island', he observed, 'are before conventionality, and share some of the liberal features that are thought peculiar to the women of Paris and New York'.[125] This is a revealing appraisal, which sees in the avant-garde modernism of Paris and New York a rediscovery of the easy and spirited spontaneity of 'primitive' society.

It is this easy and spirited spontaneity that characterizes Nora Burke. Despite the fact that she marries 'a man with a bit of a farm, and cows on it, and sheep on the back hills',[126] she never surrenders to a life of quiet domesticity. Although it is not overtly stated, there is a tantalizing implication that Nora has enjoyed, or perhaps enjoys, the fantasy of a number of extra-marital sexual liaisons, or, at the very least, flirtatious encounters. She admits to Michael Dara that 'it's a power of men I'm after knowing' (p. 49) as freely as she tells the tramp of the sexual inadequacies of her own husband:

> Maybe cold would be no sign of death with the like of him, for he was always cold, every day since I knew him, – and every night, stranger –. (p. 35)

If Patch Darcy and Michael Dara are likely conquests of hers, she also speaks fondly and in innuendo of 'the men do be reared in the Glen Malure' who know how to 'drive a mountain ewe' (p. 47).[127] There is a certain inevitability, then, about Nora's exit with the tramp at the end.

Yet Synge was acutely aware that there was a world of difference between the modish posturing of modernist Paris, fatigued by the stifling mores of bourgeois society, and the unconventional behaviour he experienced in rural Ireland which survived in spite of over-zealous colonial attempts to 'enlighten' it. He was not, after all, a mere dilettante momentarily fascinated by the exotic in Gaelic culture. On the contrary, he expended a great deal of his creative energy studying the ancient language and literature, travelling in the congested districts and highlighting the plight of the worst off.

What Synge can be credited with in a play like *Shadow of the Glen* is the fashioning of a distinctly Irish modernism which, like its metropolitan European counterpart, is critical of bourgeois values. But, crucially, this critique is levelled from the vantage point of one who empathizes with the plight of a culture which has been submerged by the enlightenment project rather than of one who has become bloated with it. If European modernism fetishizes the primitive to redeem a jaded bourgeois existence, Synge is concerned to retrieve and energize the liberational possibilities of Gaelic culture, in order to oppose the unquestioning adoption of metropolitan values and the concomitant dismissal of residual folk practices as disabling and backward.

Griffith, on the other hand, found this link between Gaelic culture and avant-garde modernism deeply disturbing and refused to recognize the possibility of the connection. 'To take the widow of Ephesus', he gibed, 'and rechristen her Mrs. Burke, and relabel Ephesus Wicklow, is not a brilliant thing'. As far as he was concerned the play was no better than 'the decadent cynicism that passes current in the Latin Quartier and the London salon'.[128] Unlike Synge, Griffith was less discerning in his embrace of bourgeois values. That his political position was shifting to the right to embrace a conservative nationalism at odds with Rooney's anti-imperial republicanism has been pointed out already. His political agenda, therefore, depended on the acceptance of a fixed and narrow definition of national identity encapsulated in his belief that 'nationality is the breath of art'.[129] He was, after all, less interested in generating an alternative

Irish polity than in replicating metropolitan models in an Irish context. That Gaelic culture as represented on the stage of the national theatre could be recruited to critique his programme of *embourgeoisement* was deeply disturbing to him. Central to Griffith's project was a need to idealize and confine the possibilities of Irish identity as expressed in representations of the peasantry. In this way radical gestures which questioned the priorities of enlightenment conventions – such as the behaviour of Synge's unconventional Nora – could only ever be configured as decadent and exotic, rather than something which could be generated from within the dynamics of Irish culture. The rediscovery and mobilization of recalcitrant cultural energies undertaken by Synge, therefore, was as much discouraged by conservative elements within nationalism, like Griffith, as it was by colonial cultural watchdogs, like Mahaffy and Atkinson.

Griffith's dismissal of *The Shadow of the Glen* – a play deeply indebted to Gaelic literary and folk traditions – as 'unIrish' is reminiscent of other attempts to refashion the peasant as a model of Victorian virtue. We have seen, repeatedly, how in the wake of the claims of Mahaffy and Atkinson there was a concerted attempt to refashion the peasant as a model of Victorian virtue. Figures as diverse as Cardinal Logue, Dr O'Hickey and Douglas Hyde all felt obliged to recast the Irish peasant as a paragon of virtue. Lady Gregory was sufficiently influenced by prevailing attitudes to excise sexual references from *Cuchulain of Muirthemne* and the Moore/Yeats *Diarmuid and Grania* was roundly criticized for publicizing one of the more 'vulgar' Irish legends. The importance of Synge lies in his resolute resistance to such patronizing views of the peasantry, which had become fashionable among a Dublin middle-class anxious to be seen to measure up to Victorian moral standards. He could see that this strategy merely served to perpetuate the notion that the Irish were unable to generate their own moral terms of reference. He took great delight in deflating such unrealistic peasant representations by providing a more rounded appraisal and drawing attention to the subversive cunning of the Irish peasantry, who were not above feigning virtue to their own advantage when benevolent visitors came calling:

> Even among the old people, whose singular charm I have tried to interpret . . . it is possible to find many individuals who are far from admirable either in body or mind. One would hardly stop to assert a fact so obvious if it had not become the fashion in Dublin, quite recently, to reject a fundamental doctrine of theology, and to exalt the Irish peasant into a type of almost absolute virtue, frugal, self-sacrificing, valiant, and I know not what. There is some truth to this estimate, yet it is safer to hold with the theologians that, even west of the Shannon, the heart of man is not spotless, for though the Irish peasant has many beautiful virtues, it is idle to assert that he is totally unacquainted with the deadly sins, and many minor rogueries. He has however . . . a fine sense of humour and the greatest courtesy. When a benevolent visitor comes to his cottage, seeking a sort of holy family, the man of the house, his wife and all their infants, too courteous to disappoint him, play their parts with delight.[130]

The budding playwright bravely decided against 'a purely fantastic, unmodern, ideal, spring-dayish, Cuchulainoid National Theatre' and opted instead for a more interrogative drama that would confront the harsh realities of Irish life. He was anxious to avoid what he called the 'insincere cult of joy' and expressed the hope that Ireland would benefit if Irish writers dealt 'manfully, directly, and decently with the entire reality of life'.[131] These were views penned shortly after the first production of *The Shadow* and could just as easily have been included as programme notes for that play. The play does indeed confront the 'insincere cult of joy' that informed contemporary views of rural life and is deliberately anti-pastoral in thrust. As in most of Synge's work, sound anthropological observation is the basis of much of his insight. In an early essay which partly inspired *The Shadow*, Synge painted a bleak picture of environmentally determined rural depression which belied the emerging stereotypes of ideal Irish bucolic simplicity. Writing of the tragic plight of a woman he met, and who was to inspire the character Peggy Cavanagh in *The Shadow of the Glen*, Synge described how 'we hear every day of the horrors of overcrowding, yet these desolate dwellings on the hill with here an old widow dying far away from her friends and there a single woman with all the whims of over-wrought virginity have perhaps a more utter, if higher sort of misery'.[132] By equating the devastating side-effects of rural loneliness with the pressing problems of urban overcrowding, Synge cleverly disabled the simplistic urban/rural binary current at the time, and uncovered a hidden world of rural suffering.

There is no shortage of characters who suffer the 'oppression of the hills' in *The Shadow of the Glen*. The story of Patch Darcy's insanity is a recurring motif throughout the play. We hear of how, in a fit of madness, he ran naked into the black hills 'talking queer talk' (p. 35) only to perish in the cold of night. Dan Burke, Nora informs us, was 'always up on the hills . . . thinking thoughts in the dark mist' (p. 35). Peggy Cavanagh, who once 'had the lightest hand at milking a cow that wouldn't be easy', lives out her final years in a squalid old house 'with no teeth in her mouth, and no sense' (p. 51). Nora, too, suffers from the isolation of rural life. She constantly talks of being lonely, especially since the demise of Patch Darcy, who would never pass the house 'night or morning' without speaking to her (p. 47).

Yet Synge is careful to point out that Nora's loneliness is not so much caused by the oppression of the hills as by the oppression of her patriarchal husband and her imprisonment in the house. Her enslavement is clearly configured in relation to her confinement within the domestic space, rather than as a consequence of the oppressive hills:

> I do be thinking in the long nights it was a big fool I was that time, Michael Dara, for what good is a bit of a farm with cows on it, and sheep on the back hills, when you do be sitting, looking out from a door the like of that door, and seeing nothing but the mists rolling down the bog, and the mists again, and they rolling up the bog, and hearing nothing but the wind crying out in the bits of broken trees were left from the great storm, and the streams roaring with the rain? (p. 49)

From the inside of the house Nora's imagination is only open to a bleak, ominous and threatening nature of dark mists, crying wind, broken trees, wild storms and flooding streams. The only activities available to her are the repetitive tasks of domestic duties:

> It's a bad night, and a wild night, Michael Dara, and isn't it a great while I am at the foot of the back hills, sitting up here boiling food for himself, and food for the brood sow, and baking cake when the night falls? (p. 49)

Such a miserable existence 'at the foot of the back hills' is further compounded by our knowledge that old Dan is 'always up on the hills' and likely to be in a position of surveillance over her daily routine.

Nora's articulation of her own domestic imprisonment is all the more significant when one takes into account the important changes taking place in the social practices and gender relations of rural Irish society at this time. Throughout this study the important role played by self-help movements like the IAOS in modernizing Irish rural society from the 1890s onwards has been noted. At a time of significant land transfer from large landowners to tenant farmers, the IAOS played a vital role in educating new landowners in modern farming methods. But if the methods of Irish farming were fundamentally altered, so too were the traditional social practices associated with rural farming life. What has not been fully appreciated is that, through agencies like the co-operative movement and publications like the *Irish Homestead*, the modernization of rural society was as much predicated on the adoption of middle-class moral values as it was on the encouragement of modern scientific methods. Week in, week out, the *Irish Homestead* urged a programme of social reform which constantly pitted a desirable middle-class propriety against the perceived uncouthness of traditional practices. It was not uncommon to find advice like the following proffered on a weekly basis.

> A stranger passing along our Irish roads is sometimes painfully struck with the air of neglect and indeed of slovenliness which many of our wayside cottages present. The thatch in many cases is rotten, overgrown with weeds. The doors and windows are ill-fitting and ill-painted. A manure heap or a pool of filthy water not infrequently lies between the highway and the cottage door. There is a dismal absence of whitewash; the walls of stone or of clay are exposed in all their uncouthness to the critical eye of the traveller and his judgement upon the habits of the owner and the inmates is, in consequence, far from complimentary.
>
> Now there is no reason why this should be so. There is absolutely no reason why our cottages, inside and outside, should not be homes in which self-respecting men and women could physically live.[133]

With the on-the-ground infrastructure of the co-operative societies at its disposal one cannot underestimate the influence the *Irish Homestead* had in reforming and modernizing what it classed as outdated and vulgar social practices. Furthermore, many of the reforms endorsed by the *Homestead* and the co-operative movement had serious repercussions for gender relations in turn-of-the-century Ireland. A great number of these new practices had the effect of restricting women to the domestic space, and cutting them off from activities outside the home, as well as curtailing expressions of female desire. The feminization of the domestic space and the concomitant restriction of female possibility which took place as a result of the industrial revolution in eighteenth-century Britain,[134] happened in Ireland towards the end of the nineteenth century, but within a narrative of national revival. The following extract from the *Irish Homestead* is one of countless examples of how the home was constructed as an essentially female space at this time:

> We know that in towns the slatternly ways and thrifty habits of the women are often largely responsible for the dissipation and disorders of the men. Nothing will more effectually impel a man to seek the light and warmth of a public house bar than a gloomy and cheerless fireside at home, the sight of an untidy wife and unwashed, neglected children.[135]

Here the twin ideals of temperance and the domestication of women are made mutually dependent, and the principle is established that male vice is inversely proportional to female domesticity.[136] This contention, that relative female autonomy and possibility were restricted with the modernization of Irish rural practices from the 1890s onwards, has been corroborated by Joanna Bourke in her recent study, *Husbandry to Housewifery*:

> In Ireland between 1890 and 1914 the position of women within the paid labour markets deteriorated. Married women were increasingly dependent on their husband's wage. Economic opportunities for unmarried women collapsed. Even forms of paid employment for women shifted into the home. Thus reforming organizations invested in home industries rather than in factory production. Rural women entered the fields only in times of peak agricultural demand, if at all. Unwaged domestic production became more important . . . [E]conomic growth exacerbated inequality within the household, making women worse off in *relation to men* than they had been in 1891.[137]

Bourke's central point here seems to be that the wholesale adoption of enlightenment notions of progress was responsible for the social and familial restriction of women from the turn of the century onwards. In the light of this analysis, Nora's radical gesture of defiance can be read as a warning against a modernization project based upon the uncritical acceptance of bourgeois enlightenment values, rather than as a critique of residual atavistic attitudes to women. Just as Synge, with his keen sociologist's eye and his heightened sense of justice, criticized the wholesale acceptance of the CDB's solutions to Irish economic problems, so too, in this play, did he warn against the importation of rigid patriarchal values which were being rapidly instituted in a modernizing Ireland.

Nora's escape, after all, is not from the lonesome 'oppression of the hills'. She absconds with the tramp not to embrace the delights of town life, but to rediscover the delights of nature, which, from inside her domestic prison, had only registered as dark and threatening:

> Come along with me now, lady of the house, and it's not my blather you'll be hearing only, but you'll be hearing the grouse, and the owls with them, and the larks and the big thrushes when the days are warm, and it's not from the like of them you'll be hearing a talk of getting old like Peggy Cavanagh, and losing the hair off you, and the light of your eyes, but it's fine songs you'll be hearing when the sun goes up, and there'll be no old fellow wheezing the like of a sick sheep close to your ear. (p. 57)

In breaking free from the patriarchal oppressions of Dan Burke and his aspiring surrogate, Michael Dara, she not only escapes from the confinement of having to 'boil food for himself, and food for the brood sow', but also asserts her right to make 'a talk with the men passing' (p. 57). Synge, employing a typical revivalist manoeuvre, uses the fragmentary resonances of the 'imperiousness and freedom of the women' in Gaelic society to critique a stifling Victorian female identity, and provides another parable for the possibilities of an alternative Irish modernity. This critique of Victorian mores and Synge's experimental use of Irish dialect combine to produce a distinct and pioneering Irish modernist aesthetic which is often mistaken in critical discourse for a belated romanticism. In so doing, he managed to overcome at an artistic level one of the enduring dilemmas of the Irish revival: how to reconcile the endeavour to preserve and reanimate the fragments of a submerged native culture and the impulse to engage with the liberating innovations of metropolitan modernity. His answer was, quite simply, to configure native culture not as a quaint premodern vestige, but as a vital constituent of a rival, non-metropolitan modernity. This strategy had the advantage of opening up moribund ancestral cultural forms to innovation once again, and of allowing for the development of an Irish sensibility which did not feel compelled to adopt uncritically all metropolitan ideas. The restriction of female possibility as represented in *The Shadow of the Glen*, then, can be read as a warning against the wholesale adoption of Victorian bourgeois values, rather than a critique of vestigial primitive attitudes to women. Likewise, Nora's departure can be interpreted as a radical rediscovery of the possibilities of a salient Gaelic impulse to critique the oppressions of metropolitan patriarchy as it was gaining a more secure foothold in rural Irish life. Undoubtedly some revivalist energies were working to promote a restricted role for women at this time, as is evidenced in some of the views expressed in the *Irish Homestead*. Significantly, though, a vigorous critique of these changes in gender relations was also provided from within the broad church of the Irish revival, most notably in the writings of J. M. Synge.

Sinn Féin/Abbey Theatre

Like most of the other leading revival figures, Synge engaged passionately with the material condition of Ireland as much as he was concerned with the state of Irish culture. He believed in the self-help idea and worked to encourage the development of local expertise as well as discouraging an unquestioning deference to imposed solutions to Irish problems. Synge was also astutely aware of the subtleties and complexities of the language revival project and was not afraid to criticize the shortcomings of the Gaelic League. He was conscious of the paradox that the language revival was being led by non-native speakers, whose dependence on rigid rules of standard grammar often mystified and discouraged the most fluent native speakers who were largely unschooled in written Irish. It was out of this insight that he decided to fashion his own dramatic art using Hiberno-English dialect, in a way that would subordinate standard English grammar to the syntax and idiom of the Irish language. His first stage play, in a similar manner, also subordinated bourgeois Victorian moral values to the recalcitrant possibilities of Gaelic culture. In so doing he developed an Irish modernist aesthetic that could critique Victorian norms, not from the point of view of a romantic, anti-modern traditionalism but out of a belief in the potential of traditional forms to be newly created. That Arthur Griffith should emerge as Synge's most vocal critic is hardly surprising given his visible political shift to the right, away from William Rooney's anti-imperial republicanism and towards an embrace of a conservative bourgeois nationalism. The debate surrounding Synge's *Shadow of the Glen*, therefore, stands as a defining moment marking the effective breakdown in the coalition of energies underpinning Cumann na nGaedheal and precipitating the emergence of Sinn Féin and the Abbey Theatre as analogous, if distinct, national forces: the former, a political organization with roots in a cultural movement; the latter, an artistic enterprise deeply implicated in politics.

REVIVING THE REVIVAL

This book opened with one of the most quoted passages of Yeats's *Auto-biographies*:

> The modern literature of Ireland, and indeed all that stir of thought which pre-pared for the Anglo-Irish war, began when Parnell fell from power in 1891. A disillusioned and embittered Ireland turned from parliamentary politics; an event was conceived; and the race began, as I think, to be troubled by that event's long gestation.

Much recent analysis dismisses this account of a 'spontaneous' Irish revolution ignited by the flame of revival literature as a flight of Yeatsian hubris which typically situates the poet himself at the vortex of Irish historical dynamics.[1] As we have seen repeatedly, the various cultural disputes surrounding some of the pioneering productions of the theatre movement were symptomatic of a wider struggle to gain control over the representations of the nation. Plays like *The Countess Cathleen*, *Diarmuid and Grania* and *The Shadow of the Glen* did not reveal *the* submerged Irish essence, as Yeats would have it, but were attempts to construct a version of Irishness which did not necessarily enjoy popular allegiance.

But, if Yeats was disingenuous in that famous quotation about the level of empathy between poets, patriots and populace during the revival, he was surely right in his estimation of the post-Parnell period as a key moment of innovation which was to have a profound influence on Irish cultural politics over the coming decades. He was also right in his contention that the closest thing to a unified movement within Irish life at that time was not to be found in the meeting rooms of parliamentary politics but within the branch organi-zations and societies of the broad self-help alliance. Once again Yeats was less than honest in claiming the credit for this.[2] In fact, the widespread success of these initiatives owed as much to the selfless efforts of mass organizers such as Hyde, Gregory, Plunkett, Finlay, Russell and countless others, as to the work of the aloof Yeats. Nevertheless, the extent to which the self-help movements transformed the social, economic and cultural practices of turn-of-the-century Ireland in a progressive and democratic fashion has yet to be fully recognized. The manner in which they attempted to lead a programme of social and cul-tural change that was not anathema to Irish cultural distinctiveness was, per-haps, their greatest achievement and a vitally important contribution to Irish decolonization. The emergence of a self-help platform outside the control of parliamentary politics was crucial to these innovations. Also of significance was the split within the Anglo-Irish ascendancy, generally along generational lines, between those older voices committed to the colonial enterprise in Ireland and a group of younger figures eager for a *rapprochement* with national culture and nationalist politics. The Mahaffy/Atkinson affair stands out as an important moment in the articulation of these generational differences. It is useful to recall this controversy, if only to break down the widespread perception, which informs much cultural analysis, of the Anglo-Irish as a solidly homogeneous grouping without internal ideological tensions.

With the outbreak of the Boer War, Ireland witnessed the emergence of a non-clandestine separatist politics which won significant levels of popular support, mounted a challenge to the newly reuniting Irish Parliamentary Party and laid the foundations of Sinn Féin. The key difference between the two political strands rested on attitudes to imperialism, with the separatists vigorously opposing British royalism and army recruitment, and the IPP conceding its preference for home rule within the empire. In this climate of tension between the parliamentarians and the separatists, the Irish Literary Theatre clearly aligned itself with the latter by staging Moore's play, *The Bending of the Bough*. This production effectively intervened in the political ferment of its moment by articulating the emerging gulf between the home rulers and the separatists at a politically sensitive time.

One of the lesser-recognized features of the revival is the extent to which it witnessed the emergence of a loose cadre of intellectuals who subscribed to a broad civic nationalism and who drew, in turn, on the ideas of co-operation, republicanism, socialism and anti-imperialism. This group included figures as diverse as James Connolly, William Rooney, W. B. Yeats, George Moore, Frank Fay, Horace Plunkett, George Russell and Lady Gregory. All subscribed to a pluralist conception of Irish culture, in so far as they encouraged the development of a national literature in both the Irish and English languages. This belies a generally held view of the period as an ethnic contest or 'battle of two civilizations'. As we have seen, there were some notable Anglo-Irish supporters of the Irish language, including Douglas Hyde, Alice Milligan and W. B. Yeats. Likewise, the championing of an Irish literature in the English language was not an entirely Anglo-Irish project. Important revivalists like William Rooney and Frank Fay were able apologists for this enterprise. Rooney was also a trenchant critic of D. P. Moran's exclusive 'Irish Ireland' ethnic nationalism. It may be more useful, therefore, to configure this period as one of conflict between a broad civic republican cultural politics and a more chauvinistic nationalism than as a battle between two clear-cut ethnic categories. This contention is further strengthened on a consideration of the contribution of J. M Synge to the revival. Acutely interested in both the material and the cultural condition of Ireland, Synge broadly supported the initiatives of the co-operative movement. He also had a profound grasp of the subtleties and complexities of the language revival project and, although a committed Irish language expert, was not afraid to criticize the shortcomings of the Gaelic League. His play, *The Shadow of the Glen*, provided a vigorous critique of the conservative bourgeois ideas being embraced at that moment by Arthur Griffith, and was instrumental in the dissolution of the Cumann na nGaedheal consensus which presaged the founding of Sinn Féin and the Abbey Theatre.

But, despite the importance of the revival to the evolution of modern Ireland and its institutions, much of the recent scholarship of the period has insisted on analysing it in terms of the personal relationships between the main protagonists. The bulk of the scholarly work carried out over the last decade or so has been author-centred and has produced major biographies as well as collections of letters and diaries of important revival figures such as W. B. Yeats, Lady Gregory, J. M. Synge, George Moore, Alice Milligan, Douglas Hyde and Maud Gonne. Vital and all as this scholarship is, it inevitably creates a view that the period's significance can be encapsulated in the coming together of a number of highly motivated, quirky and egotistical creative geniuses. The narrative often presented is of a vaguely comical movement, which witnessed moments of collective and individual brilliance, farcical collaborations, madcap schemes and petty rivalries. It would seem that the pattern set out by George Moore's seminal account of the period, *Hail and Farewell*, has made a lasting impression. There has been much interest in the individual self-fashioning of the leading figures during the revival but little recent analysis of the material impact the movement had on Irish culture and society in general, notwithstanding the fact that the imprint of revivalist thought and initiative is everywhere traceable in the cultural and social make-up of contemporary Ireland. Moreover, as this book has attempted to demonstrate, the revival was characterized by a rich and complex ferment of political and cultural thinking and no small amount of liberational energy. Now, at a century's remove from the momentous events of that period, it may be an opportune moment to begin a renewed analysis of a legacy that has been neglected, misrepresented and trivialized in recent years. At a time when the homogenizing pressures of globalization on local cultures have registered as a major concern within cultural criticism, the achievements, as well as the failures, of the Irish revival may have much to teach us about the cultural dynamics of Ireland in the twenty-first century.

NOTES

Introduction

1. Lionel Pilkington, *Theatre and the State in Twentieth-Century Ireland* (London: Routledge, 2001), p. 1.
2. Paul Gilroy has written interestingly about the viability of problematizing the relationship between tradition and modernity. See *The Black Atlantic: Modernity and Double Consciousness* (Cambridge MA: Harvard University Press, 1993), pp. 187–223.
3. David Lloyd, *Ireland After History* (Cork: Cork University Press/Field Day, 1999), p. 2.
4. This territory has been well covered by studies such as: Robert Hogan and James Kilroy, *Laying the Foundations: 1902–1904* (Dublin: Dolmen Press, 1976); Brenna Katz-Clarke, *The Emergence of the Irish Peasant Play at the Abbey Theatre* (Essex: Bowker Publishing, 1982); D. E. S. Maxwell, *A Critical History of Modern Irish Drama 1891–1980* (Cambridge: Cambridge University Press, 1984); Adrian Frazier, *Behind the Scenes: Yeats, Horniman and the Struggle for the Abbey Theatre* (Berkeley: University of California Press, 1990); Robert Welch, *The Abbey Theatre 1899–1999: Form and Pressure* (Oxford: Oxford University Press, 1999), and Christopher Morash, *A History of Irish Theatre 1601–2000* (Cambridge: Cambridge University Press, 2002).
5. W. B. Yeats, 'The Man and the Echo', *Collected Poems* (Dublin: Gill and Macmillan, 1933), p. 393.
6. For recent treatments of this play see Pilkington, pp. 30–34; Mary Trotter, *Ireland's National Theatres: Political Performance and the Origins of the Irish Dramatic Movement* (Syracuse: Syracuse University Press, 2001), pp. 93–7, and Nicholas Grene, *The Politics of Irish Drama: Plays in Context from Boucicault to Friel* (Cambridge: Cambridge University Press, 1999), pp. 63–72.

Revival Connections

1. Lady A. Gregory, 'Ireland Real and Ideal', *Nineteenth Century* 44 (Nov. 1898), p. 771.
2. Ibid., p. 772.
3. Ibid., p. 773.
4. The Kiltartan branch was founded on 16 July 1899. The meeting which Yeats and Hyde attended took place on 27 July 1899. See the *Daily Express*, 31 July 1899, and *An Claidheamh Soluis*, 29 July 1899.
5. The *United Irishman* was first published on 4 March 1899 and the first edition of *An Claidheamh Soluis* appeared two weeks later on 18 March 1899.
6. Both Plunkett and Hyde agreed to act as guarantors for the Irish Literary Theatre. The controversy centred on the production of Yeats's play, *The Countess Cathleen*, which opened on 8 May 1899.

7.   Gregory, 'Ireland, Real and Ideal', p. 773.
     This chapter will concentrate on the origins of the Irish Literary Theatre, the
     Gaelic League and the IAOS. The genesis of Sinn Féin will be dealt with fully in
     chapter 3. Although the Gaelic Athletic Association (founded in 1884) ranks as
     an important self-help popular movement which shares many characteristics
     with those mentioned here, its genesis in the early 1880s is beyond the scope of
     this study.
8.   R. F. Foster, 'Thinking from Hand to Mouth: Anglo-Irish Literature, Gaelic
     Nationalism and Irish Politics in the 1890s', in *Paddy and Mr. Punch: Connections
     in Irish and English History* (London: Penguin Press, 1993), p. 262.
9.   Ibid., p. 280.
10. Ibid., p. 268.
11. The cultural nationalists, he contends, 'held themselves above the detail of mate-
     rial benefits' (Ibid., p. 268).
12. Malcolm Brown, *The Politics of Irish Literature from Thomas Davis to W. B. Yeats*
     (London: Allen and Unwin, 1972), p. 348.
13. Desmond Roche, *Local Government in Ireland* (Dublin: Institute of Public Admin-
     istration, 1982), p. 46.
14. D. P. Moran, 'Is the Irish Nation Dying?', *New Ireland Review* (Dec. 1898), p. 345.
15. Irish was secured in the curriculum by the Intermediate Education (Ireland)
     Amendment Act of 1900. Janet Egleson Dunleavy and Gareth W. Dunleavy, *Dou-
     glas Hyde: A Maker of Modern Ireland* (Berkeley: University of California Press,
     1991), p. 211.
16. See the *Irish Homestead*, 10 Sept. 1898, p. 767 and 17 Dec. 1898, p. 1031, for
     details of these criticisms. The *Freeman's Journal* was anti-Parnellite pre-1900
     and pro-Irish Party after reunification. The *Irish Daily Independent* was Parnellite
     before 1900 and critical of the Irish Party after reunification. F. S. L. Lyons, *The
     Irish Parliamentary Party 1890–1919* (Westport: Greenwood Press, 1975), p. 269.
17. The phrase is Tom Garvin's. See *The Evolution of Irish Nationalist Politics* (Dublin:
     Gill and Macmillan, 1981), p. 88.
18. In relation to the agitation for a Catholic university, David Miller has noted that
     Parnell 'deferred to ecclesiastical wishes in this matter, and the continued def-
     erence of his successors in the national leadership [became] one of the conven-
     tions of Irish politics'. David Miller, *Church State and Nation in Ireland 1898–1921*
     (Dublin: Gill and Macmillan, 1973), p. 31. For a more recent account of the uni-
     versity question, see Senia Paseta, *Before the Revolution: Nationalism, Social Change
     and Ireland's Catholic Elite, 1879–1922* (Cork: Cork University Press, 1999), pp.
     5–27.
19. The *Irish Daily Independent*, established in 1891, was among the first of the new
     wave of nationalist publications. Its editorial policy was Parnellite and it set itself
     up as an alternative to the *Freeman's Journal* – the Irish Parliamentary Party organ.
     After this appeared, a plethora of weekly and fortnightly newspapers that were
     implicitly or explicitly linked to the emerging cultural movements came on the
     scene. The *Irish Homestead*, the newspaper of the IAOS, began publishing in 1895
     and was edited successively by Fr Tom Finley, H. F. Norman and George Russell.
     1899 saw the appearance of *An Claidheamh Soluis*, the Gaelic League's bilingual
     journal, which was edited by Eoin MacNeill (until 1903 when Patrick Pearse took
     over). Within weeks Arthur Griffith's *United Irishman* appeared. The important

work carried out by newspapers in 'imagining communities' has been ably
pointed out by Benedict Anderson in *Imagined Communities: Reflections on the Origins and Spread of Nationalism* (London: Verso, 1991), pp. 34–5.

20.   Luke Gibbons, *Transformations in Irish Culture* (Cork: Cork University Press, 1996), p. 8.

21.   'Since the hewing down of that great overshadowing tree [Parnell] other growths have had a chance of stretching towards the sunlight, and new forces, the Society of Agricultural Co-operation and the Gaelic League, that I will try [sic], in this quiet moment, to show the character of our Sancho-Quixote.' Gregory, 'Ireland, Real and Ideal', p. 770.

22.   'If his rebellion against fact has thus lamed the Celt even in spiritual work, how much more must it have lamed him in the world of business and politics! The skilful and resolute appliance of means to ends which is needed both to make progress in material civilisation, and also to form powerful states, is just what the Celt has least turn for.' Matthew Arnold, 'On the Study of Celtic Literature', *Poetry and Ireland since 1800*, ed. Mark Storey (London: Routledge, 1988), p. 66. 'In the Celticism of Matthew Arnold, for instance, Irish identity was reduced to a cultural imaginary, in a restricted aesthetic sense, all the more to remove it from more quotidian matters of power and self-determination.' Luke Gibbons, *Transformations*, p. 9.

23.   Gregory, 'Ireland, Real and Ideal', p. 775.

24.   As has been noted, Lady Gregory had a hand in the setting up of a co-operative society in her own parish and subscribed to many of Douglas Hyde's beliefs: 'Dignity and power of expression were to a great extent lost to the tongue that, like all other tongues, expressed the spirit of the race. It went out of fashion . . . It was not understood that the really uncultured Irishman is the man who has lost the Gaelic tradition and culture and has not yet gained the tradition and culture of England.' (Ibid., p. 776) She also pointed out how little the Irish Members of Parliament had achieved for the language: 'Nationalist MPs in neglecting [the Irish language] lost a great opportunity. Had they been able to carry on those stormy home rule debates in their native tongue at Westminster, they would soon not only have been allowed but implored to carry their oratory to College Green' (Ibid., p. 778).

25.   Ibid., p. 770.

26.   Gauri Viswanathan, *Outside the Fold: Conversion, Modernity, and Belief* (Princeton: Princeton University Press, 1998), p. 4.

27.   Gregory, 'Ireland Real and Ideal', p. 769.

28.   Ibid., p. 781.

29.   One can identify the influence of Yeats on her thinking here. He remarked of their excursions to collect folklore in the late 1890s that: 'When we passed the door of some peasant's cottage, we passed out of Europe as that word is understood. "I have longed," she said once, "to turn Catholic, that I might be nearer to the people, but you have taught me that paganism brings me nearer still."' W. B. Yeats, *Autobiographies* (Dublin: Gill and Macmillan, 1955), p. 400.

30.   Ibid., pp. 201–2.

31.   Yeats relates how 'he began to say violent and paradoxical things to shock provincial sobriety' at this time. Ibid., p. 95.

32.   Yeats saw Dowden as 'an image of Romance'. Ibid., p. 86.

33. This review was originally published in the *Dublin University Review*, Nov. 1886. See W. B. Yeats, *The Uncollected Prose by W. B. Yeats*, vol. 1, ed. J. P. Frayne (London: Macmillan, 1970), pp. 88–9.

34. Declan Kiberd, *Inventing Ireland* (London: Jonathan Cape, 1995), p. 160.

35. Ann Saddlemyer, '"The Noble and the Beggar-man": Yeats and Literary Nationalism', in *The World of W. B. Yeats: Essays in Perspective*, eds. Robin Skelton and Ann Saddlemyer (Dublin: Dolmen Press, 1965), p. 25. 'WBY inherited his father's view of respectable Dublin and of Dowden, who was cast as the symbol of all the city's shortcomings.' R. F. Foster, *W. B. Yeats: A Life, I: The Apprentice Mage 1865–1914* (Oxford: Oxford University Press, 1997), p. 29.

36. Standish O'Grady wrote about the poor reception of his book *History of Ireland: Heroic Periods*. 'Naturally I was a good deal laughed at; I did not mind that, but certainly was disappointed that so few people bought the book. Nevertheless time worked in my favour, and after a few years the whole impression, a score or so each year, was quite bought up.' See 'A Wet Day' *A Celtic Christmas: Being the Christmas Number of the* Irish Homestead, Dec. 1899, p. 9.

37. W. B. Yeats, *Autobiographies*, p. 200.

38. Yeats has recounted how 'these two societies were necessary because their lectures must take the place of an educated popular Press, which we had not . . . and create a standard of criticism'. *Autobiographies*, p. 200. A June meeting in the Rotunda of the NLS, attended by Hyde, issued a statement of purpose which read in part, 'Every Irish movement of recent years has drawn a great portion of its power from the literary movement started by Davis, but that movement is over, and it is not possible to live forever upon the past. A living Ireland must have a living literature.' John O'Leary rather than Hyde was Yeats's first choice for president but in the end Hyde was chosen as 'a good neutral figurehead'. Dunleavy and Dunleavy, *Douglas Hyde*, p. 181.

39. Foster, *W. B. Yeats I*, p. 119; *United Ireland* (2 Apr. 1892).

40. Conor Cruise O'Brien, 'Passion and Cunning: An Essay on the Politics of W. B. Yeats', in *Passion and Cunning: Essays on Nationalism, Terrorism and Revolution* (1965; New York: Simon and Schuster, 1988), p. 16.

41. Richard Ellmann, *Yeats: The Man and the Masks*, 2nd ed. (1948; London: Penguin, 1979), p. 107.

42. Brown, *Politics of Irish Literature*, p. 353.

43. Brown notes that this move by Hyde was 'in defiance of Yeats's advice' (Ibid., p. 353). Nevertheless as the Dunleavys have remarked, '[f]or Douglas Hyde, the radical and revolutionary doctrine of deanglicisation, delivered at a time when for many people the alternatives appeared to be only acquiescence or violence, made his National Literary Society presidential address the most important speech of his career'. Dunleavy and Dunleavy, *Douglas Hyde*, p. 185.

44. Philip Marcus, *Yeats and the Beginning of the Irish Renaissance*, 2nd ed. (Syracuse: Syracuse University Press, 1987), p. 198.

45. M. Brown, *Politics of Irish Literature*, p. 354.

46. A maxim of O'Leary's. See Ellmann, *Man and the Masks*, p. 46.

47. W. B. Yeats, *Uncollected Prose 1*, p. 361. Yeats was equally disenchanted, for similar reasons, with the type of criticism practiced by the Young Irelanders: 'one well-known anthology was introduced by the assertion that such love-poetry was superior to "affected and artificial" English love-songs like "Drink

to me only with thine eyes" – "affected and artificial," the very words used by English Victorians who wrote for the newspapers to discourage capricious, personal writing'. *Autobiographies*, p. 204.

48. Ibid., p. 205.
49. See W. B. Yeats, *Autobiographies*, pp. 224–8; Brown, *Politics of Irish Literature*, pp. 353–61; Ellmann, *Man and Masks*, pp. 106–10; Foster, *W. B. Yeats I*, pp. 118–24.
50. W. B. Yeats, *Autobiographies*, p. 228. Foster also notes that, when the productions of the Library of Ireland 'fell into WBY's clutches as a reviewer, he showed little mercy'. *W. B. Yeats I*, p. 124.
51. Ellmann, *Man and Masks*, p. 109.
52. Saddlemyer, 'The Noble and the Beggar-Man', p. 26.
53. W. B. Yeats, *Autobiographies*, p. 206.
54. Peter Quinn, 'Yeats and Revolutionary Nationalism: The Centenary of '98,' *Éire-Ireland* 15.3 (1980), p. 47.
55. W. B. Yeats, *Autobiographies*, p. 410.
56. See Frazier, *Behind the Scenes*, pp. xv–xix.
57. The right to picket and demonstrate openly was not established until the Trade Union Act of 1906. Ironically Yeats was to find himself on the wrong side of such street politics during the most controversial period of the theatre movement.
58. Foster, *W. B. Yeats I*, p. 181.
59. W. B. Yeats, *Autobiographies*, pp. 367–8.
60. Foster, *W. B. Yeats I*, p. 181.
61. Yeats had been elected to this position in 1897. Quinn, 'Yeats and Revolutionary Nationalism', p. 57.
62. W. B. Yeats, *Autobiographies*, p. 356.
63. Ibid., p. 366.
64. Ibid., p. 560. 'but if Ireland would not read literature it might listen to it, for politics and the Church had created listeners. I wanted a Theatre' (p. 396).
65. W. B. Yeats, 'The Irish Literary Theatre', Dublin *Daily Express* (14 Jan 1899). *Uncollected Prose 2*, p. 141.
66. Douglas Hyde, 'The Necessity for De-Anglicising Ireland', in *Poetry and Ireland Since 1800*, ed. M. Storey, (London: Routledge, 1988), pp. 82–3.
67. *An Claidheamh Soluis*, 29 Apr. 1899, p. 105. Significantly this appeared ten days before the inaugural production of the Irish Literary Theatre.
68. Ibid.
69. Ibid.
70. Trotter, *Ireland's National Theatres*, p. 54. The main theatres in question were the Royal, the Gaiety and the Queen's. See also D. E. S. Maxwell, *A Critical History of Modern Irish Drama 1891–1980* (Cambridge: Cambridge University Press, 1984), p. 10.
71. *United Irishman*, 3 Mar. 1899.
72. *Irish Daily Independent*, 19 Oct. 1901.
73. Katz Clarke, *The Emergence of the Irish Peasant Play*, p. 15.
74. Hyde's essay is ambiguous in many ways. For example he avoids the awkward question of how a member of the Anglo-Irish ascendancy could 'cultivate what was most racial' and become part of the Celtic nation at the same time.
75. *An Claidheamh Soluis*, 29 Apr. 1899, p. 105.

76.   'To sum up the position – the cheap price of English periodical literature, the lack of Anglo-Irish reading matter to counteract the wholesale consumption of the former, the absence of a healthy or defined Irish taste – the consequence of our up-bringing – and the fog that exists with regard to what Irish literature really is doesn't leave one much to learn as to the why and wherefore of the state of things complained of' [the popularity of English literature in Ireland] (Ibid., p. 106).

77.   W. B. Yeats, *Autobiographies*, p. 101.

78.   As Tomlinson reminds us, the notion of an authentic culture always has some degree of invention or fabrication attached to it: firstly because the contents of a culture are constantly changing; and secondly because cultures are never purely local – there are always traces of cultural borrowings. Cultures are therefore protean entities with shifting and permeable boundaries. See John Tomlinson, *Cultural Imperialism* (London: Pinter, 1991), pp. 90–92.

79.   This point was tacitly acknowledged in the opening statement of the Irish Literary Theatre, which expressed a wish to find an audience 'trained to listen by its passion for oratory'. Lady Gregory, *Our Irish Theatre* (New York: Capricorn Books, 1965), p. 9.

80.   W. B. Yeats to Lady Gregory, 4 August 1900, *The Collected Letters of W. B. Yeats, vol. II: 1896–1900*, eds Warwick Gould, Deirdre Toomey, John Kelly and Ronald Schuchard (Oxford: Clarendon, 1997), p. 631. Subsequent references will denote this collection as *Letters 2*.

81.   The amount of press space devoted to drama during this period was quite remarkable. Commentary on contemporary events in the theatre was not confined to reviews and it was not uncommon for entire articles to be dedicated to theatre matters. The Dublin *Daily Express* in particular gave considerable attention to the Irish Literary Theatre while under the ownership of Horace Plunkett (1898–1899).

82.   Brendan MacAodha, 'Was This a Social Revolution?', in *The Gaelic League Idea*, ed. Seán Ó Tuama (Cork: Mercier, 1972), p. 20.

83.   Kevin Nowlan, 'The Gaelic League and other National Movements', in Ó Tuama ed., *The Gaelic League Idea*, p. 44.

84.   Douglas Hyde, 'Necessity for De-Anglicising', p. 78.

85.   MacAodha, 'Was This a Social Revolution?', p. 20.

86.   *An Claidheamh Soluis*, 5 May 1899.

87.   See Colm Ó Cearúil, *Aspail Ar Son na Gaeilge: Timirí Chonradh na Gaeilge 1899–1923* (Baile Átha Cliath: Conradh na Gaeilge, 1995).

88.   Pádraig Ó Fearaíl, *The Story of Conradh na Gaeilge* (Baile Átha Cliath: Clódhanna Teo, 1975), p. 14.

89.   W. B. Yeats letter to the *Leader*, 26 Aug. 1900, *Letters 2*, p. 564. Although presumably Patrick Pearse, Joseph Conrad, Franz Kafka and Samuel Beckett, among others, would have disagreed.

90.   Ó Fearaíl, *The Story of Conradh na Gaeilge*, p. 14.

91.   Dunleavy and Dunleavy, *Douglas Hyde*, p. 328.

92.   Ibid., p. 225.

93.   The inauguration of the Irish Literary Theatre in May 1899 occasioned a debate on the nature of Irish literature in *An Claidheamh Soluis* which ran for several months. This is the moment when lines were first drawn between

Gaelic literature and Anglo-Irish literature as intellectuals began to develop clear (and rival) notions of an Irish national literature for the first time.

94. Patrick Pearse's only case as a barrister involved a Niall MacGiolla Bhríde, who was fined for having his name in Irish on his cart. 'The judge decided that the Irish language had no standing in law. From the point of view of the Gaelic League this judgement effectively labelled Irish a foreign language.' Ó Fearaíl, *The Story of Conradh na Gaeilge*, p. 29. It is interesting that Irish now takes precedent in law over English.

95. Ibid., p. 21.

96. Tomás Ó Fiaich, 'The Great Controversy', in Ó Tuama (ed.) *The Gaelic League Idea*, p. 63.

97. This is the first time the term 'compulsory Irish' was used.

98. Cited in Ó Fearaíl, *The Story of Conradh na Gaeilge*, p. 35.

99. Much admired by Sean O'Casey, who dedicated *Drums Under the Windows* to him.

100. Tomlinson, *Cultural Imperialism*, p. 90.

101. The annual competitive convention of the Gaelic League founded in 1897.

102. This issue will be dealt with in some detail in chapter 4.

103. Kevin Whelan, 'The Memories of "The Dead"', *The Yale Journal of Criticism* 15.1 (2002), p. 60.

104. *An Claidheamh Soluis*, 18 March 1899, pp. 8–9.

105. The hostility of both Parnellites and anti-Parnellites to the co-operative movement has already been noted above. F. S. L. Lyons wrote that: 'His parliamentary career . . . had not been such as to give him the reputation of a sound party man . . . While claiming still to be a unionist, he had with devastating frankness condemned unionism as a whole for its sterile approach to Irish economic problems and for interpreting Lord Salisbury's prescription for Ireland of "twenty years of resolute government" in terms of a purely negative policy of repression'. 'Sir Horace Plunkett: A Centenary Appreciation of his life and Work', *Irish Times*, 24 Oct. 1954. Margaret Digby records that, 'as early as 1896 he spoke in favour of an amnesty for political prisoners with both front benches against him'. *Horace Plunkett: An Anglo-American Irishman* (Oxford: Blackwell, 1949), p. 88.

106. Trevor West, *Horace Plunkett: Co-operation and Politics, An Irish Biography* (Gerrards Cross: Colin Smythe, 1986), pp. 55–9; Andrew Gailey, *Ireland and the Death of Kindness: The Experience of Constructive Unionism 1890–1905* (Cork: Cork University Press, 1987), p. 157.

107. West, *Horace Plunkett*, p. 93.

108. The most significant of these was Wyndham's Land Act of 1903.

109. George Russell, *Co-operation and Nationality* (Dublin: Maunsel, 1912), pp. 13–14.

110. Lyons, 'Sir Horace Plunkett'.

111. Plunkett's diary entry (Plunkett Foundation, Oxford) for 22 Feb. 1899 reads: 'Dinner party with an object – vis the further promotion of co-operation between the practical men and the dreamers of Ireland'. George Moore, W. B. Yeats, Edward Martyn, Lady Betty Balfour and Lady Gregory were guests. I am grateful to Trevor West for this reference.

112. West, *Horace Punkett*, pp. 25–6.

113. 'A house wanting a particular piece of work done would get a score or so of hands from among the neighbours. Such a party, brought together by the necessity for mutual aid, was called a *meitheal* (mahil). In the part of the country that I am familiar with (a district of the Midlands not yet denuded by emigration) the tradition of mutual aid still survives in mahils for outdoor work that needs many hands (turf cutting generally). Again, groups of farmers here and there put money together to buy spraying-machines. They speak of this as a "join".' Padraic Colum, 'Concerning a Creamery', *Dana: An Irish Magazine of Independent Thought*, Nov. 1904, p. 205. I am grateful to Desmond Fitzgibbon for this reference.
114. George Russell, 'Irish Clergymen and Irish Civilisation', *Irish Homestead*, 7 Oct. 1905.
115. In 1901 Plunkett sponsored a competition for the co-operative society which did most 'to make their parish a place where no Irishman would like to emigrate from'. *Irish Homestead*, 9 Nov. 1901, p. 744.
116. IAOS annual report 1901, pp. 39–41.
117. Trevor West, 'Horace Plunkett's Social Philosophy', *Plunkett Foundation, Year Book of Agricultural Co-operation* (Oxford: Plunkett Foundation, 1981), p. 12.
118. *A Celtic Christmas: Being the Christmas Number of the* Irish Homestead, Dec. 1897, p. 4.
119. George Russell, 'Village Libraries', *Irish Homestead*, 31 Mar. 1906.
120. West, *Horace Plunkett*, p. 68.
121. Ibid., p. 63.
122. Ibid., p. 75.
123. See James Connolly Heron (ed.), *The Words of James Connolly* (Cork: Mercier, 1986), p. 32.
124. Letter from AE to Charles Weekes, 14 May 1901, *Letters from AE*, ed. Alan Denson (London: Abelard-Schuman, 1961), p. 36.

Gael, Catholic, Celt or Comrade?

1.   Ó Fiaich, 'The Great Controversy', p. 64 .
2.   Douglas Hyde, 'A University Scandal', *New Ireland Review*, Dec. 1899, repr. (Dublin: Eblana Press, 1899), p. 3.
3.   Norma Borthwick, *The Irish Language and Irish Intermediate Education I: Answers to Queries*, Gaelic League Pamphlet no. 11 (Dublin: Gaelic League, 1901), p. 4.
4.   J. P. Mahaffy, 'The Education in Hungary', cited in R. B. McDowell and W. B. Stanford, *Mahaffy: A Biography of an Anglo-Irishman* (London: Routledge and Kegan Paul, 1971), p. 105.
5.   J. P. Mahaffy, *Evidence to Vice Regal Inquiry*, Gaelic League Pamphlet no. 12 (Dublin: Gaelic League, 1901), p. 2.
6.   Cited in McDowell and Stanford, *Mahaffy*, p. 105.
7.   Hyde's initial evidence to the Vice-Regal commission runs to 28 pages and his subsequent written submission is 32 pages long, making his by far the most extensive contribution.
8.   Anthony Traill, 'Hands Off Trinity', *Nineteenth Century* 45 (March 1899), p. 512.
9.   Douglas Hyde, *The Irish Language and Intermediate Education III: Dr. Hyde's Evidence*, Gaelic League Pamphlet no. 13 (Dublin: Gaelic League, 1901), p. 2.
10. Hyde, *Irish Language III*, p. 5.

11. Hyde, *Irish Language III*, p. 11.

12. Dunleavy and Dunleavy, *Douglas Hyde*, pp. 200–1.

13. In his opening remarks to Atkinson the chairman states: 'I believe it was only this morning that you were aware you were to be examined?' To which Atkinson replied: 'yes'. *The Irish Language and Irish Intermediate Education IV: Dr. Atkinson's Evidence*, Gaelic League Pamphlet no. 14 (Dublin: Gaelic League, 1901), pp. 1–2.

14. Edward Said, *Orientalism: Western Concepts of the Orient* (1978; London: Penguin, 1991), pp. 132–8.

15. Said, *Orientalism*, p. 133.

16. Atkinson, *Dr. Atkinson's Evidence*, p. 2.

17. 'In pre-print Europe, and, of course elsewhere in the world, the diversity of spoken languages . . . was immense . . . Nothing served to 'assemble' related vernaculars more than capitalism, which, within the limits imposed by grammars and syntaxes, created mechanically reproduced print-languages capable of dissemination through the market.' Anderson, *Imagined Communities*, pp. 43–5.

18. A form of standardized Irish did of course exist among the learned during the classical period, 1200–1650.

19. This issue will be discussed more fully in Chapter 4.

20. Atkinson, *Dr. Atkinson's Evidence*, p. 6.

21. Ibid., p. 13–14.

22. Ibid., p. 15.

23. Douglas Hyde, *The Irish Language and Irish Intermediate Education VI: Dr. Hyde's Reply to Dr. Atkinson*, Gaelic League Pamphlet no. 16 (Dublin: Gaelic League, 1901), p. 3.

24. Hyde, *The Irish Language VI*, p. 4.

25. Ibid., p. 16.

26. Dr Michael O'Hickey pointed out in his evidence that Atkinson's concern with coarseness and indecency did not extend to English writers such as Chaucer, Shakespeare, Fielding and Smollett. See *The Irish language and Irish Intermediate Education VII: Dr. O'Hickey's Reply to Dr. Mahaffy, Mr. Gwynn and Dr. Atkinson*, Gaelic League Pamphlet no.17 (Dublin: Gaelic League, 1901), p. 7.

27. Hyde, *The Irish Language VI*, p. 24. Atkinson had resolved that he 'would not pay the slightest attention to the testimony of foreigners in respect to this matter of Irish children's education' (*Dr. Atkinson's Evidence*, p. 9.) even though, as Pederson pointed out, he was himself an Englishman.

28. *An Claidheamh Soluis*, 18 Mar. 1899, p. 8.

29. Ó Fiaich, 'The Great Controversy', p. 69.

30. O'Hickey, *Dr. O'Hickey's Reply*, p. 5.

31. Ó Fiaich, 'The Great Controversy', p. 70.

32. W. B. Yeats, 'Windlestraws', *Samhain* 1901, repr. (London: Frank Cass, 1970), p. 9.

33. W. B. Yeats, 'The Academic Class and the Agrarian Revolution', Dublin *Daily Express* (11 Mar. 1899); *Uncollected Prose by W. B. Yeats* vol. 2, eds. J. P. Frayne and C. Johnson (Macmillan: London, 1975), pp. 148–52.

34. W. B. Yeats, 'The Academic Class', p. 148.

35. J. P. Mahaffy, 'The Recent Fuss about the Irish Language,' *Nineteenth Century* 46 (Aug. 1899), p. 221.

36.   Kiberd, *Inventing Ireland*, p. 160.
37.   Nowlan, 'Gaelic League and Other National Movements', p. 44.
38.   Ibid., p. 44.
39.   *An Claidheamh Soluis* (1 April 1899).
40.   J. M. Synge, *The Aran Islands* (London: Penguin, 1992), p. 38.
41.   Synge, *Aran Islands*, p. 50.
42.   From 1850 Cardinal Cullen transformed the Irish Catholic Church from 'a Latin-American type institution into one of the most efficiently marshalled Churches in Europe'. Joseph Lee, *The Modernisation of Irish Society 1848–1918* (1973; Dublin: Gill and Macmillan, 1979), p. 44. See also, Emmet Larkin, 'The Devotional Revolution in Ireland, 1850–75', *American Historical Review* 77 (1972), pp. 625–52.
43.   Hyde, *Dr Hyde's Reply*, p. 14.
44.   O'Hickey, *Dr. O'Hickey's Reply*, p. 8.
45.   Ó Fiaich, 'The Great Controversy', p. 69.
46.   'But of late years this Trinity College public has been occuping [sic] a space which is ever growing smaller and smaller, relatively [sic] to the whole mass of educated public opinion in Ireland, and everyone can see for himself that it is *not* from Trinity College or its pupils, *but wholly outside of them*, that all the vigorous movements of the intellectual life of the Ireland of to-day have arisen.' Hyde, 'A University Scandal', p. 2.
47.   In 1897 the youngest of the Senior Fellows of TCD was 70 years old. Stanford and McDowell, *Mahaffy*, p. 194.
48.   As Terry Eagleton has argued: 'Nineteenth-century Ireland's premier scholarly institution, Trinity College Dublin, passed from being an intellectual centre in mid-century, when men like Isaac Butt and Thomas Davis used national sentiment to bridge the gap between ideas and political life, to becoming something of an academic enclave by the end of the century. Scholars like Edward Dowden retreat to a more cloistered intellectual style, in the teeth of a Gaelic nationalism which helped to maroon them from the public sphere. The movement is mirrored in the career from mid-century to *fin-de-siècle* of the historian W. E. H. Lecky, youthful liberal nationalist turned crusty conservative scholar.' *Scholars and Rebels in Nineteenth-Century Ireland* (Oxford: Blackwell, 1999), p. 3.
49.   W. B. Yeats, at this time, was forthright in his criticisms of Trinity's anti-national tendencies: 'Trinity College, which desires to be English, has been the mother of many verse-writers and of few poets; and this can only be because she set herself against the national genius, and taught her children to imitate alien styles and choose out alien themes, for it is not possible to believe that the educated Irishman alone is prosaic and uninventive.' *A Book of Irish Verse* (1895; London: Methuen, 1920), p. xxix.
50.   F. H. O'Donnell, *Souls For Gold! Pseudo-Celtic Drama in Dublin* (London: n.p., 1899), p. 7.
51.   In the dedication Lady Gregory wrote: 'I left out a good deal I thought you would not care about for one reason or another.' *Cuchulain of Muirthemne* (Gerrards Cross: Colin Smythe, 1970), p. 5.
52.   Synge's *The Shadow of the Glen* will be discussed in detail in Chapter 5.
53.   Gregory, 'Ireland, Real and Ideal', p. 770.

54. The Catholic temperance movement re-emerged at the turn of the century. Father James Cullen began working towards the foundation of the Pioneer Branch of the Total Abstinence Association of the Sacred Heart in 1898. This Catholic 'self-help' movement boasted 150,000 members by 1909 and by 1914 the figure was 270,000. See Elizabeth Malcolm, *Ireland Sober, Ireland Free: Drink and Temperance in Nineteenth Century Ireland* (Dublin: Gill and Macmillan, 1986), pp. 293–321.

55. Cited in Elizabeth Malcolm, 'Popular Recreation in Nineteenth Century Ireland', *Irish Culture and Nationalism 1750–1950*, eds. Oliver MacDonagh, W. F. Mandle and Pauric Travers (London: Macmillan, 1983), p. 40.

56. Lady Gregory records that 'on Garlic Sunday men used to ride races naked, on unsaddled horses out into the sea; but that wild custom had long been done away with by decree of the priests'. *Our Irish Theatre*, p. 4.

57. This is a theme ably explored by Brian Friel in his play *Dancing at Lughnasa* (London: Faber and Faber, 1990).

58. 'Some Protestant nationalists undoubtedly hoped that the language would replace the Catholic religion as a primary symbol of Irish nationality. They longed for a means of identifying with the Ireland of the Catholic majority while nurturing the hope of eventually bringing their own co-religionists into the national fold as well.' David Miller, *Church, State and Nation* (Dublin: Gill and Macmillan, 1973), p. 38.

59. For example: John Rhys, *Lectures on the Origin and Growth of Religion as Illustrated by Celtic Heathendom* (London: Williams and Norgate, 1898); Henri D'Arbois de Jubainville, *Le cycle mythologique irlandais* (Paris: Thorin, 1884); Kuno Meyer, *The Voyage of Bran Son of Febal* (London: David Nutt, 1895).

60. In the summer of 1897 Lady Gregory took Yeats with her to visit the peasants' cottages in the neighbourhood. He began to make a large collection of folklore and stories, part of which he used in a series of articles in English reviews. See Foster, *W. B. Yeats 1*, pp. 170–1.

61. W. B. Yeats, 'The Prisoner of the Gods,' *Nineteenth Century* (Jan. 1898). *Uncollected Prose 2*, pp. 74–87.

62. Philip Marcus, *Yeats and the Beginning of the Irish Renaissance*, 2nd ed. (Syracuse: Syracuse University Press, 1987), p. 28.

63. Gregory, *Our Irish Theatre*, pp. 8–9. For an account of the drafting of this founding document, see Foster, *W. B. Yeats I*, pp. 183–5.

64. Yeats's interest in a darker Celticism is evident from early poems, most obviously 'The Stolen Child'.

65. Of particular influence was the Dublin *Daily Express*, owned at this time by Horace Plunkett, which gave strong support to the Irish Literary Theatre and more often than not took its literary cue from Yeats.

66. Dublin *Daily Express*, 12 Jan. 1899.

67. 'The Irish Literary Theatre', Dublin *Daily Express*, 14 Jan. 1899. *Uncollected Prose 2*, pp. 139–41. One of the most important things about this article is that it set the agenda for almost all of the Dublin papers, most of which were later vocal in their condemnation of contemporary drama.

68. W. B. Yeats, 'The Irish Literary Theatre', p. 140.

69. In his famous article 'What Should be the Subjects of National Drama?' John Eglinton accused Yeats of succumbing to the worst excesses of aestheticism. He felt that Yeats's preoccupation with 'the ancient legends of Ireland' could only

produce a form of *belles lettres* rather than a genuinely national literature. First published Dublin *Daily Express*, 18 Sept. 1898.

70.   W. B. Yeats, 'The Irish Literary Theatre', pp. 140–1.

71.   'The resuscitation of our national language is a work in which every one of us should help; at the same time we would regret any insistence on a knowledge of Gaelic as the test of patriotism.' *United Irishman* editorial, 4 Mar. 1899 (first edition of the paper).

72.   *United Irishman*, 4 Mar. 1899.

73.   Despite the early misgivings of the *United Irishman*, Griffith did support Yeats in the ensuing controversy and offered the presence and support of 'a lot of men from the quays' who would 'applaud anything the church did not like'. W. B. Yeats, *Uncollected Prose 2*, p. 337; *Autobiographies*, p. 279. The founder of Sinn Féin was to become one of the most trenchant critics of the theatre movement during its first decade and as formidable an opponent of Yeats as Gavan Duffy.

74.   W. B. Yeats, 'The Irish Literary Theatre', p. 141.

75.   Hyde must have been a particularly inspirational model for Yeats, challenging and discrediting, as he did, his former teachers.

76.   'An American publisher of great experience said to me the other day: "I have noticed that quite a number of young men, who have come to the States from your Dublin University, try literature or art, but that they always take to commerce in the end . . .". I answered, so far as I remember, "Trinity College, Dublin, makes excellent scholars, but it does not make men with any real love for ideal things or with any fine taste in the arts".' *Uncollected Prose 2*, p. 151.

77.   Robert Hogan and James Kilroy, *Literary Theatre*, pp. 30–1. The authors also cite the personal rancour directed against Yeats by F. Hugh O'Donnell as a reason for the controversy.

78.   The following evening, 9 May 1899, Edward Martyn's Ibsenesque play, *The Heather Field*, was staged and received with uncritical applause. See Adrian Frazier, *George Moore, 1852–1933* (New Haven: Yale University Press, 2000), p. 271.

79.   All quotes from *The Countess Cathleen* are taken from W. B. Yeats, *Poems*, revd. and rptd. (1895; London: Fisher Unwin, 1901). Subsequent references will be noted parenthetically. As the 1899 reprint of *Poems* had gone to print before the inaugural performance of *The Countess Cathleen*, it is plausible to assume that the 1901 text best reflects the version used in performance. See Colin Smythe, 'The Countess Cathleen: a Note', *Yeats Annual 3* (1985), pp. 193–7.

80.   Brown, *Politics of Irish Literature*, p. 143.

81.   Frazier, *Behind the Scenes*, p. 10.

82.   O'Donnell, *Souls For Gold!* , p. 1.

83.   Ibid., p. 1.

84.   Ibid., p. 5. He continues: 'Mr. Yeats seems to see nothing in the Ireland of old days but an unmanly, an impious and renegade people, crouched in degraded awe before demons, and goblins and sprites and sowlths and thivishes, – [sic] just like a sordid tribe of black devil-worshippers and fetish-worshippers on the Congo or the Niger.' (p. 7)

85.   Respectability, morality and cleanliness were also advocated by the *Irish Homestead*. Significantly, days before the first production of *The Countess Cathleen*, the *Homestead* began a crusade to clean up Irish cottages and change peasant practices: 'But it must be confessed that our Irish villages and cabins in many dis-

tricts retain their primitive characteristics of untidiness and dirt, and would seem to indicate an utter lack of feeling for beauty, which yet cannot be truly said of a people who have the loveliest folk-tales and songs in Europe, which are even now creating a new literature and a new spiritual influence in the thought of these islands . . . The members of the co-operative societies ought to make it their boast that they are clean and not on a level with the Fiji Islanders in their home life. They ought to be proud of their faith and show their faith by their works, by a more cheerful social life and by improved arrangements in their cottages.' *Irish Homestead*, 29 April 1899, p. 311. That Yeats should represent the peasantry as immoral and degenerate at a time when profound modernizing changes were taking place in Irish social practices annoyed many nationalists.

86. Leon Ó Broin, *Revolutionary Underground: The Story of the Irish Republican Brotherhood* (Dublin: Gill and Macmillan, 1976), p. 98.
87. *Daily Nation*, 6 May 1899. The slogan of the paper was: 'To create and foster public opinion in Ireland and make it racy of the soil'.
88. 'And we hope very earnestly that . . . those Irish Catholics, who may form a portion of the audience, will so give expression to their disapproval as to effectually discourage any further ventures of a similar kind.' *Daily Nation*, 6 May 1899.
89. Joseph Holloway, *Joseph Holloway's Abbey Theatre: A Selection from His Unpublished Journal 'Impressions of a Dublin Playgoer'*, eds. Robert Hogan and Michael J. O'Neill (Illinois: S. Illinois University Press, 1967), p. 7.
90. *Freeman's Journal*, 10 May 1899.
91. Richard Ellmann, *James Joyce*, rev. ed. (1959; Oxford: Oxford University Press, 1982), p. 69. Joyce recalls the opening night of *The Countess Cathleen* in *Portrait of the Artist as a Young Man*: '[Stephen] was alone at the side of the balcony, looking out of jaded eyes at the culture of Dublin in the stalls and at the tawdry scene-cloths and human dolls framed by the garish lamps of the stage. A burly policeman sweated behind him and seemed at every moment about to act. The catcalls and hisses and mocking cries ran in rude gusts around the hall from his scattered fellowstudents.' (London: Penguin, 1992), p. 245.
92. *Daily Nation*, 10 May 1899.
93. The University Act of 1879 provided for the dissolution of the Queen's University and its replacement by the Royal University of Ireland, a purely examining body. The university question was revived as a live issue in the wake of the Local Government Act of 1898 and was to remain a contentious issue until a solution was achieved in 1908. See T. W. Moody, 'The Irish University Question of the Nineteenth Century', *History: The Journal of the Historical Association* 43 (1958), pp. 90–109.
94. 'During the famine of '48 demons did walk the land with the soup can, and, unfortunately, some few of our race, overcame with hunger, bartered their souls for food; but what numbers died on the road side when they need only have renounced their religion to get full and plenty, and I make a present of the compliment to Mr. Yeats and his "Express" supporters of the comparison of "selling to the souper and selling to the Devil". [*sic*] . . . Why tell our Irish youth that their ancestors were a lower lot (according to Mr. Yeats) than the aborigines of the south seas?' Letter to editor, *Daily Nation*, 10 May 1899.
95. Frazier, *Behind the Scenes*, p. 19.
96. *Daily Nation*, 10 May 1899.

97. *Irish Daily Independent*, 15 May 1899.
98. Brown, *Politics of Irish Literature*, p. 294.
99. More than likely in response to Yeats's lecture to the Irish Literary Society the previous week.
100. *An Claidheamh Soluis*, 29 Apr. 1899.
101. *An Claidheamh Soluis*, 6 May 1899. Yeats responded to this attack in the *Leader*, 1 Sept. 1900.
102. *An Claidheamh Soluis*, 20 May 1899.
103. Ibid.
104. Ibid. Pearse later changed his mind in relation to an Irish literature in English and by 1912 he was claiming Synge's *Playboy of the Western World* as a masterpiece. Ruth Dudley Edwards, *Patrick Pearse: The Triumph of Failure* (1977; Dublin: Poolbeg, 1990), p. 102.
105. Another example of his ongoing attempt to interest the younger generation of the ascendancy in things Irish.
106. Hogan and Kilroy, *Literary Theatre*, p. 58; Reported in the *Daily Express*, 1 June 1899, p. 5.
107. Hogan and Kilroy, *Literary Theatre*, p. 59.
108. More than likely Pearse's article in *An Claidheamh Soluis* quoted above.
109. Hogan and Kilroy, *Literary Theatre*, p. 59.
110. 'Trinity College and the Literary Theatre', *Daily Express*, 1 Jun. 1899, p. 5; Hogan and Kilroy, *Literary Theatre*, p. 60.
111. Hogan and Kilroy, *Literary Theatre*, p. 60.
112. Ironically Murray was later to become one of the exemplars of Irish Ireland as expounded by Daniel Corkery. *Synge and Anglo-Irish Literature* (Cork: Mercier, 1966), p. 14.
113. *An Claidheamh Soluis*, 24 June 1899.
114. Ibid.
115. Ibid.
116. 'What is Irish National Literature?', *An Claidheamh Soluis*, 1 July 1899, p. 248. In fact the article was more a statement of what Irish literature was *not*, rather than a clear statement of what it actually was.
117. *An Claidheamh Soluis*, 1 July 1899, p. 248. The question of 'What is Irish National Literature?' was further debated in an editorial the following week (still provoked by T. C. Murray's letter). Certain prerequisites for a national literature were outlined here. Firstly, a national literature must have the freedom of choice of subject, and secondly, the freedom of mode. 'The choice of subject must not be limited by any restrictions of place or theme.' This he believes is the shortcoming of the Anglo-Irish writers who must keep to Irish subjects or the 'Celtic note' in order to be considered national. *An Claidheamh Soluis*, 8 July 1899, p. 264.
118. W. B. Yeats to the Editor of the *Gael* (New York), August 1899, *Letters 2*, pp. 445–6.
119. Other notable speakers included: Douglas Hyde, whose speech was not reported, as he spoke in Irish; J. F. Taylor, who criticized Trinity College for its neglect of the language, history and literature of Ireland; Standish O'Grady, who introduced a note of reality by reminding the audience that 'their people were perishing and disappearing out of the country at a rate of 25,000 per annum'; and R. A. Ander-

son, who reiterated the point that 'the success of co-operation depended, not so much on the making of money as upon the making of character'.

120. Reprinted in the Dublin *Daily Express*, 17 May 1899.
121. See *Irish Homestead*, 'The "Legitimate Interests" of the Traders', 10 Sept. 1898, 767: 'The Enemies of Co-operation', 17 Dec. 1898, p. 1031; *Freeman's Journal*, 19 Jan. 1899 and 23 Jan. 1899.
122. *Workers' Republic*, 27 Aug. 1898; *The Words of James Connolly*, ed. James Connolly Heron (Cork: Mercier, 1986), p. 32.
123. *Workers' Republic*, 5 Aug. 1899, Heron ed., p. 21.
124. *Workers' Republic*, 1 Oct. 1898, Heron ed., p. 45.
125. *The Harp*, Sept. 1908, Heron ed., p. 51.
126. For example: 'We are socialists because we see in socialism not only the modern application of the social principle which underlay the Brehon Laws of our ancestors but because we recognise in it the only principle by means of which the working class can in their turn emerge into the dignity of freemen with a right to live as MEN and not as mere profit-making machines for the service of another.' *Workers' Republic*, 13 Aug. 1898, Heron ed., p. 34.
127. P. Berresford Ellis, 'Introduction', *James Connolly: Selected Writings* (London: Pluto Press, 1988), p. 37. See also Gregory Dobbins, 'Scenes of Tawdry Tribute: Modernism, Tradition and Connolly', *New Voices in Irish Criticism*, ed. P. J. Mathews (Dublin: Four Courts Press, 2000), pp. 3–12.
128. Gregory Dobbins, 'Whenever Green is Red: James Connolly and Postcolonial Theory', *Nepantla: Views from South* 1.3 (2000), p. 619.
129. Paul Gilbert, 'The Idea of a National Literature', *Literature and the Political Imagination*, eds. John Horton and Andrea T. Baumeister (London: Routledge, 1996), p. 212.

Stirring Up Disloyalty

1. Maud Gonne MacBride, A *Servant of the Queen* (1938; London: Victor Gollancz, 1974), p. 280.
2. Donal P. McCracken, *The Irish Pro-Boers* (Johannesburg: Perskor, 1989), p. 42.
3. '. . . her theatre was a country and her audience all of its people'. Margaret Ward, *Maud Gonne: A Life* (1990; London: Pandora, 1993), p. 1.
4. Padraic Colum, *Arthur Griffith* (Dublin: Brown and Nowlan, 1959), p. 51.
5. McCracken, *Irish Pro-Boers*, p. 44.
6. Ibid., p. xviii.
7. Ibid., p. 44.
8. Quoted in Robert Mitchell Henry, *Evolution of Sinn Féin* (Dublin: Talbot Press, n.d.), p. 56.
9. McCracken, *Irish Pro-Boers*, p. 45; *United Irishman*, 2 Sept. 1899; *Workers' Republic*, 2 Sept. 1899.
10. Colum, *Arthur Griffith* (Dublin: Brown and Nowlan, 1959), p. 52. Yet Connolly's involvement with Griffith in the Transvaal Committee in many ways prefigured his alliance with Pearse and the Irish Volunteers in 1916.
11. McCracken, *Irish Pro-Boers*, p. 47.
12. *United Irishman*, 7 Oct. 1899, p. 3.
13. *United Irishman*, 7 Oct. 1899, p. 3.

'Majuba Hill' is a reference to the first Anglo-Boer war, which began in 1880. 'After a series of skirmishes, a small, badly-led British force was defeated by Joubert at Majuba Hill on the Transvaal–Natal border in March 1881. A legend was then created that under South African conditions the Boers could always beat the inefficient red-coated British soldiers.' Eversley Belfield, *The Boer War* (1975; London: Leo Cooper, 1993), p. 157.

14. McCracken, *The Irish Pro-Boers*, p. 47. On 28 November the *Irish Daily Independent* reported that 'rows between civilians and soldiers in Limerick are becoming rather frequent of late arising out of friction over the Boer War'. McCracken, *Irish Pro-Boers*, p. 54.

15. *Hansard* LXXVII, 25 Oct. 1899, col. 622.

16. *Hansard* LXXVII, 25 Oct. 1899, col. 622.

17. W. B. Yeats to Michael Davitt, 2 Nov 1899, *Letters 2*, pp. 464–5.

18. McCracken, *Irish Pro-Boers*, p. 51.

19. Ibid., p. 51.

20. Maud Gonne Mac Bride, *A Servant of the Queen* (1938; London: Victor Gollanez, 1974), p. 292.

21. Ward, *Maud Gonne*, p. 58.

22. See *TCD: A College Miscellany*, 10 Mar. 1900, p. 42.

23. '. . . ostensibly to receive a degree from the University of Dublin, but really to identify Ireland with the war'. Colum, *Arthur Griffith*, p. 52.

24. Patrick Keatinge, *A Place Among the Nations: Issues of Irish Foreign Policy* (Dublin: Institute of Public Administration, 1978), p. 28.
'The result when it came was close, but decisive and not unexpected. The Tories, their numbers swollen by defecting Liberal Unionists [led by Chamberlain], were able to defeat the home rule bill on its second reading by thirty votes. Gladstone thereupon resigned and the subsequent general election, returned a strong Conservative and Liberal Unionist majority in Britain.' F. S. L. Lyons, *Ireland since the Famine* (1971; London: Fontana, 1973), p. 187.

25. McCracken, *Irish Pro-Boers*, p. 63.

26. Maud Gonne records Pat O'Brien's explanation of Davitt's absence: '"It's not Davitt's fault he's not here, but his wife is expecting a baby and if he got arrested it would upset her badly."' *Servant of the Queen*, p. 299.

27. Sean O'Casey was present at the scene and described it as follows: 'When they streamed into Dame Street, they mingled with a tremendous crowd, cheering fiercely, and waving hundreds of Boer, Irish, French and American flags. Some way after the head of the crowd was a brake, a long car, benched on both sides, drawn by two frightened hearse horses. A stout, short, stocky man, whose face was hidden by a wide-awake hat, was driving them. Several other men, pale-faced and tight-lipped, sat on the seats, facing each other; and with them was a young woman with long lovely yellow hair, smiling happily, like a child out on her first excursions.' *Autobiographies 1: Pictures in the Hallway* (1942; London: Macmillan, 1992), p. 365.

28. Roy Foster records that Yeats 'had given Gonne a public letter of support for her Boer victory meeting'. *Freeman's Journal*, 18 Dec. 1899. Foster, *W. B. Yeats 1*, p. 223.

29. W. B. Yeats to Maud Gonne, c.15 Dec 1899, *Letters 2*, p. 477. This letter was published in the *Freeman's Journal* on 18 Dec 1899.

30. Similarly, Carlton Younger reports of this incident that: 'Griffith struggled with a police officer – who was trying to seize a Boer flag from a small boy. George Lyons saw the officer and his horse sprawling in the road, while Griffith triumphantly waved the flag in one hand, the officer's sword in another.' *Arthur Griffith* (Dublin: Gill and Macmillan, 1981), p. 15.

31. James Joyce, *Ulysses*, intro. by Declan Kiberd (London: Penguin, 1992), p. 206.

32. F. S. L. Lyons, *The Irish Parliamentary Party 1890–1919*, (Westport CT: Greenwood Press, 1975), p. 89.

33. Ibid., p. 96.

34. F. S. L. Lyons, *Ireland since the Famine*, p. 261.
'When John Redmond visited Australia as a young man in 1883 he maintained that it was "undesirable that two countries so closely connected geographically and socially, and having so many commercial and international ties, should be wholly separated, or that any dismemberment of the Empire, which Ireland has had her share in building up, should take place". Although he was later to talk to American audiences rather ambiguously about "national independence", he was sincere and consistent in insisting that independence should take place within an imperial framework.' Keatinge, p. 33.

35. *United Irishman*, 10 Feb. 1900, p. 4.

36. *United Irishman*, 10 Feb. 1900, p. 4.

37. McCracken, *Irish Pro-Boers*, p. 72.

38. Anthony J. Jordan, *Major John MacBride 1865–1916* (Westport: Westport Historical Society, 1991), p. 37. MacBride had the support of the Transvaal Committee and the IRB. McCracken, *Irish Pro-Boers*, p. 72.

39. 'What especially annoyed O'Brien was the intrusion into his native Mayo of his archenemy, Tim Healy, campaigning on MacBride's side.' McCracken, *Irish Pro-Boers*, p. 72.

40. McCracken, *Irish Pro-Boers*, p. 74.

41. 'We are anxious to get plays in Irish, and can we do so will very possibly push outward into the western counties, where it would be an important help to the movement for the revival of the Irish language on which the life of the nation may depend.' W. B. Yeats, 'Plans and Methods', *Beltaine* (1900).

42. See Frazier, *George Moore*, pp. 283–6, 289–92.

43. W. B. Yeats to Susan Mary Yeats, 1 November 1899, *Letters 2*, p. 462.

44. W. B. Yeats, *Irish Literary Society Gazette*, January 1900, *Uncollected Prose 2*, pp. 196–7.

45. W. B. Yeats, *Beltaine* (1900), p. 23.

46. James Pethica, *Lady Gregory's Diaries 1892–1902* (Gerrards Cross: Colin Smythe, 1996), p. 226.

47. Ibid., p. 226.

48. Like Standish O'Grady, Alice Milligan's youthful education 'contained nothing of Ireland' and she was anxious to make up the deficit in adult life. Sheila Turner Johnston, *Alice: A Life of Alice Milligan* (Omagh: Columnpoint Press, 1994), p. 99.

49. Colum, *Arthur Griffith*, p. 31.

50. Turner Johnston, *Alice*, p. 90.

51. *Shan Van Vocht*, Jan. and Aug. 1897.

52. Turner Johnston, *Alice*, p. 92.

53. Dublin *Daily Express*, 21 Jan. 1899. Hogan and Kilroy, *Literary Theatre*, pp. 53–4.

54. *The Passing of Conall*, possibly by Fr Eugene O'Growney, contained a scene in Irish of St Patrick at Tara which was translated by 'Padraic' of the New York Gaelic movement. The Belfast Gaelic League was a pioneer of Gaelic drama and on 7 May 1898 produced three *tableaux vivants* on the themes of Meadhbh, Diarmad and Gráinne and Gráinne Mhaol in a production which perhaps marks the birth of Gaelic drama. P. Ó Siadhail, *Stair Dhrámaíocht na Gaeilge 1900–1970* (Conamara: Cló Iar-Chonnachta, 1993), p. 20.

55. William J. Feeney, ed., *Maeve: A Psychological Drama in Two Acts by Edward Martyn and* The Last Feast of the Fianna *by Alice Milligan* (Chicago: De Paul University, 1967), p. 42.

56. Alice Milligan, 'The Last Feast of the Fianna', *Beltaine* (1900), p. 18.

57. Milligan, 'The Last Feast', p. 21.

58. 'Some very beautiful music – ancient Irish airs supplied by the Gaelic League and orchestrated by Mrs. C. Milligan-Fox, sister of the authoress of the play – was contributed in the form of a double-string quartet with fine effect.' *Irish Daily Independent*, 20 Feb. 1900, p. 6. Hogan and Kilroy, *Literary Theatre*, p. 72.

59. Hogan and Kilroy, *Literary Theatre*, p. 74.

60. Welch, *The Abbey Theatre*, p. 9.

61. Trotter, *Ireland's National Theatres*, p. 24.

62. Lady Gregory records the affair in her diary entry for 24 Feb. 1900. Pethica, *Lady Gregory's Diaries*, p. 246.

63. *Beltaine* 1900, p. 12.

64. *Beltaine* 1900, p. 13.

65. Feeney, *Maeve and The Last Feast of the Fianna*, p. 12. All quotations from the play will be taken from this edition. Subsequent references will be noted parenthetically.

66. *Freeman's Journal*, 20 Feb. 1900, p. 5. Hogan and Kilroy, *Literary Theatre*, p. 71.

67. *Freeman's Journal*, 20 Feb. 1900, p. 5. *Irish Times*, 20 Feb., p. 6. Hogan and Kilroy, *Literary Theatre*, pp. 71–3.

68. *United Irishman*, 24 Feb. 1900, p. 6. Hogan and Kilroy, *Literary Theatre*, p. 73.

69. Pethica, *Lady Gregory's Diaries*, p. 247.

70. Malcolm Brown, *George Moore: A Reconsideration* (Seattle: University of Washington Press, 1955), p. 147.

71. Pethica, *Lady Gregory's Diaries*, 24 Feb. 1900, p. 247.

72. Ibid., 31 Dec. 1899, p. 223.
    For a full account of this saga see George Moore, *Ave* (New York: Appleton and Co., 1914), pp. 170–340; Frazier, *George Moore*, pp. 278–81. John Freeman, *A Portrait of George Moore* (1922; London: T. Werner Laurie, 1971), pp. 132–41. William J. Feeney, 'Introduction', *The Bending of the Bough*, Irish Drama Series vol. 3 (Chicago: De Paul University, 1969). On the changes made to a *Tale of a Town*, see Sister Marie-Thérèse Courtney, *Edward Martyn and the Irish Theatre* (New York: Vantage Press, 1956), pp. 101–18.

73. On 28 Nov. 1899 Yeats wrote to Lady Gregory: 'Moore has really very much improved the play.' *Letters 2*, p. 472. On 21 Jan. 1900 Lady Gregory records that George Moore 'has *signed* the re-written 'Tale of a Town' & called it 'the bending of a bough' [sic]. Pethica, *Lady Gregory's Diaries*, p. 227.

74. Brown, *George Moore*, p. 149.

75. Moore, *Ave*, p. 315.

76. Ibid., p. 305.
77. Ibid., p. 306
78. Brown, *George Moore*, p. 149.
79. Ibid., p. 383.
80. *Fortnightly Review* 67.1 (Feb. 1900), pp. 317–24.
81. Feeney, 'Introduction', p. 6.
82. Standish O'Grady, 'The New Irish Movement', *Fortnightly Review* 61.362 (Feb. 1897), pp. 170–9.
83. Feeney, 'Introduction', p. 7.
84. Macnee remarks in an obvious reference to Fenian rebels: 'There are the hillside men; some of them have walked twenty miles to cheer Mr. Dean.' (p. 61)
85. W. B. Yeats, *Autobiographies*, p. 430.
86. In a letter to George Russell Yeats wrote: 'Moore has written a tremendous scene in the third act & I have worked at it here & there through out.' Early Nov. 1899, *Letters 2*, p. 464.
87. 'The Bending of the Bough was the first play dealing with a vital Irish question that had appeared in Ireland.' Gregory, *Our Irish Theatre*, p. 27.
88. W.B Yeats to George Russell, Nov 1899, *Letters 2*, p. 464.
89. W. B. Yeats to Lady Gregory, 21 Dec. 1899, *Letters 2*, p. 480.
90. W. B. Yeats to Lady Gregory, 31 Jan. 1900, *Letters 2*, p. 492.
91. Pilkington, *Theatre and the State*, p. 21.
92. *Freeman's Journal*, 21 Feb., p. 5. Hogan and Kilroy, *Literary Theatre*, p. 75.
93. *Irish Daily Independent*, 21 Feb., p. 5. Hogan and Kilroy, *Literary Theatre*, p. 76.
94. *United Irishman*, 24 Feb. 1900, p. 5.
95. *Irish Times*, 21 Feb. 1900, p. 6. Hogan and Kilroy, *Literary Theatre*, p. 78.
96. ARDMAN   I can send them some cart-loads of seed potatoes – an early kind, you know for those impoverished nursery gardens to the west of your town.
      LAWRENCE: That will do very nicely, my dear mayor. Potatoes do not stir up any dangerous fermentation of ideas. (p. 65)
97. *Freeman's Journal*, 23 Feb. 1900. Hogan and Kilroy, *Literary Theatre*, p. 80.
98. Hogan and Kilroy, *Literary Theatre*, p. 82. Moore's address was also published as 'The Irish Literary Renaissance and The Irish Language', *New Ireland Review* 13.2 (April 1900), pp. 65–72.
99. On George Moore's tongue-in-cheek recollection of his sudden enthusiasm for the Irish language, see *Ave*, pp. 340–1.
100. Moore, 'The Irish Literary Renaissance', p. 72.
101. Hogan and Kilroy, *Literary Theatre*, p. 84.
102. '. . . if any such denationalising system was introduced into Parliament they would require their parliamentary representatives to use obstruction, insult, and every old weapon with which they had met the stranger in the past.' Hogan and Kilroy, *Literary Theatre*, p. 84.
103. *An Claidheamh Soluis*, 3 Mar. 1900, p. 808.
104. Ward, *Maud Gonne*, p. 61.
105. *Freeman's Journal*, 8 Mar. 1900, p. 6. See James H. Murphy, *Abject Loyalty: Nationalism and Monarchy in Ireland During the Reign of Queen Victoria* (Cork: Cork University Press, 2001), p. 277.
106. *Hansard LXXVII*, 8 March 1900, col. 402.
107. *Freeman's Journal*, 17 Mar. 1900, p. 6.

108. *United Irishman*, 24 Mar. 1900, p. 4.
109. 'In George's street the people were bludgeoned that Pile [the Lord Mayor] might progress. In Parliament street the police were overpowered by the people, who seized the carriage, and but for the arrival at the double-quick of reinforcements, things would have gone badly with the Freemason.' *United Irishman*, 24 Mar. 1900, p. 4.
110. *United Irishman*, 17 Mar. 1900, p. 7.
111. Ibid.
112. 12 Mar. 1900, Pethica, *Lady Gregory's Diaries*, p. 255.
113. 17 March 1900, Pethica, p. 264.
114. Ibid., p. 267 (n. 192).
115. Letter to *United Irishman*, 17 Mar. 1900, p. 7.
116. W. B. Yeats to *Freeman's Journal*, 20 Mar. 1900. *Letters 2*, p. 503.
117. *Letters 2*, p. 503. In a letter to Lady Gregory on 29 March 1900, Yeats recounts that he has 'just heard that the Irish Party have accepted my proposition of a meeting of protest against the Act of Union but whether they mean to make it in Dublin or at a mere meeting of the party, where it will be useless, I don't know . . . O'Brien, as well as Dillon, has now stolen Moore's thunder, & made a speech about "Chamberlain's recruiting sergeant", & Moore's "smart" friends are cutting him. He is in fine spirits as a result.' *Letters 2*, p. 506.
118. W. B. Yeats to *Freeman's Journal*, 3 Apr. 1900, *Letters 2*, pp. 508–9. Yeats expanded on this letter in an article, 'Noble and Ignoble Loyalties', published in the *United Irishman* on 21 April 1900. Here he argued that the cheers that Queen Victoria received on the streets of Dublin should not be taken as a sign of the loyalty of the Irish people. Referring also to her visits of 1853 and 1861 he noted that: 'Her visits to Ireland have indeed been unfortunate for English power, for they have commonly foreshadowed a fierce and sudden shaking of English power in Ireland. I do not think this last visit will be more fortunate than the others, for I see all round me, among the young men who hold the coming years in their hands, a new awakening inspiration and resolve!'
119. James Joyce, 'Ireland: Island of Saints and Sages', *Occasional, Critical, and Political Writing*, p. 118.
120. *United Irishman*, 7 Apr., p. 5. Margaret Ward records that 'despite workers having a day off in her honour and those in Guinness's brewery discovering an extra shilling in their pay packets, Victoria's entry into Dublin on 4 April, was less than triumphant. Silent people stared at her carriage. A counter-demonstration by the Transvaal Committee was quickly broken up by the police.' *Maud Gonne*, p. 61.
121. Henry, *Evolution of Sinn Féin*, p. 63. Ward, *Maud Gonne*, p. 62.
   Percy French made ample use of this episode in his skit, 'The Queen's After-Dinner Speech', which appeared in the Dublin *Daily Express* on 18 Apr. 1900 (p. 6): 'And that other wan,' sez she, / 'That Maud Gonne,' sez she, / 'Dhressin' in black,' sez she, / 'To welcome me back,' sez she, / 'Though I don't care,' sez she, / 'What they wear,' sez she, 'An' all that gammon,' sez she, / 'About me bringin' famine,' sez she. / 'Now Maud Gonne will write,' sez she, / 'That I brought the blight,' sez she, / 'Or altered the saysons,' sez she, / 'For some private raysins,' sez she.
122. Maud Gonne, 'The Famine Queen', *United Irishman*, 7 Apr. 1900, p. 5.
123. Ward, *Maud Gonne*, p. 62.

124. Ibid., p. 62.
125. Gonne Mac Bride, *Servant of the Queen*, p. 291.
126. Margaret Ward, *In Their Own Voice: Women and Irish Nationalism* (Dublin: Attic Press, 1995), p. 19.
127. 'At the Vice-Regal Lodge in Phoenix Park, Victoria the Famine Queen gave a treat to 15,000 school-children. Convent schools vied with the Protestant ascendancy in sending the largest contingents of children, shepherded by holy nuns. Obviously we could not interfere with nuns and children, and the Unionist papers revelled in picture and print descriptions of the spontaneous display of loyalty.' Gonne, *Servant of the Queen*, p. 294.
128. Ward, *Maud Gonne*, p. 62.
129. Gonne Mac Bride, *Servant of the Queen*, p. 295.
130. W. B. Yeats to Lady Gregory, 10 April 1900, *Letters 2*, p. 512.

A Battle of Two Civilizations?

1. 'First published in the *Daily Mail* for 31 Oct. 1899, the poem subsequently appeared in a variety of versions: on tobacco jars, ashtrays, packages of cigarettes, pillowcases, plates and many other forms . . . there is no doubt that, both as a fund-raiser and morale-raiser, it was no mean contribution to the war effort.' The poem raised £250,000 to aid soldiers and their families. *Rudyard Kipling: The Man, His Work and His World*, ed. John Gross (London: Weidenfeld and Nicolson, 1972), p. 84.
2. Colum, *Arthur Griffith*, p. 58.
3. P. S. O'Hegarty, *A History of Ireland Under the Union 1801–1922* (London: Methuen, 1952), p. 639. This remains a useful source of contemporary material.
4. Colum, *Arthur Griffith*, p. 57.
5. *United Irishman*, 15 Mar. 1900; O'Hegarty, p. 638.
6. O'Hegarty, *Ireland Under the Union,* p. 638. 'The Home Ruler acknowledges the right of England to govern this country, while he demands facilities for purely local Irish matters in Ireland, and for that purpose seeks the erection of a legislative body in Dublin. In return for this concession, he guarantees the loyalty and devotion of the Irish people to England and their readiness to share in the turpitude of the British Empire.'
7. Ibid., p. 638.
8. Colum, *Arthur Griffith*, p. 64.
9. O'Hegarty, *Ireland Under the Union*, p. 639.
10. For details of anti-recruitment activities, see Cumann na nGaedheal document dated 1 Nov. 1902, NLI Lo. P114. The festival names were supplied by W. B. Yeats. See Colum, *Arthur Griffith*, p. 58. On 3 Dec. 1903 Padraic Colum's *The Saxon Shillin'* was played before Craobh Liam Ua Maolruanaigh (William Rooney branch, 36 Penton St, North London) at the Wellington Hall in Islington, Cumann na nGaedheal programme, NLI P.2127. The programme makes mention of three other London branches: Irish National Club branch, 54 Chancery Lane; Erin's Hope branch 29 Fentimar Rd, Clapham; Clarence Mangan branch, 47 Uxbridge St, Notting Hill.
11. Lyons, *Culture and Anarchy*, p. 57.

12.   See Conor Cruise O'Brien, 'The Irish Mind: A Bad Case of Cultural National-
       ism', *Passion and Cunning*, pp. 192–8, and *States of Ireland* (1972; Herts: Pan-
       ther, 1974), pp. 74–8; John Hutchinson, *The Dynamics of Cultural Nationalism:
       The Gaelic Revival and the Creation of the Irish Nation State* (London: Allen and
       Unwin, 1987), pp. 173–8; Roy Foster, 'Thinking from Hand to Mouth', *Paddy
       and Mr Punch* (London: Penguin, 1993); Deirdre Toomey, 'Moran's Collar: Yeats
       and Irish Ireland', *Yeats Annual* 12 (1996), pp. 45–83; Stephen Regan, 'W. B.
       Yeats and Irish Cultural Politics in the 1890s', *Cultural Politics at the* Fin de Siè-
       cle, eds. Sally Ledger and Scott McCracken (Cambridge: Cambridge University
       Press, 1997), p. 77; Harry White, *The Keeper's Recital: Music and Cultural His-
       tory in Ireland, 1770–1970* (Cork: Cork University Press/Field Day, 1998),
       pp. 94–124.
13.   Margaret O'Callaghan, 'Language, Nationality and Cultural Identity in the Irish
       Free State, 1922–7: The *Irish Statesman* and the *Catholic Bulletin* Reappraised',
       Irish Historical Studies 24 (1984), pp. 226–45.
14.   As Gregory Dobbins has pointed out, Connolly's idea of Irishness was based on
       'the collective desire to resist colonial rule by retaining some degree of a cultur-
       ally specific difference. But unlike so many adherents of the Gaelic Revival, Con-
       nolly did not articulate such cultural difference in mythical, religious, or most
       importantly, racial terms' ('Whenever Green is Red', p. 618).
15.   Deirdre Toomey, 'Moran's Collar, p. 48.
16.   The *New Ireland Review* began publishing in December 1898, was edited by
       Father Tom Finlay and associated with University College. Father Finlay, pro-
       fessor of metaphysics, was deeply involved in Plunkett's co-operative movement.
       Moran's articles appeared between December 1898 and August 1900 and were
       published as *The Philosophy of Irish Ireland* in 1905.
17.   D. P. Moran, 'Is the Irish Nation Dying?', *New Ireland Review*, Dec. 1898, p. 213.
18.   D. P. Moran, 'The Future of the Irish Nation', *New Ireland Review*, Feb. 1899, p.
       346.
19.   Moran, 'Future of the Irish Nation', p. 352.
20.   D. P. Moran, 'The Battle of Two Civilizations', *New Ireland Review*, Aug. 1900, p.
       334.
21.   Moran, 'Battle of Two Civilizations', p. 335.
22.   Trevor West, *Horace Plunkett*, p. 3. On the co-operative movement Moran wrote:
       'There is a certain body, largely tainted with Unionism, I believe, who preach a
       propaganda of industrial co-operation and economic progress which, whatever
       its shortcomings may be, no man can reasonably oppose, and which every man
       is at liberty to improve upon if he can.' 'The Gaelic Revival', p. 265.
23.   Moran, 'Future of the Irish Nation', p. 355.
24.   Ibid., p. 356.
25.   Ibid., p. 354.
26.   *Leader*, 8 Sept. 1900, p. 28.
27.   Patrick Maume, *D. P. Moran* (Dublin: Dundalgan Press, 1995), p. 18.
28.   Moran, 'Is the Irish Nation Dying?', p. 212. On the question of national charac-
       ter, Moran saw the 'ignorant peasants' as 'the most interesting portion of the pop-
       ulation. In them are yet to be seen, undeveloped and clouded perhaps, the
       marks of the Gaelic race . . . They still possess the unspoiled raw material for the
       making of a vigorous and a real Irish character' (p. 210).

29. *Leader*, 17 Oct. 1903, p. 119.
30. Patrick Maume warns against the tendency to rely on the Irish Ireland articles in appraisals of Moran and argues that in his later journalistic career Moran's 'most valuable characteristics were his commitment to debate, the acuteness of his observations, and his business enterprise'. Yet the Irish Ireland articles were crucially important to the intellectual ferment of the period in question here. *D. P. Moran*, p. 55.
31. Moran, 'Battle of Two Civilizations', p. 328.
32. Moran's adverse reaction to *The Countess Cathleen* has been discussed in chapter 2.
33. Moran, 'Future of the Irish Nation', p. 353. If this was insulting to Yeats and his friends, it was also calculated to insult Arthur Griffith and William Rooney, who were, after all, long-time members of the Celtic Literary Society.
34. Ibid., pp. 328–9.
35. Ibid., p. 329.
36. Brian Maye, *Arthur Griffith* (Dublin: Griffith College, 1997), pp. 60–2.
37. *United Irishman*, 10 June 1899, Maye, *Arthur Griffith*, pp. 60–1.
38. Henry, *Evolution of Sinn Féin*, p. 59.
39. 'At this time Arthur Griffith played a distinctly secondary role. Rooney did not even nominate him for membership of the Celtic [Literary Society] till Oct. 1895. At the end of 1896 Griffith emigrated to South Africa and did not return till 1898 . . . In later years Griffith was to demonstrate an almost superstitious reverence for Rooney.' Richard Davis, *Arthur Griffith and Non-Violent Sinn Féin* (Dublin: Anvil Books, 1974), p. 7. Cumann na nGaedheal 'suffered a staggering blow through the death of William Rooney, and for a time it seemed as though the blow would prove a fatal one'. *United Irishman*, 1 Nov. 1902.
40. Arthur Griffith, 'Preface', *Poems and Ballads by William Rooney* (Dublin: United Irishman, n.d. [1903?], p. ix.
41. Griffith, 'Preface', p. ix.
42. 'The constitution and proceedings of the society have importance in that the Celtic was to a large extent a forerunner and model of other societies which later amalgamated to form an early strand of the Sinn Féin movement.' Davis, *George Russell*, p. 5.
     'By far the most conscientious worker in this society was William Rooney. He was the founder and inspirer, and indeed, until the return of Griffith [from South Africa], he was the *factotum*, and seemed to carry all the responsibility on his own shoulders.' George Lyons, *Some Recollections of Griffith and his Times* (Dublin: Talbot Press, 1923), p. 3.
43. Davis, *George Russell*, p. 5.
44. 'Fear na Muintire', 'Hi Fiachra' and Criadhaire' in his poetry; 'Shel Martin', 'Sliabh Ruadh', 'Glenn an Smoil', 'Knocksedan', 'Killeste', 'Feltrim', 'Ballinascorney' and 'Baltrasna' in his prose.
45. I am indebted to Patrick Bradley for much of this biographical detail: 'William Rooney – A Sketch of His Career', *Poems and Ballads by William Rooney*, pp. xiii–xlvi.
46. 'If an Irish landlord evicts a tenant farmer he is denounced by the Home Rule press as an enemy to Ireland, but an Irish employer can lock out and attempt to starve thousands of true Irishmen, as was done in the building trade in 1896, in

the tailoring trade in 1900, and in the engineers of Inchicore in 1902; and not a member of parliament would take up the fight for the workers, or bother himself about them.' James Connolly, 'Election Address, 1903', Heron ed., p. 82.

47. Bradley, 'William Rooney', p. xxxviii.
48. William Rooney, 'The Development of the National Ideal', *United Irishman*, 13 Jan. 1900, p. 2.
49. Rooney, 'Development of the National Ideal', pp. 2–3.
50. Moran, 'Battle of Two Civilizations', p. 334.
51. William Rooney, 'Gaelicism in Practice', Lecture to Celtic Literary Society, 4 Jan. 1901, *Prose Writings* (Dublin: M.H. Gill, 1909), p. 148.
52. William Rooney, 'Our Native Parliament', *Prose Writings*, p. 157.
53. Quoted by Bradley, 'William Rooney', p. xxv.
54. Moran, 'Future of Irish Nation', p. 347. Rooney had published poems entitled 'The Return of Owen Roe' and 'Sarsfield's Ride' in the *United Irishman*. See *Poems and Ballads by William Rooney*. James Joyce was also highly critical of Rooney's poetry: 'we find in these pages a weary succession of verses, "prize" poems – the worst of all. They were written, it seems, for papers and societies week after week, and they bear witness to some desperate and weary energy.' James Joyce, 'An Irish Poet', *Occasional, Critical, and Political Writing*, ed. Kevin Barry (Oxford: Oxford University Press, 2000), p. 62.
55. William Rooney, 'Is There an Anglo-Irish Literature?', *Prose Writings*, pp. 230–1.
56. 'He pointed out how the Rev. Dr. O'Hickey and many another acknowledged that it was the writings of Davis that first helped to make them as Irish as they are; to Davis we, in a large measure, owe such men as Douglas Hyde, W. B. Yeats, and many another writer in Irish and English.' Bradley, 'William Rooney', p. xliv.
57. W. B. Yeats, *Letters 3*, p. 72. In a letter to Lady Gregory on 21 May 1901, Yeats confided that Rooney's 'death has plunged everybody into gloom'.
58. Rooney, 'Is There an Anglo-Irish Literature?', pp. 231–2. Rooney argued that for Anglo-Irish writers to use Irish 'would be as untrue of them as it would be of Aodh O'Donnell or Shane O'Neill if one made these talk English' (p. 227).
59. Ibid., p. 232.
60. As we have seen in Chapter 2, Yeats had already broached the subject of an Irish literature in English in an address to the Trinity College Historical Society in the wake of the *Countess Cathleen* affair. See Hogan and Kilroy, *Literary Theatre*, pp. 58–60.
61. W. B. Yeats, letter to the *Leader*, 26 Aug. 1900, *Letters 2*, p. 564.
62. W. B. Yeats, *Letters 3*, p. 23.
63. Rooney, 'Is There an Anglo-Irish Literature?', pp. 231–2.
64. W. B. Yeats, letter to the *Leader*, 26 Aug. 1900, *Letters 2*, p. 564. Indeed, D. P. Moran was himself a good illustration of this maxim in that he presented the vast bulk of his work in the English language.
65. In a letter to Douglas Hyde in July 1901, W. B. Yeats wrote in praise of Gregory's work on Cuchulain. This was eventually published as *Cuchulain of Muirthemne* in April 1902. W. B. Yeats, *Letters 3*, p. 97.
66. Lady Gregory, 'Dedication', *Cuchulain of Muirthemne* (1902; Gerrards Cross: Colin Smythe, 1970), p. 5. 'Her familiarity with the Gaelic text at this early point is indicative of her efforts with both the language and its literature, and lends considerable weight to her claim to have been considering translating the Tain

for some time prior to broaching the subject with Yeats in Nov. 1900.' Pethica, *Lady Gregory's Diaries*, p. 202n.

67.   Diary entry 20 Nov. 1900, Ibid., p. 290.

68.   'I remember on one occasion, when she was asked to sing the English version of that touching melody, "The Red-haired Man's Wife," she replied, "I will sing it for you; but the English words and the air are like a quarrelling man and wife: the Irish melts into the tune, but the English doesn't," an expression scarcely less remarkable for its beauty than truth.' William Carleton, 'Introduction to Traits and Stories of the Irish Peasantry', *The Works of William Carleton* vol. 2 (1881; New York: Books for Libraries Press, 1970), p. 646.

69.   Daniel Murphy, 'Foreword', *Cuchulain of Muirthemne*, p. 8.

70.   W. B. Yeats, *Autobiographies*, p. 455.

71.   W. B. Yeats, 'Preface', *Cuchulain of Muirthemne*, p. 12.

72.   Lady Gregory, *Seventy Years 1852–1922* (Gerrards Cross: Colin Smythe, 1974), p. 390.

73.   Yeats remarks that Lady Gregory was motivated to write *Cuchulain of Muirthemne* because 'An eminent Trinity College professor had described ancient Irish literature as "silly, religious, or indecent", and she thought such work necessary for the dignity of Ireland'. *Autobiographies*, p. 456

74.   Gregory, 'Dedication', p. 6.

75.   Ibid., p. 5.

76.   See W. B. Yeats, *Letters 3*, p. 163n.

77.   W. B. Yeats, *Letters 3*, p. 165n. One recalls the comments of Professor Atkinson before the Vice-Regal Commission on the Irish language: 'I would allow no daughter of mine of any age to see [Irish literature].' See Chapter 2.

78.   Letter to Lady Gregory, 24 Mar. 1902: 'I have just noticed with some alarm the bit of bowdlerizing (how do you spell that word) on page 20 . . . I beg of you to insert in your notes something like the sentence I send you. The original incident is so well known & has so many folk lore ramifications that people will notice its absence & suspect your text everywhere else.' *Letters 3*, p. 164.

79.   See *Towards a National Theatre: The Dramatic Criticism of Frank J. Fay*, ed. Robert Hogan (Dublin: Dolmen Press, 1970).

80.   Frank Fay, 'Mr. Yeats and the Stage', *United Irishman*, 4 May 1901, Hogan, *Towards a National Theatre*, p. 51.

81.   Fay, 'Yeats and the Stage', p. 50.

82.   F. Fay, 'The Irish Literary Theatre', *United Irishman*, 23 Nov. 1901, Hogan, *Towards a National Theatre*, p. 84.

83.   For Moore's support of Gaelic drama see 'The Irish Literary Theatre', *Samhain* (1901), p. 13. In 'The Culture Hero in Dublin Myths' Moore launched a scathing attack on Mahaffy, lampooning the professor and the 'folklore' surrounding him. Moore's aim was to highlight his colonial provincialism: 'he also reminds me of a distinguished butler, and the large blandness of the Professor . . . encourages the idea of a servant; there is just that mixture of kindness and shrewdness in the Professor's shallow eyes that we take note of in the eyes of a particular type of family servant . . . A title astonishes him as it astonishes a valet.' *Leader*, 20 July 1901, pp. 329–331.

84.   George Moore, *Salve* (London: Heinenman, 1912), p. 107. Hogan and Kilroy, *Literary Theatre*, p. 107.

85. 'Central Branch Sgóruidheacht – Address by Mr. W. B. Yeats', *An Claidheamh Soluis*, 27 Oct. 1900, pp. 516–7.
86. W. B. Yeats, *Letters 2*, p. 570n. Adrian Frazier contends that George Moore may also have had a hand in the shaping of the play. *George Moore*, p. 295
87. W. B. Yeats, letter to Lady Gregory, 21 May 1901, *Letters 3*, p. 72.
88. Letter to W. B. Yeats, 24 May 1901, *Letters 3*, p. 74n. As a result of the *Countess Cathleen* controversy and his protests against Queen Victoria, Yeats succeeded in alienating himself from both mainstream Catholic nationalist and Protestant unionist opinion. In a letter to Lady Gregory, he tells of the difficulty he experienced in selling his books to Dublin booksellers: 'Memory of the *Countess Cathleen* dispute accounts for a good deal. Bullen found the protestant booksellers little better & asked me if TCD disliked me. Magee, the college publisher said "What is he doing here. Why doesn't he go away and leave us in peace." He seems to have suspected me of some deep revolutionary design.' Letter to Lady Gregory, 21 May 1901, *Letters 3*, p. 71. Further evidence of Yeats's unpopularity at the time is suggested by his appeal to Arthur Griffith to publicize the fact that his *Land of the Heart's Desire* had been a 'real success' in America. 16 July 1901, *Letters 3*, p. 88. An article was subsequently published in the *United Irishman* to publicize Yeats written by Frank Fay. See 'The Land of Heart's Desire', Hogan, pp. 69–71.
89. Stephen Gwynn, 'The Irish Literary Theatre and Its Affinities', *Fortnightly Review* (1901), pp. 1058–9. Hogan and Kilroy, *Literary Theatre*, p. 39.
90. For an account of the tensions between Moore and Yeats during the writing of this play, see George Moore, *Ave*, pp. 358–78; W. B. Yeats, *Letters 3*, pp. 585–90; Frazier, *George Moore*, pp. 293–9; Anthony Farrow, 'Introduction', *Diarmuid and Grania* (Chicago: DePaul University, 1974), pp. 1–18.
91. '[The actors] could not even pronounce the proper names either correctly or uniformly wrong.' *Leader*, 2 Nov 1901, p. 155.
92. Philip Marcus, *Standish O'Grady* (Lewisburg: Bucknell University Press, 1970), p. 60.
93. Marcus, *Standish O'Grady*, p. 44.
94. Farrow, 'Introduction', *Diarmuid and Grania*, p. 10.
95. John Eglinton, W. B. Yeats, AE and William Larminie, *Literary Ideals in Ireland* (London: Fisher Unwin, 1899), p. 27.
96. Standish O'Grady, *All Ireland Review* (Oct. 1901), p. 244. Hogan and Kilroy, *Literary Theatre*, p. 101.
97. 'An Irish Play and an English Afterpiece', *Leader*, 2 Nov. 1901, p. 155.
98. 'Diarmuid and Grania', *Leader*, 2 Nov. 1901, p. 157.
99. Frank Fay, 'The Irish Literary Theatre', *United Irishman*, 26 Oct. 1901. Hogan, *Towards a National Theatre*, p. 72.
100. Frank Fay, 'The Irish Literary Theatre', *United Irishman*. 2 Nov. 1901. Hogan, *Towards a National Theatre*, p. 78.
101. Frank Fay, 'The Irish Literary Theatre', *United Irishman*, 23 Nov. 1901. Hogan, *Towards a National Theatre*, p. 84.
102. James Joyce, 'The Day of the Rabblement', *Occasional, Critical, and Political Writing*, pp. 50–2.
103. Frank Fay, 'The Irish Literary Theatre, *United Irishman*, 2 Nov. 1901. Hogan, p. 79.
104. See Emer Nolan, *James Joyce and Nationalism* (London: Routledge, 1995), p. 47.
105. Ellmann, *James Joyce*, p. 61.

106. Ibid., p. 87.
107. W. B. Yeats, *Collected Letters vol. III*, eds. John Kelly and Ronald Schuchard (Oxford: Clarendon Press, 1994), p. 657.
108. James Joyce, 'The Day of the Rabblement', p. 51. Yeats responded to Joyce's allegations in a letter to the young writer: 'The qualities that make a man succeed do not shew in his work, often for quite a long time. They are much less qualities of talent than qualities of character – faith (of this you have probably enough), patience, adaptability (without this one learns nothing), and a gift for growing by experience & this is perhaps the rarest of all.' W. B. Yeats to James Joyce, *c.* 15 Nov. 1902, *Letters 3*, p. 250.
109. Ellmann, *James Joyce*, p. 170.
110. 'Politics and Cattle Disease', *Freeman's Journal*, 10 Sept 1912. See *Occasional, Critical, and Political Writing*, pp. 206–8.
111. Joyce, *Ulysses*, p. 122. All subsequent references to the text will be cited parenthetically.
112. West, p. 74
113. *Freeman's Journal*, 5 March 1904; West, p. 74.
114. The controversy surrounding the publication of Plunkett's book is examined in chapter 1.
115. Ellmann, *James Joyce*, pp. 169–70. Well might Russell recommend such moneymaking schemes to Joyce, given the fact that the young writer was seriously in debt at this time. This may explain Stephen's cryptic thought, 'A.E.I.O.U', in the National Library (p. 243).
116. Plunkett, *Ireland in the New Century*, p. 121
117. James Joyce, *Dubliners*, intro. Terence Brown (London: Penguin, 1992) p. 1. All subsequent references to the text will be cited parentethically.

Sinn Féin, the Abbey Theatre and *The Shadow of the Glen*

1. W. B. Yeats, *Samhain* (1903), p. 9.
2. The play was staged under the auspices of the Irish National Theatre Society in the Molesworth Hall.
3. Frank Fay, 'Mr. Yeats and the Stage', *United Irishman*, 4 May 1901. Hogan, *Towards a National Theatre*, p. 53. In August 1901 Yeats had seen the Fays' production of Alice Milligan's *The Harp that Once, The Deliverance of Red Hugh* and *Eilís agus an Bhean Dhéirce* at the Pan Celtic Congress. Foster, *W. B. Yeats 1*, p. 259.
4. See *Samhain* (1902), p. 3.
5. Davis, *George Russell*, 15.
6. W. B. Yeats to Lady Gregory, 21 May 1901, *Letters 3*, p. 72.
   'He was Griffith's greatest friend and helper in the paper. His loss was irreparable; I wondered if Griffith would be able to carry on without him . . . If he had lived his influence might have prevented Griffith accepting the disastrous Treaty of 1922.' Gonne Mac Bride, *Servant of the Queen*, pp. 312–3.
7. Davis, *George Russell*, p. 21.
8. Maye, *Arthur Griffith*, p. 95.
9. See Maye, *Arthur Griffith*, pp. 94–111; Davis, *George Russell*, pp. 17–36; Henry, *Evolution of Sinn Féin*, pp. 39–85.

10.   Davis, *Arthur Griffith*, p. 27.

11.   *United Irishman,* 3 Oct. 1903. Maye, *Evolution of Sinn Féin*, p. 96.

12.   William Rooney, 'Our Native Parliament, *Prose Writings*, p. 157.

13.   'Griffith's republican critics looked to Rooney as an alternative founder of Sinn Féin.' Maume, *The Long Gestation: Irish Nationalist Life 1891–1918* (Dublin: Gill and Macmillan, 1999), p. 42.

14.   Bulmer Hobson, *Ireland Yesterday and Tomorrow* (Tralee: Anvil Books, 1968), p. 23. The Dungannon Clubs later merged with Cumann na nGaedheal and the National Council to form Sinn Féin.

15.   Ibid., p. 20.

16.   Ibid., p. 10.

17.   This uneasy coexistence of bourgeois nationalism and republicanism would lead to repeated tensions within the movement, most obviously and tragically over the Treaty in 1922.

18.   The publication of the *Resurrection of Hungary* was funded by John Sweetman, Edward Martyn and Thomas Martin. *United Irishman* 18 Mar. 1905. Davis, *Arthur Griffith*, p. 22.

19.   The plays performed that week include *The Sleep of the King* by James Cousins, *The Laying of the Foundations* by Fred Ryan, Yeats's *A Pot of Broth*, *The Racing Lug* by James Cousins and Peadar MacFhionnlaoich's *Eilís agus an Bhean Déirce*. This was the first Samhain festival organized by Cumann na nGaedheal.

20.   *United Irishman,* 8 Nov. 1902. Robert Hogan and James Kilroy, *Laying the Foundations 1902–1904* (Dublin: Dolmen, 1976), p. 38.

21.   W. B. Yeats, 'What Ireland Needs', *Chicago Daily News*, 17 Mar. 1903. *Letters 3*, p. 327.

22.   'We cannot have too much discussion about ideas in Ireland. The discussion over the theology of "The Countess Cathleen", and over the politics of "The Bending of the Bough ", and over the morality of "Diarmuid and Grania", set the public mind thinking of matters it seldom thinks of in Ireland, and I hope the Irish Literary Theatre will remain a wise disturber of the peace.' W. B. Yeats, letter to *Freeman's Journal*, 14 Nov. 1901. *Letters 3*, p. 118.

23.   Frank Fay, 'Mr. Yeats and the Stage', *United Irishman*, 5 May 1901. Hogan, p. 52.

24.   W. B. Yeats to Lady Gregory, 9 Nov. 1903, *Letters 3*, p. 462.
      Part of the stated aim of Cumann na nGaedheal was 'to undertake the education of the people in the history, literature, and language of their country, to teach them to appreciate Irish art, and to induce them to study the resources of Ireland', *United Irishman*, 15 Mar. 1900.

25.   The National Dramatic Society was formed in August 1902. Members elected Yeats as President, AE, Maud Gonne and Douglas Hyde as Vice-Presidents and Fred Ryan as Secretary. *Letters 3*, p. 219n. It became the Irish National Theatre Society (INTS) in January 1903. R. F. Foster, *W. B. Yeats 1*, p. 288.

26.   Maud Gonne to W. B. Yeats, 28 Dec. 1902. *The Gonne–Yeats Letters 1893–1938*, eds. Anna McBride White and A. Norman Jeffares (London: Hutchinson, 1992), p. 160. The competition referred to was the Cumann na nGaedheal Samhain festival, during which prizes were awarded for essays, plays and songs. Ibid., p. 490n.

27.   Griffith's reaction was reported in a letter from Maud Gonne to W. B. Yeats, Jan. 1902. Ibid., p. 162. Fay left the following record of events: 'I found that the end-

ing though it read well did not act at all so strong. I suggested to Columb to take the piece and see if he could not make a better shot of it . . . Now miss Gonne turned up at the 3rd rehearsal . . . she told me before the company that I had ruined the piece and that Cuman no Gaedhal [sic] would be vexed and I thought my ending best and I was not playing the piece for Cuman no Gaedhal and I did not see what they had to do with it . . . I won't [be] scared of any political play that anyone in Ireland has backbone enough to write.' W. Fay to W. B. Yeats, 30 Jan. 1903. *Letters to W. B. Yeats*, vol. 1, eds. Richard J. Finneran, George Mills Harper and William M. Murphy (London: Macmillan, 1977), p. 118.

28.   It was subsequently produced by Inghinidhe na h-Éireann on 15 May 1903.

29.   W. B. Yeats, *Samhain* (1903), p. 4.

30.   *United Irishman*, 27 Dec. 1902, *Letters 3*, p. 278.

31.   W. B. Yeats to Lady Gregory, 26 Dec. 1902, *Letters 3*, p. 285.

32.   Further complicating the relationship between Yeats and Griffith was the marriage of Maud Gonne to Major John MacBride on 21 February. She was very much the linking figure between the two and following the wedding 'there were no longer meetings between [Griffith] and Yeats' (Padraic Colum, *Arthur Griffith*, p. 74).

33.   Colum, *Arthur Griffith*, p. 74. Bulmer Hobson concurred with this character assessment: 'Griffith was an excellent propagandist, but was extremely dogmatic and narrow and I found him difficult to work with. He did not appear to want co-operation, but obedience. *Ireland Yesterday and Tomorrow*, p. 4.
      'While Rooney had Thomas Davis's facility for winning the respect and co-operation of men of widely differing backgrounds and beliefs – even the egocentric novelist George Moore was prepared to follow his lead – Arthur Griffith, in reality shy, introverted and retiring, often appeared brittle and arrogant to associates from whom he was frequently estranged.' Davis, p. *Arthur Griffith*, 15.

34.   *Freeman's Journal*, 9 Apr. 1903, *Letters 3*, p. 346; *Freeman's Journal*, 13 July 1903, *Letters 3*, p. 396; *United Irishman*, 1 Aug. 1903, *Letters 3*, p. 411; *United Irishman*, 20 May 1903, *Letters 3*, p. 377 (as co-signatory).

35.   The National Council was also known as the People's Protection Committee. Its stated aim was 'to ensure that the National [sic] opinion of the country [would] not be misrepresented, and also to protect the people from being coerced into a makebelieve acquiescence in reception displays, and to protect the children of the people from being used for a similar purpose'. Attention was also drawn to the fact that the coronation oath that Edward VII had taken was 'grossly insulting' to the Catholic religion. *United Irishman*, 20 May 1903, *Letters 3*, p. 377.

36.   To the editor of the *Freeman's Journal*, 9 Apr. 1903, *Letters 3*, p. 346.

37.   Likewise, in his objection to the visit of Queen Victoria, he argued that she had used her influence 'to cherish mediocrity in music and in painting and in literature' ('Noble and Ignoble Loyalties', p. 212). This of course was a clever, if coded, challenge to the leaders of Irish nationalism not to emulate her in this regard.

38.   To the editor of the *Freeman's Journal*, 13 July 1903, *Letters 3*, p. 396. Yeats's antipathy to Edward VII was given further articulation in his poem 'In the Seven Woods', where he bluntly referred to a 'new commonness/Upon the throne'. *Collected Poems*, p. 85.

39.   *Leader,* 29 Aug. 1903, p. 5. This is reminiscent of the position adopted by the character, Henchy, in Joyce's 'Ivy Day in the Committee Room'. Set in October 1902, this story alludes to the impending visit of Edward VII. Henchy, a nationalist, welcomes the King's visit because of the 'capital' it will bring to a depressed Ireland. 'Listen to me, said Mr. Henchy. What we want in this country, as I said to old Ward, is capital. The King's coming here will mean an influx of money into this country. The citizens of Dublin will benefit by it.' James Joyce, *Dubliners,* (London: Penguin, 1992), p. 128.

40.   W. B. Yeats to *United Irishman,* 1 Aug. 1903, *Letters 3,* pp. 411–2.

41.   *Letters 3,* p. 376n.

42.   See Chantal Deutsch Brady, 'The King's Visit and the People's Protection Committee, 1903', *Éire-Ireland* 10.3 (Fall 1975), pp. 3–10.

43.   Frazier, *Behind the Scenes,* p. 50.

44.   *United Irishman,* 17 Oct. 1903.

45.   'We are willing if need be to sit at the feet of the Frank, the Teuton, the Sclav, and learn from them – to accept reproof, to accept praise – we shall accept neither from the Anglo-Saxon. With regret, therefore, we observe that Mr. W. B. Yeats includes in *Samhain* a flattering notice of the Irish National Theatre from the London *Times* . . . The Irish National Theatre Society made a false step when it went last year to play in London – it makes a second when it quotes the encomiums of London upon itself – it will make the third and fatal step when it exchanges Cathleen ni Houlihan for the Ephesian dame. We hope that . . . our greatest poet, who was a Nationalist when Respectability blushed at the name, shall still hold it his high ambition to accounted be True Brother of that company. Who sang to sweeten Ireland's wrong. *United Irishman,* 17 Oct. 1903.

46.   Arthur Walkley, *Times Literary Supplement,* repr. *Samhain* (1903), p. 34.

47.   J. M. Synge, 'Various Notes', *Prose,* p. 347.

48.   David H. Greene and Edward M. Stephens, *J. M. Synge: 1871–1909* (New York: Macmillan, 1959), p. 10.

49.   Ibid., p. 11.

50.   Synge, *Aran Islands,* p. 44. Synge's opposition to the Boer War also separated him from conventional Anglo-Irish attitudes. See Edward Stephens, *My Uncle John* (London: Oxford University Press, 1974), p. 152.

51.   J. M. Synge, 'Autobiography', *Prose,* p. 13.

52.   Kiberd, *Synge and the Irish Language* 2nd ed. (1979; Dublin: Glll and Macmillan, 1993), p. 19.

53.   In fact his many visits to the Aran Islands between 1898 and 1902 enabled him 'to become a competent speaker of the language'. Ibid., p. 43.

54.   Synge was to claim that the *Spirit of the Nation* made him 'commit my most serious literary error; I thought it excellent for a considerable time and then repented bitterly'. 'Autobiography', *Prose,* p. 13.

55.   Letter to Maud Gonne, 6 Apr. 1897, *Collected Letters of John Millington Synge, vol. 1: 1871–1907,* ed. Ann Saddlemyer (Oxford: Clarendon Press, 1983), p. 47.

56.   The co-operative movement.

57.   J. M. Synge, 'Le mouvement intellectuel irlandais', *L'Européen,* 31 May 1902, *Prose,* p. 378. Translation, Michael Egan, unpublished.

58.   Synge, 'Le mouvement', p. 378.

59. 'By 1911 it had spent £10 million and bought two and a half million acres out-right from the smallest tenants and sold them to more solvent neighbours.' West, *Horace Plunkett*, p. 32.

60. West, *Horace Plunkett*, p. 32.

61. J. M. Synge, 'Among the Relief Works', *Prose*, pp. 296–8.

62. J. M. Synge, 'The Kelp-Makers', *Prose*, p. 308.

63. Ibid., p. 307.

64. Hyde, 'The Necessity for De-Anglicising Ireland', p. 79.

65. J. M. Synge, 'Erris', *Prose*, p. 327.

66. J. M. Synge, 'Possible Remedies', *Prose*, p. 341. On the complexities of intro-ducing new innovations to the congested districts, Synge had the following to say: 'In all these works it needs care and tact to induce the people to undertake new methods of work; but the talk sometimes heard of sloth and ignorance has not much foundation. The people have traditional views and instincts about agriculture and live stock [*sic*], and they have a perfectly natural slowness to adopt the advice of an official expert who knows nothing of the peculiar condi-tions of their native place. The advice is often excellent, but there have been a sufficient number of failures in the work done by the Congested Districts Board . . . to make the conservatism of the people a sign of, perhaps, valuable pru-dence (p. 340).

67. J. M. Synge, 'Between the Bays of Carraroe', *Prose*, p. 294.

68. *Irish Homestead*, 9 Nov. 1901, p. 744. A prize fund of £45 was sponsored by Plunkett. 'The old forms of rural life, the tales told round the hearth, the songs, the music of pipes and fiddle, the dances, and all that kept the heart warm, are daily only becoming memories to the old; and a sterile social life, without beauty or interest, is taking its place.' *Irish Homestead*, 20 Oct. 1900, p. 673.

69. J. M. Synge, Letter to Stephen MacKenna, 13 July 1905, *Prose*, p. 283n.

70. Ibid., p. 283. The extent to which the plight of the landless labourers was ignored by the UIL has been pointed out by Paul Bew in *Conflict and Concilia-tion in Ireland 1890–1910* (Oxford: Clarendon, 1987), pp. 76–7.

71. West, *Horace Plunkett*, p. 32.

72. Synge, 'Erris' *Prose*, p. 327.

73. J. M. Synge, 'The Village Shop', *Prose*, p. 330.

74. See *Irish Homestead*, 'The 'Legitimate Interests of the Traders'', 10 Sept. 1898, p. 767; 'The Enemies of Co-operation', 17 Dec. 1898, p. 1031; 28 Jan. 1899. Also *Freeman's Journal*, 19 Jan. 1899; 23 Jan. 1899. See also Michael McAteer, 'Reac-tionary Conservatism or Radical Utopianism? AE and the Irish Cooperative Movement', *Éire-Ireland* 35.3/4 (Fall/Winter 2000), p. 151.

75. 'The Legitimate Interests' of the Traders', *Irish Homestead*, 10 Sept. 1898, p. 767. The article continues: 'We are not sure that their 'legitimate interests' will bear examination, and we think they would be well advised to say as little as possi-ble about them. Indeed, what their 'legitimate interests' are, and why they must not be interfered with, we have never been able to discover . . . But if the farm-ers co-operate to start stores, or even to purchase to the best advantage their seeds, implements, and manures, they are indignantly warned off as trespassers. By what right are they warned off?

76. Letter to Stephen MacKenna, 13 July 1905, *Prose*, p. 283n.

77. Kiberd, *Synge and the Irish Language*, p. 214.

78.   As recent scholars have pointed out, it is important not to overstate the decline in Gaelic literary activity in the centuries after Kinsale. Breandán Ó Buachalla has argued that a resistance to contemporary socio-political realities during the eighteenth century produced one of the richest chapters in Gaelic literary history. See 'Canóin na Creille: An file ar leaba a bháis', *Nua-Léamha: Gnéithe de Chultúr, Stair agus Polaitíocht na hÉireann c.1600–c.1900*, ed. Máirín Ní Dhonnchadha (Baile Átha Cliath: An Clóchomhar Tta, 1996), pp. 149–69. See also Philip O'Leary, *The Prose Literature of the Gaelic Revival, 1881–1921* (PA: Pennsylvania State University Press, 1994), p. 3.

79.   J. M. Synge, 'Le Mouvement', *Prose*, pp. 381–2. Unpub. trans., Michael Egan. Seumas MacManus records that the singing of the Irish songs was led 'by William Rooney and some fellow enthusiasts' and that Ethna Carbery was moved to commemorate this event in her verse, 'A Gaelic Song'. The poem begins: 'A murmurous tangle of voices/Laughter to left and right/We waited the curtain's rising/In a glare of electric light/When down through the din came, slowly/Softly, then clear and strong/The mournful minor cadence/Of a sweet old Gaelic song.' *The Story of the Irish Race* (1921; Connecticut: Devin-Adair, 1990), p. 684.

80.   This issue had already been broached by Peadar Ua Laoghaire (see below).

81.   Sean O'Casey, *Drums Under the Window*, p. 73.

82.   Maume, *D. P. Moran*, p. 8.

83.   *United Irishman*, 12 Jan. 1901.

84.   Having invested considerable time and effort in studying the language, 'he was not only competent in spoken Irish but was also conversant with the literary language in all its phases from the classical Irish of 1200 to the idiom of contemporary literature' (Kiberd, *Synge and the Irish Language*, p. 54).

85.   David Greene, *The Irish Language* (1966; Cork: Mercier Press, 1972), p. 12. 'It was at this stage [twelfth century] that the momentous decision was taken to establish a comprehensive standard literary language. We do not know who devised this language but presumably it was the poets. At any rate we have ample evidence of the thoroughness with which they did their work in the professional poetry and to a lesser extent in the prose of the next four hundred years or more, from about 1200 AD until after 1600.' Brian Ó Cuív, 'The Changing Form of the Irish Language', *A View of the Irish Language*, ed. Brian Ó Cuív, p. 27.

86.   Greene, *The Irish Language*, p. 13.

87.   Ibid., p. 27.

88.   J. M. Synge, 'Le Mouvement', p. 377.

89.   See Gearóid Denver, 'Decolonizing the Mind: Language and Literature in Ireland', *New Hibernia Review* 1.1 (Spring 1997), pp. 44–68.

90.   See 'The Poems of Geoffrey Keating' (*Prose*, pp. 356–9) and 'An Irish Historian' (*Prose*, pp. 361–3) for Synge's appraisal of one of the masters of classical Irish literature. The significance of Keating to Synge is discussed by Declan Kiberd in *Synge and the Irish Language* (pp. 54–76).

91.   Michael Cronin, *Translating Ireland* (Cork: Cork University Press, 1996), p. 149.

92.   Ibid., p. 149.

93.   Ibid., p. 155.

94.   Ibid., p. 155. The Gaelic League initially preferred the anachronistic, if strikingly distinctive, Gaelic type and harboured 'a prejudice against Roman type, which

gave rise to the most extraordinary arguments based on sentiment rather than on reason'. Learners were also hampered by the fact that Fr Dineen's landmark dictionary of 1904 'made an antiquated and cumbersome spelling the norm'. (Ó Cuív, 'The Changing Form of the Irish Language', p. 25.)

95. Patrick Pearse 'in his critical writings advocated the creation of a new literature which would take modern European literature for its model and which would be based on the living speech of the Gaeltacht'. Gearóid S. MacEoin, 'Twentieth Century Irish Literature', *A View of the Irish Language*, ed. Brian Ó Cuív (Dublin: Stationery Office, 1969), p. 60. See also Philip O'Leary, *Prose Literature*, pp. 30–3.

96. The annual competitive convention of the Gaelic League was founded in 1897. It awarded prizes for essay writing, poetry, folklore, short stories, the novel, history, Irish language primers and drama, among other cultural activities. It did more than any other institution to revive a vigorous Irish literature in Irish. It also standardized other traditional cultural practices – most notably dancing – by laying down strict rules for competition entry. Often participants in non-language competitions would have to pass a language test before being allowed to compete. 'Sar a dtosnófar ar iomaíocht an rinc déan far na hiarrthóirí go léir a scrúdú sa Ghaeilge. Ní leigfear isteach éinne go dteipfidh air san scrúdú so. [Before the commencement of the dancing competition each competitor will have completed the Irish test. Anyone who fails this test will not be allowed to compete.] Donncha Ó Súilleabháin, *Sceál an Oireachtas 1897–1924* (Baile Átha Cliath: An Clóchomhar Tta, 1984), p. 117.

97. Greene *The Irish Language*, p. 13.

98. Chief among the supporters of the revival of classical Irish was Risteard de Hindeberg. He was of the opinion that: 'Irish lost its mainstay when, after long centuries of activity, it ceased to be written, and fell entirely under the feeble guardianship of oral transmission, to suffer the rapid wearing process fated to all rude tongues lacking the back-bone of a fixed literary canon . . . This want of a living literature must be supplied as quickly as may be. Our scholars must write to provide it . . . Our native Irish speakers, of whatever province soever, can easily by training correct their vernacular to the normal [sic] of the last Classic writers . . . The head-waters are abundant to over-flowing; we have but to make a staunch joint in the broken conduit, and the flow will go on copious and sparkling like long ago.' *Irishleabhar na Gaedhilge*, 1892, pp. 142–3. Cited in Cathal Ó Háinle, 'Ó Chaint na nDaoine go dtí an Caighdeán Oifigiúil', *Stair Na Gaeilge*, eds. Kim McCone et al. (Maigh Nuad: Coláiste Phádraig, 1994, pp. 745–93).

99. 'I became fully aware of the fact that we had absolutely nothing at all in the form of a book to put in the hand of a child so as to teach him Gaelic. As a result, I decided to write a special book for our young people, a book whose language would be free from the faults which could be found with most of the language of the poets, a book with language which would suit our young people, which would appeal to them. Such was the reflection which set me to writing *Séadna*.' Peter O'Leary, *My Story*, trans. Cyril Ó Céirín (Oxford: Oxford University Press, 1987), p. 157.

100. Ó Cuív, 'The Changing Form of the Irish Language', p. 33.

101. Letter to *An Claidheamh Soluis*, 14 Dec. 1899. Cited in Brendán Delap, *Úrscéalta Stairiúla na Gaeilge* (Baile Átha Cliath: An Clóchomhar Tta, 1993), p. 17.

102. Cronin, *Translating Ireland*, p. 149.
103. Ibid., p. 149.
104. Peter O'Leary, *Papers on Irish Idiom*, cited in Cronin, *Translating Ireland*, p. 149.
105. 'Irish Prose Composition', *Leader*, 26 Oct. 1901, pp. 139–40.
106. Synge, *Aran Islands*, p. 68.
107. Ibid., p. 68.
108. Ibid., p. 85. This would tend to back up the claim made by Peadar Ua Laoghaire that 'When the two tongues were mixed, without any cultivation being done to either of them, what happened was that many people were left floundering in both languages'. *My Story*, trans. Cyril Ó Céirín, p. 150.
109. Philip O'Leary also makes this point. *Prose Literature*, p. 13.
110. J. M. Synge, *Prose*, p. 383n.
     By 1907 this frustration would develop into a total rejection of 'the incoherent twaddle that is passed off as Irish by the Gaelic League', which, he felt, had become 'gushing, cowardly and maudlin'. 'Can We Go Back into Our Mother's Womb?', *Prose*, pp. 399–400.
111. See O'Leary, *Prose Literature*, 73–90.
112. J. M. Synge, 'An Irish Historian', *Prose*, p. 361.
113. Synge, 'The Old and the New in Ireland', *Prose*, p. 383.
114. J. M. Synge, 'A Translation of Irish Romance', *Prose*, p. 372.
115. Synge, *Aran Islands*, p. 123.
116. Cronin, *Translating Ireland*, p. 141.
117. Synge, 'The Old and the New in Ireland', *Prose*, p. 385.
118. J. M. Synge, 'An Epic of Ulster', *Prose*, p. 367.
119. Synge recounts the original story upon which the play is based in *The Aran Islands*, pp. 26–28.
120. Synge, *Aran Islands*, p. 28.
121. *United Irishman*, 17 Oct. 1903, p. 1.
122. Synge, 'An Epic of Ulster', *Prose*, p. 369.
123. Declan Kiberd, *Synge and the Irish Language*, p. xix.
124. Examples of 'unconventional' female behaviour include: 'shouting down a confused babble of satire and praise' at men working at the bottom of the cliff on which they gathered (p. 25); a young woman leans 'across my knees to look nearer at some photograph that pleased her' (p. 60); Synge is surrounded by a crowd of women who 'begin jeering and shrieking at me because I am not married. A dozen screamed at a time, and so rapidly that I could not understand all they were saying, yet I was able to make out that they were taking advantage of the absence of their husbands to give me the full volume of their contempt (p. 90).
125. Synge, *Aran Islands*, p. 95.
126. All quotations from the play are taken from *J. M. Synge: Collected Works vol. III*, ed. Ann Saddlemyer, London: Oxford University Press, 1968 (p. 49). Further references will be noted parenthetically.
127. Synge makes many strong innuendoes comparing Nora to a wild mountain ewe. Interestingly, the Tramp mocks Michael's inability to control mountain ewes while Patch Darcy's proficiency in this matter is praised by Nora (p. 47). For a discussion of the importance of sheep allusions in the play, see Nicholas Grene, 'Synge's *The Shadow of the Glen*: Repetition and Allusion', in *Critical Essays on John Millington Synge*, ed. Daniel J. Casey (New York: GK Hall, 1994), pp. 81–9.

128. *United Irishman*, 17 Oct. 1903, p. 1.
129. *United Irishman*, 17 Oct. 1903.
130. J. M. Synge, 'The People of the Glens', *Prose*, p. 224n.
131. J. M. Synge to Stephen McKenna, 28 Jan. 1904, *Collected Letters of John Milling-ton Synge vol. 1 1871–1907*, ed. Ann Saddlemyer (Oxford: Clarendon Press, 1983), p. 74.
132. J. M. Synge, 'The Oppression of the Hills', *Prose*, p. 211.
133. *Irish Homestead*, 18 May 1895.
134. See Nancy Armstrong, *Desire and Domestic Fiction: A Political History of the Novel* (New York, OUP, 1987). 'To consider the rise of the domestic woman as a major event in political history is not, as it may seem, to present a contradiction in terms, but to identify the paradox that shapes modern culture. It is also to trace the history of a specifically modern form of desire that, during the early eight-eenth century, changed the criteria for determining what was most important in a female.' (p. 3)
135. *Irish Homestead*, 9 Mar. 1895, p. 13.
136. 'To her went authority over the household, leisure time, courtship procedures, and kinship relations, and under her jurisdiction the most basic qualities of human identity were supposed to develop.' Armstrong, *Desire and Domestic Fiction*, p. 3.
137. Joanna Burke, *Husbandry to Housewifery: Women, Economic Change and House Work in Ireland 1890–1914* (Oxford: Clarendon Press, 1993), p. 263. See also James MacPhearson, '"Ireland Begins in the Home": Women, Irish National Iden-tity, and the Domestic Sphere in the *Irish Homestead*, 1896–1912', *Éire-Ireland* 36.3/4 (Fall/Winter 2001), pp. 131–52.

Reviving the Revival

1. See Regan, 'W. B. Yeats and Irish Cultural Politics in the 1890s', for a discussion of this analysis.
2. Yeats writes: 'Meanwhile I had begun a movement in English, in the language in which modern Ireland thinks and does its business; founded certain societies where clerks, working men, men of all classes, could study the Irish poets, nov-elists and historians who had written in English, and as much of Gaelic litera-ture as had been translated into English'. *Autobiographies*, p. 559.

BIBLIOGRAPHY

Anderson, Benedict. *Imagined Communities: Reflections on the Origin and Spread of Nationalism.* Revised ed. 1983; London: Verso, 1991.

Armstrong, Nancy. *Desire and Domestic Fiction: A Political History of the Novel.* New York, Oxford University Press 1987.

Arnold, Bruce. 'Synge and Jack Yeats in the Congested Districts'. *Times Literary Supplement* (16 Dec. 1994): 12.

Arnold, Matthew. 'On the Study of Celtic Literature'. In *Poetry and Ireland Since 1800.* Ed. M. Storey. London: Routledge, 1988. 61–8.

Atkinson, Robert. *The Irish Language and Irish Intermediate Education IV: Dr Atkinson's Evidence*, Gaelic League Pamphlet no. 14. Dublin: Gaelic League, 1901.

Barker, Francis, Peter Hulme and Margaret Iverson (eds.). *Colonial Discourse/Postcolonial Theory.* Manchester: Manchester University Press, 1994.

Beckett, J. C. *The Making of Modern Ireland 1603–1923.* 2nd ed. 1966; London: Faber and Faber, 1981.

Belfield, Eversley. *The Boer War.* 1975; London: Leo Cooper, 1993.

Bence-Jones, Mark. *Twlight of the Ascendancy.* London: Constable, 1987.

Bew, Paul. *Conflict and Conciliation in Ireland 1890–1910.* Oxford: Clarendon,1987.

Bhabha, Homi (ed.). *Nation and Narration.* London: Routledge, 1990.

Bickley, Francis L. *J. M. Synge and the Irish Dramatic Movement.* London: Constable, 1912.

Borthwick, Norma. *The Irish Language and Irish Intermediate Education I: Answers to Queries.* Gaelic League Pamphlet no. 11. Dublin: Gaelic League, 1901.

Bourgeois, Maurice. *John Millington Synge: The Irish Theatre.* New York: Benjamin Blom, 1956.

Bourke, Joanna. *Husbandry to Housewifery: Women, Economic Change and House Work in Ireland 1890–1914.* Oxford: Clarendon Press, 1993.

Bowen, Elizabeth. *Seven Winters.* Dublin: Cuala Press, 1942.

Bowen, Zack. *Padraic Colum.* Carbondale: S. Illinois University Press, 1970.

Boyce, D. George. *Ireland 1828–1923: From Ascendancy to Democracy.* Oxford: Blackwell, 1992.

Boyd, Ernest A. *Ireland's Literary Renaissance.* Dublin: Maunsel, 1916.

Bradley, Anthony and Maryan Gialanella Valiulis. *Gender and Sexuality in Modern Ireland.* Amherst: University of Massachusetts Press, 1997.

Bradshaw, Brendan. 'Nationalism and Historical Scholarship in Modern Ireland'. *Irish Historical Studies* 26.104 (1989): 329–51.

Brady, Ciaran. *Ideology and the Historians*. Dublin: Lilliput, 1991.

Brennan, Tim. 'The National Longing for Form'. In *Nation and Narration*. Ed. H. Bhabha. London: Routledge, 1990. 44–70.

Breuilly, J. *Nationalism and the State*. Manchester: Manchester University Press, 1982.

Brown, Malcolm. *George Moore: A Reconsideration*. Seattle: University of Washington Press, 1955.

———. *The Politics of Irish Literature from Thomas Davis to W. B. Yeats*. London: Allen and Unwin, 1972.

Brown, Terence. *Ireland: A Social and Cultural History 1922–1985*. Rev. ed. 1981; London: Fontana, 1987.

———. 'Cultural Nationalism'. In *Field Day Anthology* vol. 2. Ed. S. Deane. Derry: Field Day, 1991. 516–20.

———. *The Life of W. B. Yeats*. Dublin: Gill and Macmillan, 1999.

Bushrui, Suheil B. *Yeats's Verse Plays: The Revisions 1900–10*. Oxford: Oxford University Press, 1962.

———. (ed.) *Sunshine and the Moon's Delight: A Centenary Tribute to John Millington Synge, 1871–1909*. Gerrards Cross: Colin Smythe, 1972.

Caerwyn-Williams, J. E. and P. K. Ford. *The Irish Literary Tradition*. Cardiff: University of Wales Press, 1992.

Cairns, David and Shaun Richards. *Writing Ireland: Colonialism, Nationalism and Culture*. Manchester: Manchester University Press, 1988.

Cardozo, Nancy. *Lucky Eyes and a High Heart: The Life of Maud Gonne*. New York: Bobbs and Merrill, 1978.

Carleton, William. 'Introduction to *Traits and Stories of the Irish Peasantry*'. *The Works of William Carleton,* vol. 2. New York: Books for Libraries Press, 1970. 641–53.

Casey, Daniel, J. *Views of the Irish Peasantry 1800–1916*. Hamden: Archon Books, 1977.

———. (ed.) *Critical Essays on John Millington Synge*. New York: GK Hall, 1994.

Chatterjee, Partha. *Nationalist Thought and the Colonial World: A Derivative Discourse*. London: Zed Books, 1986.

———. *The Nation and Its Fragments: Colonial and Postcolonial Histories*. Princeton: Princeton University Press, 1993.

Clark, David R. *W. B. Yeats and the Theatre of Desolate Reality*. Rev. ed. Washington: Catholic University of America Press, 1993.

Clarke, Brenna Katz. *The Emergence of the Irish Peasant Play at the Abbey Theatre*. Essex: Bowker Publishing, 1982.

——— and H. Ferrar. *The Dublin Drama League 1919–1941*. Dublin: Dolmen Press, 1979.

Clery, Arthur. 'The Gaelic League: 1893–1919'. *Studies* 8 (1919): 398–408.

Colum, Padraic. 'Concerning a Creamery'. *Dana: An Irish Magazine of Independent Thought* (Nov. 1904): 205–8.

———. *Arthur Griffith*. Dublin: Brown and Nowlan, 1959.

——. *Three Plays: The Land, The Fiddler's House, Thomas Muskerry*. Dublin: A. Figgis, 1963.

Connolly, James. *The Words of James Connolly*. Ed. James Connolly Heron. Cork: Mercier, 1966.

——. *Selected Writings*. Ed. P. Berresford Ellis. 1973; London: Pluto Press, 1988.

Connor, Steven. *Postmodernist Culture: An Introduction to Theories of the Contemporary*. Oxford: Basil Blackwell, 1989.

Coolahan, John. *Irish Education: History and Structure*. Dublin: Institute of Public Administration, 1981.

Corkery, Daniel. *The Hidden Ireland*. 1924; Dublin: Gill and Macmillan, 1967.

——. *Synge and Anglo-Irish Literature*. Cork: Mercier, 1966.

Costello, Peter. *The Heart Grown Brutal: The Irish Revolution in Literature from Parnell to the Death of Yeats 1891–1939*. Dublin: Gill and Macmillan, 1978.

Cronin, Michael. *Translating Ireland*. Cork: Cork University Press, 1996.

Cullen, Louis M. 'The Hidden Ireland: Reassessment of a Concept'. *Studia Hibernica* 9 (1969): 7–47.

Curtis, L. P. *Apes and Angels: The Irishman in Victorian Caricature*. Washington: Smithsonian Institution Press, 1971.

Daniels, William L. 'AE and Synge in the Congested Districts'. *Éire-Ireland* 11.4 (1976): 14–26.

Davis, Robert Bernard. *George Russell (AE)*. London: George Prior, 1977.

Deane, Seamus. *Celtic Revivals: Essays in Modern Irish Literature 1880–1980*. London: Faber and Faber, 1985.

——. *A Short History of Irish Literature*. London: Hutchinson, 1986.

——. (ed.) *The Field Day Anthology of Irish Writing*. 3 vols. Derry: Field Day, 1991.

——. *Strange Country: Modernity and Nationhood in Irish Writing since 1790*. Oxford: Oxford University Press, 1997.

De Burca, Marcus. *The GAA: A History*. Dublin: Cumann Lúthcleas Gael, 1980.

De Freine, Sean. *The Great Silence*. Cork: Mercier, 1978.

de Jubainville, Henri D'Arbois. *Le cycle mythologique irlandais*. Paris: Thorin, 1884.

Deutsch-Brady, Chantal. 'The King's Visit and the People's Protection Committee, 1903'. *Éire-Ireland* 10.4 (1975): 3–10.

Delap, Brendán. *Úrscéalta Stairiúla na Gaeilge*. Baile Átha Cliath: An Clóchomhar Tta., 1993.

Denver, Gearóid. 'Decolonizing the Mind: Language and Literature in Ireland'. *New Hibernia Review* 1.1 (Spring 1997): 44–68.

Digby, Margaret. Horace Plunkett: An Anglo-American Irishman. Oxford: Blackwell, 1949.

Dobbins, Gregory. 'Whenever Green Is Red: James Connolly and Postcolonial Theory', *Nepantla: Views from South* 1.3 (2000): 605–48.

Dowling, P. J. *A History of Irish Education: A Study in Conflicting Loyalties*. Cork: Mercier, 1971.

Dudley Edwards, Ruth. *Patrick Pearse: The Triumph of Failure*. 1977; Dublin: Poolbeg, 1990.

——. *James Connolly*. Dublin: Gill and Macmillan, 1981.

Duggan, G. C. *The Stage Irishman*. London: Longmans, Green & Co., 1937.

Dunleavy, Janet Egleson and Gareth W. Dunleavy. *Douglas Hyde: A Maker of Modern Ireland*. Berkeley: University of California Press, 1991.

Eagleton, Terry. *Heathcliff and the Great Hunger: Studies in Irish Culture*. London: Verso, 1995.

——. 'The Ideology of Irish Studes'. *Bullán* 3.1 (Spring 1997): 5–14.

——. *Crazy John and the Bishop and other Essays on Irish Culture*. Cork: Cork University Press/Field Day, 1998.

——. *Scholars and Rebels in Nineteenth-Century Ireland*. Oxford: Blackwell, 1999.

Edwards, Philip. 'Shakespeare and the Politics of the Irish Revival'. *The Internationalism of Irish Literature and Drama*. Ed. Joseph McMinn. Gerrards Cross: Colin Smythe, 1992.

Edwards, Ruth Dudley. *Patrick Pearse: The Triumph of Failure*. 1977; Dublin: Poolbeg, 1990.

Eglinton, John [William Kirkpatrick Magee]. 'What Should Be the Subjects of a National Drama'. In *Field Day Anthology*, vol. 3. Ed. S. Deane. Derry: Field Day, 1991. 956–63.

Ellis-Fermor, Una. *The Irish Dramatic Movement*. Rev. ed. London: Methuen, 1954.

Ellmann, Richard. *Yeats: The Man and the Masks*. 2nd ed. 1948; London: Penguin, 1979.

——. *James Joyce*. Rev. ed. 1959; Oxford: Oxford University Press, 1982.

Fanning, Ronan. *Independent Ireland*. Dublin: Helicon, 1983.

——. 'The Meaning of Revisionism'. *The Irish Review* 4, (1988) 15–19.

Fay, Frank. *Towards a National Theatre: Dramatic Criticism*. Ed. and intro. by Robert Hogan. Dublin: Dolmen, 1970.

Fay, Gerard. *The Abbey Theatre*. London: Hollis & Carter, 1958.

Feeney, William J., ed. Maeve: *A Psychological Drama in Two Acts by Edward Martyn and* The Last Feast of the Fianna *by Alice Milligan*. Chicago: De Paul University, 1967.

Fingall, Countess Elizabeth. *Seventy Years Young: Memories of Elizabeth Countess of Fingall*. 1937; Dublin: Lilliput, 1991.

Finneran, Richard, George Mills Harper and William M. Murphy (eds.). *Letters to W. B. Yeats*. 2 vols. New York: Columbia University Press, 1971.

Flannery, James W. *Miss Annie F. Horniman and the Abbey Theatre*. Irish Theatre Series no. 3. Dublin: Dolmen, 1970.

——. *W. B. Yeats and the Idea of a Theatre: The Early Abbey Theatre in Theory and Practice*. New Haven: Yale University Press, 1976.

Foster, John Wilson. *Colonial Consequences: Essays in Irish Literature and Culture*. Lilliput: Dublin, 1991.

Foster, Roy F. *Modern Ireland 1600–1972*. London: Penguin, 1989.

——. (ed.) *The Oxford History of Ireland*. Oxford: Oxford University Press, 1992.

——. *Paddy and Mr. Punch: Connections in Irish and English History*. London: Penguin, 1993.

——. *W. B. Yeats: A Life, I: The Apprentice Mage*. Oxford: Oxford University Press, 1997.

——. *The Irish Story: Telling Tales and Making it up in Ireland*. London: Allen Lane, 2001.

Frazier, Adrian. *Behind the Scenes: Yeats, Horniman, and the Struggle for the Abbey Theatre*. Berkeley: University of California Press, 1990.

——. 'Queering the Irish Renaissance: The Masculinities of Moore, Martyn, and Yeats'. In *Gender and Sexuality in Modern Ireland*. Eds. Anthony Bradley and Maryann Gialanella Valiulis. Amherst: University of Massachusetts Press, 1997. 8–38.

——. *George Moore, 1852–1933*. New Haven: Yale University Press, 2000.

Freeman, John. *A Portrait of George Moore*. 1922; London: T. Werner Laurie, 1971.

Friel, Brian. *Dancing at Lughnasa*. London: Faber and Faber, 1990.

Gaelic League. *Special Pamphlets on Education No.s 1–27*. Dublin: Gaelic League, 1900–02.

Gailey, Andrew. *Ireland and the Death of Kindness: The Experience of Constructive Unionism 1890–1905*. Cork: Cork University Press, 1987.

Garvin, Tom. *The Evolution of Irish Nationalist Politics*. Dublin: Gill and Macmillan, 1981.

——. *1922: The Birth of Irish Democracy*. Dublin: Gill and Macmillan, 1996.

Gellner, Ernst. *Nations and Nationalism*. Oxford: Blackwell, 1983.

Gibbons, Luke. 'Political Writings and Speeches 1850–1918'. In *Field Day Anthology*, vol. 2. Ed. S. Deane. Derry: Field Day, 1991. 332–9.

——. *Transformations in Irish Culture*. Cork: Cork University Press/Field Day, 1996.

Gilbert, Paul. 'The Idea of a National Literature'. In *Literature and the Political Imagination*. Eds. John Horton and Andrea T. Baumeister London: Routledge, 1996.

Gilroy, Paul. *'There Ain't No Black in the Union Jack'*. 1987; Chicago: University of Chicago Press, 1991.

——. *The Black Atlantic: Modernity and Double Consciousness*. Cambridge, MA: Harvard University Press, 1993.

Glandon, Virginia E. 'Index of Irish Newspapers 1900–1922 (Part 1)'. *Éire-Ireland* 11.4 (1976): 84–121.

——. 'The Irish Press and Revolutionary Irish Nationalism'. *Éire-Ireland* 16.1 (1981): 21–33.

——. *Arthur Griffith and the Advanced-Nationalist Press Ireland, 1900–1922*. New York: Peter Lang, 1985.

Goldring, Maurice. *Pleasant the Scholar's Life: Irish Intellectuals and the Con-struction of a Nation State*. London: Serif, 1994.

Gonne MacBride, Maud. *A Servant of the Queen*. 1938; London: Victor Gol-lancz, 1974.

Greaves, C. Desmond. *The Life and Times of James Connolly*. London: Lawrence and Wishart, 1976.

Greene, David H. 'Robert Atkinson and Irish Studies'. *Hermathena* 102 (1966): 6–15.

——. 'The Founding of the Gaelic League'. In *The Gaelic League Idea*. Ed. S. Ó Tuama. Cork: Mercier, 1972. 9–31.

Greene, David H. and Edward M. Stephens. *J. M. Synge, 1871–1909*. New York: Macmillan, 1959.

Gregory, Lady Augusta. 'Ireland Real and Ideal'. *Nineteenth Century* 44 (Nov. 1898): 769–82.

——. (ed.) *Ideals in Ireland*. London: Unicorn, 1901.

——. *Cuchulain of Muirthemne*. 1902; Gerrards Cross: Colin Smythe, 1970.

——. *Our Irish Theatre*. 1913; New York: Capricorn Books, 1965.

——. *The Collected Plays of Lady Gregory*. 4 vols. Ed. and foreword by Ann Saddlemyer. Gerrards Cross: Colin Smythe, 1970.

——. *Seventy Years: Being the Autobiography of Lady Gregory*. Ed. and foreword by Colin Smythe. Gerrards Cross: Colin Smythe, 1974.

——. *Selected Writings*. Ed. Lucy MacDiarmuid. London: Penguin, 1995.

Grene, Nicholas. *The Politics of Irish Drama: Plays in Context from Boucicault to Friel*. Cambridge: Cambridge University Press, 1999.

Gross, John, ed. *Rudyard Kipling: The Man, His Work and His World*. London: Weidenfeld and Nicolson, 1972.

Gwynn, Denis. *Edward Martyn and the Irish Literary Revival*. London: Jonathan Cape, 1930.

Gwynn, Stephen. *Experiences of a Literary Man*. London: Thornton Butter-worth, 1926.

Hand, Derek. *John Banville: Exploring Fictions*. Dublin: Liffey Press, 2002.

Henry, Robert Mitchell. *The Evolution of Sinn Féin*. Dublin: Talbot Press.

Hirsh, Edward. 'The Gallous Story and the Dirty Deed: The Two Playboys'. *Modern Drama* 26.1 (1983): 85–102.

Hobsbawm, Eric. *The Invention of Tradition*. Cambridge: Cambridge University Press, 1983.

——. *Nations and Nationalism since 1780*. Cambridge: Cambridge University Press, 1990.

Hobson, Bulmer. *Ireland Yesterday and Tomorrow*. Tralee: Anvil Books, 1968.

Hogan, Robert (ed.). *Towards a National Theatre: The Dramatic Criticism of Frank J. Fay*. Dublin: Dolmen Press, 1970.

—— and James Kilroy. *Lost Plays of the Irish Renaissance*. Dixon, CA: Prosce-nium Press, 1970.

——. *The Modern Irish Drama: A Documentary History*, vol. 1 *The Irish Literary*

Theatre 1899–1901. Dublin: Dolmen, 1975; vol. 2. *Laying the Foundations 1902–1904*. Dublin: Dolmen, 1976; vol. 3. *The Abbey Theatre: The Years of Synge 1905–1909*. Dublin: Dolmen, 1978; vol. 4. *The Rise of the Realists 1910–1915*. Eds. Robert Hogan, Richard Burnham and Daniel P. Poteet. Dublin: Dolmen, 1976.

Holloway, Joseph. *Joseph Holloway's Abbey Theatre: A Selection from His Unpublished Journal 'Impressions of a Dublin Playgoer'*. Eds. Robert Hogan and Michael J. O'Neill. Illinois: S. Illinois University Press, 1967.

Howes, Majorie. *Yeats's Nations: Gender, Class, and Irishness*. Cambridge: Cambridge University Press, 1996.

Hunt, Hugh. *The Abbey Theatre: Ireland's National Theatre 1904–1979*. Dublin: Gill and Macmillan, 1979.

Hutchinson, John. *The Dynamics of Cultural Nationalism: The Gaelic Revival and the Creation of the Irish Nation State*. London: Allen and Unwin, 1987.

Hyde, Douglas. *The Songs of Connacht*. Ed. and intro. by Breandán Ó Conaíre. Dublin: Irish Academic Press, 1985.

——. 'The Necessity for De-Anglicising Ireland'. In *Poetry and Ireland Since 1800*. Ed. M. Storey. London: Routledge, 1988. 78–84.

——. *A Literary History of Ireland*. 1899; London: Ernest Benn, 1967.

——. 'A University Scandal'. *New Ireland Review* (Dec. 1899).

——. *The Irish Language and Intermediate Education III: Dr Hyde's Evidence*. Gaelic League Pamphlet no. 13. Dublin: Gaelic League, 1901.

——. *The Irish Language and Irish Intermediate Education VI: Dr. Hyde's Reply to Dr. Atkinson*. Gaelic League Pamphlet no. 16. Dublin: Gaelic League, 1901.

——. *Casadh an tSúgáin*. Trans. Lady A. Gregory. Baile Átha Cliath: An Cló-Chumann: 1905.

Inglis, Tom. *The Catholic Church in Modern Irish Society*. Dublin: Gill and Macmillan, 1987.

Innes, C. L. *Woman and Nation in Irish Literature and Society 1880–1935*. London: Harvester Wheatsheaf, 1993.

Jackson, Alvin. 'The Failure of Unionism in Dublin, 1900'. *Irish Historical Studies* 26.104 (Nov. 1989): 376–95.

Johnston, Sheila Turner. *Alice: A Life of Alice Milligan*. Omagh: Columnpoint Press, 1994.

Jordan, Anthony J. *Major John MacBride 1865–1916*. Westport: Westport Historical Society, 1991.

Joyce, James. *Dubliners*. Intro. and notes by Terence Brown. London: Penguin, 1992.

——. *A Portrait of the Artist as a Young Man*. Intro. and notes by Seamus Deane. London: Penguin, 1992.

——. *Ulysses*. Intro. by Declan Kiberd. London: Penguin, 1992.

——. *The Critical Writings of James Joyce*. Eds. Ellsworth Mason and Richard Ellmann. London: Faber & Faber, 1959.

——. *Occasional, Critical, and Political Writing.* Ed. Kevin Barry. Oxford: Oxford University Press, 2000.

Kain, Richard M. *Susan L. Mitchell.* Lewisburg: Bucknell UP, 1972.

—— and James H. O'Brien. *George Russell (AE).* Lewisberg: Bucknell University Press, 1976.

Kavanagh, Peter. *The Story of the Abbey Theatre.* New York: Devin-Adair, 1950.

Kearney, Richard. *Transitions.* Dublin: Wolfhound Press, 1988.

Keatinge, Patrick. *The Formulation of Irish Foreign Policy.* Dublin: Institute of Public Administration, 1973.

——. *A Place Among the Nations: Issues of Irish Foreign Policy.* Dublin: Institute of Public Administration, 1978.

Kennedy, Liam. 'Modern Ireland: Post-Colonial Society or Post-Colonial Pretensions?' *The Irish Review* 13 (1992/3): 107–21.

Kiberd, Declan. *Synge and the Irish Language.* 2nd ed. 1979; Dublin: Gill and Macmillan, 1993.

——. 'The Fall of the Stage Irishman'. *Genres of the Irish Literary Revival.* Ed. R. Schleifer. Dublin: Wolfhound Press, 1980.

——. 'George Moore's Gaelic Lawn Party'. *The Way Back: George Moore's The Untilled Field and The Lake.* Ed. Robert Welch. Dublin: Wolfhound Press, 1982.

——. *Inventing Ireland.* London: Jonathan Cape, 1995.

——. *Irish Classics.* London: Granta, 2000.

Kiely, David, M. *John Millington Synge: A Biography.* Dublin: Gill and Macmillan, 1994.

Kinsella, Thomas. 'The Irish Writer'. In *Field Day Anthology*, Ed. S. Deane. Derry: Field Day, 1991. vol. 3. 625–9.

——. *The Dual Tradition.* Manchester: Carcanet Press, 1995.

Kohfeldt, Mary Lou. *Lady Gregory: The Woman Behind the Irish Renaissance.* London: André Deutsch, 1985.

Kuch, Peter. *Yeats and AE: The Antagonism that Unites Dear Friends.* Gerrards Cross: Colin Smythe, 1986.

Laffan, Michael. *The Resurrection of Ireland: The Sinn Féin Party 1916–1923.* Cambridge: Cambridge University Press, 1999.

Larkin, Emmet. 'The Devotional Revolution in Ireland, 1850–75', *American Historical Review* 77 (1972): 625–52.

Lee, Joseph. *The Modernisation of Irish Society 1848–1918.* 1973; Dublin: Gill and Macmillan, 1979.

Lloyd, David. *Nationalism and Minor Literature: James Clarence Mangan and the Emergence of Irish Cultural Nationalism.* Berkeley: University of California Press, 1987.

——. *Anomalous States: Irish Writing and the Post-Colonial Mind.* Dublin: Lilliput, 1993.

——. 'Cultural Theory and Ireland'. *Bullán* 3.1 (Spring 1997): 87–92.

——. *Ireland after History.* Cork: Cork University Press/Field Day, 1999.

Longley, Edna. *The Living Stream: Literature and Revisionism in Ireland*. Newcastle-Upon-Tyne: Bloodaxe, 1994.

Luddy, Maria. *Hanna Sheehy Skeffington*. Dublin: Historical Association of Ireland, 1995.

Lyons, F. S. L. 'Sir Horace Plunkett: A Centenary Appreciation of His Life and Work'. *Irish Times* (24 Oct. 1954).

——. *Ireland since the Famine*. 2nd ed. 1971; London: Fontana, 1973.

——. *The Irish Parliamentary Party 1890–1919*. Westport, CT: Greenwood Press, 1975.

——. *Culture and Anarchy in Ireland 1890–1939*. Oxford: Clarendon Press, 1979.

Lyons, George. *Some Recollections of Griffith and his Times*. Dublin: Talbot Press, 1923.

Lyons, J. B. *The Enigma of Tom Kettle*. Dublin: Glendale Press, 1983.

MacAodha, Brendan. 'Was This a Social Revolution'. In *The Gaelic League Idea*. Ed. S. Ó Tuama. Cork: Mercier, 1972. 20–30.

McAteer, Michael. 'Reactionary Conservatism or Radical Utopianism? AE and the Irish Cooperative Movement', *Éire-Ireland* 35.3/4 (Fall/Winter 2000): 148–62.

McCarthy, Conor. *Modernisation: Crisis and Culture in Ireland 1969–1992*. Dublin: Four Courts Press, 2000.

McCormack, W. J. *Ascendancy and Tradition in Anglo-Irish Literary History from 1789–1939*. Cork: Cork University Press, 1994.

McCracken, Donal P. *The Irish Pro-Boers 1877–1902*. Johannesburg: Perskor, 1989.

——. '"Fenians and Dutch Carpetbaggers": Irish and Afrikaner Nationalisms, 1877–1930'. *Éire-Ireland* 29.3 (Fall 1994): 109–25.

——. 'The Irish Literary Movement, Irish Doggerel and the Boer War'. *Études Irlandaises* 20.2 (Automne 1995): 97–115.

McDiarmuid, Lucy. 'Augusta Gregory, Bernard Shaw and the Shewing Up of Dublin Castle'. *Publications of the Modern Language Association* 109.1 (Jan. 1994): 26–44.

McDowell, R. B. and W. B. Stanford. *Mahaffy: A Biography of an Anglo-Irishman*. London: Routledge and Kegan Paul, 1971.

McKenna, Lambert. 'The Catholic University of Ireland'. *Irish Ecclesiastical Record*, 31 (1928).

MacKillop, J. 'Beurla on it: Yeats, Joyce and the Irish Language'. *Éire-Ireland* 15.1 (1980) 138–48.

MacManus, Seumas. *The Story of the Irish Race*. 1921; Connecticut: Devin-Adair, 1990.

McMinn, Joseph, Anne McMaster and Angela Welch (eds.). *The Internationalism of Irish Literature and Drama*. Gerrards Cross: Colin Smythe, 1992.

MacPhearson, James. '"Ireland Begins in the Home": Women, Irish National Identity, and the Domestic Sphere in the *Irish Homestead*, 1896–1912', *Éire-Ireland* 36.3/4 (Fall/Winter 2001): 131–52.

McVeagh, John and Andrew Hadfield (eds.). *Strangers to That Land: British Perceptions of Ireland from the Late Reformation to the Famine*. Gerrards Cross: Colin Smythe, 1994.

Mahaffy, J. P. 'The Recent Fuss about the Irish Language'. *Nineteenth Century* 46 (Aug. 1899): 213–22.

——. *Evidence to Vice Regal Inquiry*. Gaelic League Pamphlet no. 12. Dublin: Gaelic League, 1901.

Malcolm, Elizabeth. 'Popular Recreation in Nineteenth-Century Ireland'. In *Irish Culture andNationalism 1750–1950*. Eds. Oliver MacDonagh, W. F. Mandle and Pauric Travers. London: Macmillan, 1983. 40–55.

——. *Ireland Sober, Ireland Free: Drink and Temperance in Nineteenth-Century Ireland*. Dublin: Gill and Macmillan, 1986.

Malone, A. E. *The Irish Drama*. London: Constable, 1929.

Mansergh, Nicholas. *The Irish Question 1840–1921: A Commentary on Anglo-Irish Relations and on Social and Political Forces in Ireland in the Age of Reform and Revolution*. 3rd ed. London: Allen and Unwin, 1975.

Marcus, Philip. *Standish O'Grady*. Lewisburg: Bucknell University Press, 1970.

——. *Yeats and the Beginning of the Irish Renaissance*. 2nd ed. Syracuse: Syracuse University Press, 1987.

Martyn, Edward. *The Heather Field*. Irish Drama Series vol. 1. Chicago: De Paul University, 1966.

——. *Maeve: A Psychological Drama in Two Acts*. In Maeve: A Psychological Drama in Two Acts *by Edward Martyn and* The Last Feast of the Fianna: A Dramatic Legend *by Alice Milligan*. Ed. and intro. by W. J. Feeney. Irish Drama Series vol. 2. Chicago: De Paul University, 1967.

Mathews, P. J. (ed.) *New Voices in Irish Criticism*. Dublin: Four Courts Press, 2000.

Maume, Patrick. *Life that Is Exile: Daniel Corkery and the Search for Irish Ireland*. Belfast: Queens University, 1993.

——. *D. P. Moran*. Dublin: Dundalgan Press, 1995.

——. *The Long Gestation: Irish Nationalist Life 1891–1918*. Dublin: Gill and Macmillan, 1999.

Maxwell, D. E. S. *A Critical History of Modern Irish Drama 1891–1980*. Cambridge: Cambridge University Press, 1984.

Maye, Brian. *Arthur Griffith*. Dublin: Griffith College, 1997.

Memmi, Albert. *The Colonizer and the Colonized*. Trans. H. Greenfeld. New York: Orion Press, 1965.

Meyer, Kuno. *The Voyage of Bran Son of Febal*. London: David Nutt, 1895.

Miller, David W. *Church State and Nation in Ireland 1898–1921*. Dublin: Gill and Macmillan, 1973.

——. 'The Roman Catholic Church in Ireland 1898–1918'. In *Reactions to Irish Nationalism 1865–1914*. Ed. Alan O'Day. London: Hambledon, 1987.

Moody, T. W. 'The Irish University Question of the Nineteenth Century'. *History* 43.148 (1958): 90–109.

Moore, George. *The Bending of the Bough*. Ed. and intro. William J. Feeney. Irish Drama Series vol. 3. Chicago: De Paul University, 1969.

——. 'A Preface to "The Bending of the Bough"'. *Fortnightly Review* 67.398 (1 Feb. 1900): 317–24.

——. 'The Irish Literary Renaissance and the Irish Language'. New Ireland Review (April 1900): 65–72.

——. *Hail and Farewell*. 3 vols. In *Ave, Salve, Vale*. Ed. Richard Allen Cave. 2nd ed. Gerrards Cross: Colin Smythe, 1976.

Moore, George, and W. B. Yeats. *Diarmuid and Grania*. Ed. William J. Feeney with intro. by Anthony Farrow. Irish Drama Series vol. 10. Chicago: De Paul University, 1974.

Moran, D. P. 'Is the Irish Nation Dying?'. *New Ireland Review* (Dec. 1898): 208–14.

——. 'The Future of the Irish Nation'. *New Ireland Review* (Feb. 1899): 345–359.

——. 'The Pale and the Gael'. *New Ireland Review* (June 1899): 230–44.

——. 'Politics, Nationality and Snobs'. *New Ireland Review* (Nov. 1899): 129–43.

——. 'The Gaelic Revival'. *New Ireland Review* (Jan. 1900): 257–72.

——. 'The Battle of Two Civilizations'. *New Ireland Review* (Aug. 1900): 323–37.

——. *The Philosophy of Irish Ireland*. Dublin: James Duffy and Co., 1905.

Morash, Christopher. *A History of Irish Theatre 1601–2000*. Cambridge: Cambridge University Press, 2002.

Morgan, Austen. *James Connolly: A Political Biography*. Manchester: Manchester University Press, 1988.

Morrissey, Thomas J. *Towards a National University: William Delaney s.j. (1895–1924), An Era of Initiative in Irish Education*. Dublin: Wolfhound Press, 1983.

Murphy, Brian P. 'The Canon of Irish Cultural History: Some Questions'. *Studies* 27.305 (1988): 90–109.

——. 'Father Peter Yorke's "Turning of the Tide" (1899): The Strictly Cultural Nationalism of the Early Gaelic League'. *Éire-Ireland* 23.1 (Spring 1988): 35–44.

——. *Patrick Pearse and the Lost Republican Ideal*. Dublin: James Duffy, 1991.

Murphy, James H. *Abject Loyalty: Nationalism and Monarchy in Ireland During the Reign of Queen Victoria*. Cork: Cork University Press, 2001.

Murray, Christopher. *Twentieth-Century Irish Drama: Mirror Up to Nation*. Manchester: Manchester University Press, 1997.

Newey, V., and A. Thomson (eds.) *Literature and Nationalism*. Liverpool: Liverpool University Press, 1991.

Nolan, Emer. *James Joyce and Nationalism*. London: Routledge, 1995.

Nowlan, Kevin. 'The Gaelic League and Other National Movements'. In *The Gaelic League Idea*. Ed. S. Ó Tuama. Cork: Mercier, 1972. 41–51.

O'Brien, Conor Cruise. *The Shaping of Modern Ireland*. London: Routledge & Kegan Paul, 1970.

——. *States of Ireland*. 1972; Hertsfordshire: Panther, 1974.

——. 'Passion and Cunning: An Essay on the Politics of W. B. Yeats'. In *Passion and Cunning: Essays on Nationalism, Terrorism and Revolution*. New York: Simon and Schuster, 1988. 8–61.

——. *Ancestral Voices*. Dublin: Poolbeg, 1994.

Ó Broin, Leon. *Revolutionary Underground: The Story of the Irish Republican Brotherhood*. Dublin: Gill and Macmillan, 1976.

Ó Buachalla, Breandán. 'Canóin na Creille: An file ar leaba a bháis', *Nua-Léamha: Gnéithe de Chultúr, Stair agus Polaitíocht na hÉireann c.1600–c.1900*. Ed. Máirín Ní Dhonnchadha. Baile Átha Cliath: An Clóchomhar Tta., 1996. 149–69.

Ó Buachalla, Séamas. *A Significant Irish Educationalist: The Educational Writings of P. H. Pearse*. Cork: Mercier, 1980.

——. (ed.) *The Letters of P. H. Pearse* (Gerrards Cross: Colin Smythe, 1980).

O'Callaghan, Margaret. 'Language, Nationality and Cultural Identity in the Irish Free State, 1922–7: *The Irish Statesman* and the *Catholic Bulletin* Reappraised'. *Irish Historical Studies* 24 (1984): 226–45.

O'Casey, Sean. *Three Plays*. London: Pan Books, 1980.

——. *Drums Under the Window*. 1945; London: Macmillan, 1981.

——. *Autobiographies*. 2 vols. New York: Carroll and Graf, 1984.

Ó Cearúil, Colm. *Aspail Ar Son na Gaeilge: Timirí Chonradh na Gaeilge 1899–1923*. Baile Átha Cliath: Conradh na Gaeilge, 1995.

Ó Conaire, Pádraic Óg. *Liam Ó Maolruanaidh 1873–1901*. Baile Átha Cliath: Clódhanna Teo., 1975.

Ó Cuív, Brian (ed.) *A View of the Irish Language*. Dublin: Stationery Office, 1969.

O'Donnell, Frank H. *Souls for Gold! Pseudo-Celtic Drama in Dublin*. London: Nassau Press, 1899.

O'Driscoll, Robert, (ed.). *Theatre and Nationalism in Twentieth Century Ireland*. Toronto: University of Toronto Press, 1971.

Ó Fearaíl, Pádraig. *The Story of Conradh na Gaeilge*. Baile Átha Cliath: Clódhanna Teo., 1975.

O'Faolain, Sean. 'Daniel Corkery'. *The Dublin Magazine* 11.2: 49–61.

Ó Fiaich, Tomás. 'The Great Controversy'. In *The Gaelic League Idea*. Ed. S. Ó Tuama. Cork: Mercier, 1972. 63–75.

O'Grady, Standish. 'The New Irish Movement'. *Fortnightly Review* 61.362 (Feb. 1897): 170–9.

——. 'A Wet Day'. *A Celtic Christmas: Being the Christmas Number of the Irish Homestead* (Dec. 1899): 9.

Ó Háinle, Cathal. 'Ó Chaint na nDaoine go dtí an Caighdeán Oifigiúil'. In *Stair Na Gaeilge*. Eds. Kim McCone et al. Maigh Nuad: Coláiste Phádraig, 1994. 745–93.

O'Hegarty, P. S. *A History of Ireland Under the Union 1801–1922*. London: Methuen, 1952.

O'Hickey, Michael. *The Irish language and Irish Intermediate Education VII: Dr. O'Hickey's Reply to Dr. Mahaffy, Mr. Gwynn and Dr. Atkinson.* Gaelic League Pamphlet no.17. Dublin: Gaelic League, 1901.

O'Leary, Peter. *My Story*. Trans. Cyril Ó Céirin. Oxford: 1915, OUP, 1987.

O'Leary, Philip. 'Poor Relations: Gaelic Drama and the Abbey Theatre, 1899–1913'.*Journal of Irish Literature* 18.1 (Jan 1989): 3–24.

———. *The Prose Literature of the Gaelic Revival, 1881–1821: Ideology and Innovation*. PA: Pennsylvania State University Press, 1994.

Oram, Hugh. *The Newspaper Book: A History of Newspapers in Ireland 1649–1983*. Dublin: MO Books, 1983.

O'Riordan, Michelle. *The Gaelic Mind and the Collapse of the Gaelic World*. Cork: Cork University Press, 1990.

Ó Siadhail, Pádraig. *Stair Dhramaíocht na Gaeilge*. Indreabhán, Conamara: Cló Iar-Chonnachta: 1993.

Ó Súilleabháin, Donncha. *Scéal an Oireachtas 1897–1924*. Baile Átha Cliath: An Clóchomhar Tta., 1984.

O'Sullivan, Seumas. *Essays and Recollections*. Dublin: Talbot Press, 1944.

Ó Tuama, Seán (ed.). *The Gaelic League Idea*. Cork: Mercier, 1972.

———. 'Synge and the Idea of a National Literature'. In *J. M. Synge Centenary Papers, 1971*. Ed. Maurice Harmon. Dublin: Dolmen Press, 1972.

———. *Repossessions: Selected Essays on the Irish Literary Heritage*. Cork: Cork University Press, 1995.

Parry, Benita. 'Problems in Current Theories of Colonial Discourse'. *Oxford Literary Review* 9.1 (1987): 27–57.

Pašeta, Senia. *Before the Revolution: Nationalism, Social Change and Ireland's Catholic Elite, 1879–1922*. Cork: Cork University Press, 1999.

Pearse, Patrick H. *Political Writings and Speeches*. Dublin: Phoenix Publishing, 1924.

———. *The Letters of P. H. Pearse*. Ed. Seamus O'Buachalla. Gerrards Cross: Colin Smythe, 1980.

———. *A Significant Irish Educationalist: The Educational Writings of P. H. Pearse*. Cork: Mercier, 1980.

Pethica, James. *Lady Gregory's Diaries 1892–1902*. Gerrards Cross: Colin Smythe, 1996.

Pilkington, Lionel. *Theatre and State in Twentieth Century Ireland*. London: Routledge, 2001.

Plunkett, Horace. 'The Working of Woman Suffrage in Wyoming', *Fortnightly Review* 47 (1890): 656–69.

———. *Ireland in the New Century*. Foreword by Trevor West. 1904; Dublin: Irish Academic Press, 1983.

Quinn, Antoinette. 'Cathleen ni Houlihan Writes Back: Maud Gonne and Irish National Theatre'. In *Gender and Sexuality in Modern Ireland*. Eds.

Anthony Bradley and Maryann Gialanella Valiulis. Amherst: University of Massachusetts Press, 1997, 39–59.

Quinn, Peter. 'Yeats and Revolutionary Nationalism: The Centenary of '98'. *Éire-Ireland* 15.3 (1980): 47–64.

Regan, Stephen. 'W. B. Yeats and Irish Cultural Politics in the 1890s'. In *Cultural Politics at the* Fin de Siècle. Eds. Sally Ledger and Scott McCracken. Cambridge: Cambridge University Press, 1997.

Renan, Ernest. *The Poetry of the Celtic Races, and other Studies.* Trans. with intro. and notes by William G. Hutchinson. Kennikat Series in Irish History and Culture. Port Washington: Kennikat Press, 1970.

Rhys, John. *Lectures on the Origin and Growth of Religion as Illustrated by Celtic Heathendom.* 3rd ed. London: Williams and Norgate, 1898.

Robinson, Lennox. *Ireland's Abbey Theatre.* Port Washington: Kennikat Press, 1968.

——. (ed.) *The Irish Theatre.* New York: Haskell House, 1971.

Roche, Anthony. 'The Two Worlds of Synge's *Well of the Saints*'. In *Critical Essays on J. M. Synge.* New York: GK Hall, 1994. 98–107.

——. *Contemporary Irish Drama from Beckett to McGuinness.* Dublin: Gill and Macmillan, 1994.

Roche, Desmond. *Local Government in Ireland.* Dublin: Institute of Public Administration, 1982.

Rooney, William. *Poems and Ballads by William Rooney.* Intro. Patrick Bradley. Dublin: United Irishman, n.d.[1903?].

——. *Prose Writings.* Dublin: MH Gill, 1909.

Russell, George. *Co-operation and Nationality.* Dublin: Maunsel and Co., 1912.

——. *Some Passages from the Letters of AE to W. B. Yeats.* Dublin: Cuala Press, 1936.

——. *The Living Torch.* Ed. with intro. by Monk Gibbon. London: Macmillan, 1937.

——. *Letters from AE.* Ed. Alan Denson with foreword by Dr. Monk Gibbon. London: Abelard-Schuman, 1961.

——. *Selections from the Contributions to the* Irish Homestead *by G. W. Russell – AE.* Ed. Henry Summerfield. Gerrards Cross: Colin Smythe, 1978.

Saddlemyer, Ann. '"The Noble and the Beggar-man": Yeats and Literary Nationalism'. In *The World of W. B. Yeats.* Eds. Robin Skelton and Ann Saddlemyer. Dublin: Dolmen, 1965. 22–39.

——. (ed.) *Theatre Business: The Correspondence of the First Abbey Theatre Directors – William Butler Yeats, Lady Gregory and J. M. Synge.* Gerrards Cross: Colin Smythe, 1982.

——. *In Defense of Lady Gregory, Playwright.* Dublin: Dolmen Press, 1966.

Said, Edward W. *Orientalism: Western Concepts of the Orient.* 1978; London: Penguin, 1991.

——. *Nationalism, Colonialism and Literature: Yeats and Decolonisation.* Field Day Pamphlet no. 15. Derry: Field Day, 1988.

Shaw, George Bernard. *The Shewing Up of Blanco Posnet and Fanny's First Play*. Ed. Dan H. Laurence. London: Penguin, 1987.

——. *John Bull's Other Island*. Ed. Dan H. Laurence. London: Penguin, 1987.

Shuiblaigh, Máire Nic. *The Splendid Years*. Dublin: Duffy, 1955.

Skelton, Robin and Ann Saddlemyer (eds.). *The World of W. B. Yeats: Essays in Perspective*. Dublin: Dolmen Press, 1965.

Smith, David M. "'I Thought I Was Landed!": The Congested Districts Board and the Women of Western Ireland'. *Éire-Ireland* 31.3 & 4 (Winter 1996): 209–27.

Smyth, Gerry. *Decolonisation and Criticism: The Construction of Irish Literature*. London: Pluto Press, 1998.

Smythe, Colin. 'The Countess Cathleen: A Note', *Yeats Annual* 3 (1985): 193–7.

Society of Jesus. *A Page of Irish History: The Story of University College Dublin, 1883–1909*. Dublin: 1930.

Storey, Mark (ed.). *Poetry and Ireland Since 1800: A Source Book*. London: Routledge, 1988.

Summerfield, Henry. *That Myriad-Minded Man: A Biography of George William Russell 'AE', 1867–1935*. Gerrards Cross: Colin Smythe, 1975.

Synge, John Millington. *Collected Works*. 4 vols. Ed. Robin Skelton. London: Oxford University Press, 1962–8.

——. *Some Letters of John M. Synge to Lady Gregory and W. B. Yeats*. Ed. Ann Saddlemyer. Dublin: Cuala Press, 1971.

——. *The Collected Letters of John Millington Synge*. 2 vols. Ed. Ann Saddlemyer. Oxford: Clarendon Press, 1983, 1984.

——. *The Aran Islands*. London: Penguin, 1992.

Temple-Thurston, Barbara. 'The Reader as Absentminded Beggar: Recovering South Africa in Ulysses'. *James Joyce Quarterly* 28.1 (Fall 1990): 247–56.

Tomlinson, John. *Cultural Imperialism*. London: Pinter, 1991.

Toomey, Deirdre. 'Moran's Collar: Yeats and Irish Ireland'. *Yeats Annual* 12 (1996): 45–83.

Towey Mitchell, Joan. 'Yeats, Pearse and Cuchulain'. *Éire-Ireland* 11.4 (1976): 51–65.

Traill, Anthony. 'Hands Off Trinity'. *Nineteenth Century* 45 (Mar. 1899): 512–24.

Trotter, Mary. *Ireland's National Theatres: Political Performance and the Origins of the Irish Dramatic Movement*. Syracuse: Syracuse University Press, 2001.

Turner-Johnston, Sheila. *Alice: A Life of Alice Milligan*. Omagh: Colourpoint Press, 1994.

Tymoczko, Maria. 'Amateur Political Theatricals, Tableaux Vivants, and *Cathleen ni Houlihan*'. *Yeats Annual* 10 (1993): 33–64.

——. *The Irish Ulysses*. Berkeley: University of California Press, 1994.

Vance, Norman. *Irish Literature: A Social History. Tradition, Identity and Difference*. Cambridge: Basil Blackwell, 1990.

Veeser, H. Aram (ed.). *The New Historicism*. London: Routledge, 1989.

Viswanathan, Gauri. *Outside the Fold: Conversion, Modernity, and Belief*. Princeton: Princeton University Press, 1998.

Ward, Margaret. *Unmanageable Revolutionaries*. London: Pluto Press, 1983.

——. *Maud Gonne: Ireland's Joan of Arc*. London: Pandora, 1990.

——. *In their Own Voice: Women and Irish Nationalism*. Dublin: Attic Press, 1995.

Wa Thiong'o, Ngugi. *Decolonising the Mind: The Politics of Language in African Literature*. London: Heinemann, 1966.

Watson, George. *Irish Identity and the Literary Revival*. 2nd ed. 1979; Washington DC: Catholic University of America, 1994.

Welch, Robert. *The Abbey Theatre 1899–1999: Form and Pressure*. Oxford: Oxford University Press, 1999.

West, Trevor. *Horace Plunkett's Social Philosophy*. Oxford: Plunkett Foundation, 1981.

——. *Horace Plunkett: Co-operation and Politics, An Irish Biography*. Gerrards Cross: Colin Smythe, 1986.

Whelan, Kevin. 'The Memories of "The Dead"'. *The Yale Journal of Criticism* 15.1 (2002): 59–97.

White, Anna MacBride, and A. Norman Jeffares (eds.). *The Gonne–Yeats Letters 1893–1938: 'Always Your Friend'*. London: Hutchinson, 1992.

White, Harry. *The Keeper's Recital: Music and Cultural History in Ireland, 1770–1970*. Cork: Cork UP/Field Day, 1997.

White, Hayden. 'New Historicism: A Comment'. In *The New Histories*. Ed. H. A. Veeser. London: Routledge, 1989. 293–302.

Wilde, Sir William. *Irish Popular Superstitions*. Dublin: Irish Academic Press [facsimile reprint], 1853.

Willson, David Harris. *A History of England*. 2nd ed. Hinsdale: Dryden Press, 1972.

Worth, Katharine. *The Irish Drama of Europe from Yeats to Beckett*. Atlantic Highlands: Humanities Press, 1978.

Yeats, William Butler. *A Book of Irish Verse*. 1895; London: Methuen, 1920.

——. (ed.) *Beltaine* (1899–1900).

——. (ed.) *Samhain* (1901–1906, 1908/9).

——. *Poems*. 1895; London: Fisher Unwin, 1901.

——. *Collected Poems*. Dublin: Gill and Macmillan, 1933.

——. *Autobiographies*. Dublin: Gill and Macmillan, 1955.

——. *Essays and Introductions*. Dublin: Gill and Macmillan, 1961.

——. *The Uncollected Prose of W. B. Yeats*. 2 vols. Eds. J. P. Frayne and Colton Johnson. London: Macmillan, 1970–75.

——. *Collected Plays*. Dublin: Gill and Macmillan, 1982.

——. *The Collected Letters of W. B. Yeats*. Ed. John Kelly. 3 vols. Oxford: Clarendon Press, 1986.

Younger, Carlton. *Arthur Griffith*. Dublin: Gill and Macmillan, 1981.

NEWSPAPERS AND JOURNALS

An Claidheamh Soluis
Church of Ireland Gazette
Daily Nation
Dublin *Daily Express*
Freeman's Journal
Irish Homestead
Irish Independent
Irish Times
The Leader
New Ireland Review
Nineteenth Century
Sinn Féin
TCD: A College Miscellany
United Irishman

INDEX